57   annual property expense
80   Retainer contract

NOTHING DOWN
How to Buy Real Estate With Little or No Money Down

by Robert G. Allen

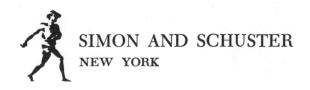

SIMON AND SCHUSTER
NEW YORK

Published by Simon and Schuster
A Division of Gulf & Western Corporation
Simon & Schuster Building
Rockefeller Center
1230 Avenue of the Americas
New York, New York 10020

SIMON AND SCHUSTER and colophon are
trademarks of Simon & Schuster

Designed by Jeanne Joudry
Art by David E. Canaan

Manufactured in the United States of America

11 12 13 14 15 16 17 18 19 20

Library of Congress Cataloging in Publication Data

Allen, Robert G.
Nothing down, how to buy real estate with little or
no money down.

Bibliography: p.
Includes index.
1. Real estate investment. I. Title.
HD1379.A38   332.6′324   79–16915

ISBN 0–671–24748–4

To my father
John L. Allen
the greatest man
I know

Contents

Introduction

Have you heard any loud noises lately?

If you listen closely, you can hear them. It's happening all around you. It is the noise caused as more and more Americans drop from lower-middle class income to upper-lower class income! Obviously, I don't mean gross income. The income I'm talking about is the net take-home pay—adjusted for inflation.

What's happening to us? Will we have enough money to keep us warm, well-fed, and happy? Or will inflation and skyrocketing prices force us to cut our shopping list until we can't even afford to fill a sack at the supermarket?

What does *your* future look like?

It depends on what kind of decisions you make today.

You've tried to figure out how to beat spiralling inflation that is draining your pocketbook. You've listened to friends; read books. And the message you've received has been that investing in real estate may be the answer to your problem.

So you pored over the classified ads section of the newspaper, marking all the possible finds with a red felt-tip pen. But you became slowly confused. What does all the lingo mean? You weren't sure which offers were good deals. You snapped the lid back on your felt-tip pen and tossed the newspaper into the fireplace. So much for real estate.

But don't give up! In the pages that follow, you will learn how to get from where you are now to where you want to be financially, and you'll learn how to get there in the shortest possible amount of time. You'll learn how to find the best buys. How to negotiate. How to deal with realtors. How to manage your properties.

Best of all, you'll learn how to do it with the least amount of your own

11

money. Maybe *none* of your own money. You'll learn how to buy with nothing down.

Some parts of this book may tax your patience. But stick with it. The principles in this book are valid and vital. I know. I've done it; I've tried, I've failed, I've learned from my mistakes, and I've succeeded.

I want to share that knowledge with you. I want to help you begin a journey toward financial independence that will bring you the means for a promising future of wealth and security, and ultimate freedom.

—ROBERT G. ALLEN

CHAPTER ONE

Guns and Butter: A Guide to Sensible Investing

WHILE IN a large city several months ago I saw something I'll never forget: a ragged toothless man with a stubby beard was digging methodically through a garbage can, sorting through its grubby contents. From time to time he would find a discarded treasure, hold it up with stained fingers to examine it from every angle, verify its value, pocket it hastily, and continue his feverish search. I wondered then how, in the richest country in the world, there could still be those who so very obviously did not share in any of the wealth, let alone the basic comforts of life.

Since then, I have often reflected about this nameless beggar's plight. As bad as it was, I have concluded that his situation is not unlike that of tens of millions of his fellow Americans who, in a figurative sense, are daily digging through the garbage cans of their jobs, searching for financial security and freedom from financial bondage.

Think about this: According to the latest government statistics, seventy-five out of one hundred Americans sixty-five years of age and older have incomes less than $675 per month. You can't call that financial independence! What happened to the hundreds of thousands of dollars that must have slipped through the fingers of these hard-working men *and* women during those fifty-odd years while they were earning a living? They vanished. They're gone forever. Your dollars are among them.

It gets worse: It has been said that only 2 percent of all 65-year-olds are financially independent. The exact government figures show that only 2 percent of Americans over age 65 make more than twenty-five thousand dollars a year. The rest of the hopeful retirees, 98 percent of the total,

13

must rely upon the good graces of the government, the church, or their relatives for at least a portion of the necessities of life. Many of them literally become desperate beggars, digging in the dumps. Is this the American dream? Is this what you are working for?

I once saw a television commercial that portrayed an elderly gentleman standing on the docks in New York City. Behind him, in the harbor, a beautiful ocean liner is putting out to sea filled with rejoicing vacationers. The old gentleman looks directly into the television screen and says, referring to the departing ship: "When I had the money, I didn't have the time. Now, I have all of the time in the world, and I don't have the money."

Have you ever stopped to consider what will stop the same fate from happening to you?

There are three major reasons why so many Americans never achieve financial independence:

1. Few Americans understand exactly how inflation destroys a long-range plan.

2. Few Americans have learned how and where to invest their money so that it will ensure long-range growth.

3. Few Americans have ever prepared a written long-range financial blueprint that includes specific goals and objectives. Their financial daydreams never amount to more than a hill of beans.

You are as familiar as I am with the results. Inflation hits all of us—hard. And the prospects are not bright. This same inflationary monster has prevented over three-fourths of the population from ever qualifying for a mortgage on a new home.

Then add insult to injury—consider taxes. The average person has to work 2.75 hours of every 8-hour business day just to pay the taxes—a figure released recently by the Tax Foundation, a nonprofit research organization. Federal taxes eat up 1 hour and 46 minutes; it takes 59 minutes worth of work to pay state and local taxes.

The government takes its slice of our paycheck on the front end; inflation steals its portion from the back end. We are caught in the squeeze, wondering where to turn for help. If we try to make more money to get ahead of inflation, we find ourselves in higher tax brackets, resulting in higher tax bills. It's an endless treadmill. Inflation and taxflation.

Combine all of this, and the chance that you and I will someday become virtual beggars is overwhelming: those odds are 98 percent against us. If either of us hope to reach retirement with any more than just a couple of hundred dollars in our pockets, it is imperative that we face some facts today.

To conquer inflation, it is urgent that you mount a frontal attack.

You must invest for the future. Now! You can't wait until tomorrow. Every day you wait means ground lost.

You must invest your money in something that grows faster than inflation!

There is only one problem with the word investment. Most people are locked into the mistaken assumption that "It takes money to make money." "The rich get richer and the poor get poorer." "Money talks."

It has been estimated that over 70 percent of the wealth of this country is concentrated in the hands of less than 20 percent of the population. Have you ever wondered why? Perhaps you are beginning to believe that you are hopelessly enslaved in the lower 80 percent. The fact remains that some of us seem to be able to accumulate wealth while the rest of us have to "eat the wolf at the door" in order to survive from month to month. I think one of the causes of this dilemma can be illustrated by referring to a theory that I learned years ago in an under-graduate economics class. It is called the Guns and Butter theory.

In simple terms the theory states that each of us has a limited source of income. We may spend our precious dollars for guns or butter, or a combination of both. Guns are classified as capital goods such as stocks, machinery, precious gems, gold, land, real estate and other capital investments that appreciate and grow in value. Butter is classified as consumer goods such as stereos, televisions, fancy cars, and other "Keeping-up-with-the-Joneses" items that depreciate and lose value over time. The more we spend on guns, the less we are able to spend on butter, and vice versa.

Each decision requires a sacrifice. By definition, investing (buying guns) is the limiting of current consumption (buying butter) for future profit. However, he who invests his dollars wisely in guns today will discover that tomorrow his investments will generate enough return to buy him all the butter he will ever need or want. Conversely, he who invests his dollars in butter today will live to see the day when his investments will be worthless and there will be no more dollars with which to buy more butter. If you doubt me, ask any retired person who had planned to retire handsomely solely on a fixed pension.

Are you a guns or a butter spender? Let me give you an example of a client who came to me four years ago with a guns or butter decision. He had just sold a small orchard and had $4,000 that was burning a hole in his pocket. He and his wife had seriously considered spending the bulk of their nest-egg for new carpets, draperies and some other butter items for their home. "After all," they reasoned, "don't we deserve some pleasure out of life?" I convinced them, instead, to buy a small $15,000 three-bedroom home as an investment (a good price by-the-way). He used his precious money as a down payment and rented the home out in order to make the mortgage payments. Now, only four years later, the home is worth about $40,000. His $4,000 investment had grown to almost $30,000. If, on the other hand, he had spent his money on butter, how much would you give him for his used carpets and drapes today?

Every one of us is faced with guns or butter decisions each day. Money spent is money invested. Remember, it takes money (invested in guns) to make money. The (guns-minded) rich (or poor) get richer and the (butter-minded) poor get poorer. Money (spent on guns) talks (the loudest).

What kinds of investments can you make if you are committed to spending your money on guns? I don't think I have to remind you that real estate stands head and shoulders above any other form of investment. And for good reason.

Real estate is a hedge against inflation because even old structures increase in value as the cost of construction materials rises. And that increase in value often supersedes even the most glaring increases in inflation.

A group of Harvard and MIT researchers recently revealed a startling report entitled "The Nation's Housing Needs 1975 to 1985," in which they stated that the median price of a new home in 1970 was $23,400; by 1976, the price for the same new home was $44,200. And, if the same trend continues into the 1980s, the report predicted the average cost of a new home then will be $78,000—affordable by only the most affluent. We are even now, seeing the realization of this prediction.

Those of you who have not yet invested in real estate probably absorbed the last paragraph with shock and dismay over inflation's impact. If you are still renting while hoping things will get better, you have a long wait. Those more sophisticated real estate investors may have reacted with a sigh, "Oh, if I had only bought real estate in 1970!" And then there are those few who neither rent nor lament, but invest. To them, the report confirmed some very important conclusions:

1. The cost of real estate will continue to increase in the future.
2. The sooner one invests, the faster his investment will grow.

3. The dramatic rise in the cost of new real estate will soon make the American dream of owning a home an impossibility for more and more Americans.

4. As home prices rise, the demand for apartment buildings will increase along with rent.

5. Unlike the stock market, the real estate market will not experience broad price fluctuations. You will see, instead, a consistent increase in prices.

6. To be conservative in today's market is the biggest gamble of all. If your only investment for the future is a savings account, the odds and inflation are against you.

At this point, you should be asking yourself, "How does an ordinary person, with limited knowledge and skill, become an investor in real estate?"

This book is the answer to that question. And there are dozens of other books on the market that are excellent. One of the best is entitled *How I Turned $1,000 into Three Million in Real Estate in My Spare Time,* by William Nickerson. Another is *How You Can Become Financially Independent by Investing in Real Estate,* by Albert J. Lowry.

Each of us has a different threshold of risk and debt. But, whether you are a renter, a lamenter or an investor, you need to do something *now* to prepare for your future. Buy a second home, a small apartment building, a piece of land. Talk to your banker, your realtor, your local builder. Do it now!

I met a man recently who had made the decision to do something. About three years ago he began buying single-family homes at the rate of one house per month. He looked for well-built homes in good neighborhoods that were for sale with little or no down payment. He leased the homes to good, solid families who paid enough rent to cover mortgage payments and expenses. His portfolio now consists of over fifty homes. He has no cash flow. But you don't need a degree in math to realize that in five years, at even the most conservative estimate, his homes will be worth at least $1,000,000 more than he paid for them. Now, that's an easy million!

You know the old adage, "They ain't makin' any more land." One day, you and I will meet and lament, "Oh, had we only bought more real estate in the 1970s." But there are many kinds of real estate to invest in. Which one is right for you? Let's explore the advantages and disadvantages of each one and help you decide which investment you'll make.

CHAPTER TWO

They're Not Making Any More Land

S̲o REAL estate is the best investment; but what is real estate? Real estate is all around you. It's the home you live in. It's the building you work in. It's the factory or warehouse you see next to the freeway. It's the store where you shop. It's the playground where your children play. It's the field where your uncle plants his wheat crop. It's the mountain cabin where you spend your summer vacation.

Real estate is everywhere, because the common denominator of all real estate is land. And land is everywhere. And it's all going up in value. And the reason real estate increases in value is because, as Mark Twain put it, "They ain't makin' any more land." But they are making more and more people every year to populate that land.

It's important to know that real estate is increasing in value; but it's critical to know that certain kinds of real estate are a better investment than others. Land can be utilized several different ways, and some kinds of property are increasing in value faster than others because of the way they're used. This story should illustrate my point:

Three wealthy old poker buffs were playing a very important game. The stakes were high, and after several hours of playing, the three of them had been dealt equally good hands. The antes increased, and finally each of them ran out of cash and began to gamble with the deeds to their various real estate holdings. The rancher from Montana began the last round of raises by pledging his entire 10,000-acre ranch, including all of his cattle and equipment. The oil baron from Oklahoma met the challenge by pledging his entire 2,000 acres of oil-producing wells with

all of his oil derricks and equipment. The wealthy Texan ended the
bidding by offering his seven acres of ground in Texas.

"Seven acres!" gasped the other two partners. "Here we have pledged
thousands of acres, and you expect us to accept your measly *seven
acres*?!"

"Yup," replied the Texan. "My land is right in the middle of downtown
Dallas."

Obviously, some ground is more valuable than other ground. And the
shorter the supply, the higher the sales price and the quicker the property
will increase in value.

There are four major categories of land use. *Undeveloped land* is
located away from civilization centers and has no immediate development potential. It is the kind of ground that is only good for holding the
earth together.

Recreational ground has little use except for limited recreational value.
Recreational property is not a sound investment.

Neither is *agricultural land*. You can tell how much the farmer is
making from his land investment by the number of farmers who are
selling out. As the story goes, one farmer went to his bank and withdrew
$100 in one-dollar bills. He then stood in front of the bank and sold each
dollar bill for $.75. When someone asked him why he was doing it, he
replied, "Well, it sure beats farming."

The fourth type of land utilization is *urban/suburban*. Urban/suburban
land increases in value because it is near population centers and because
of the various uses to which it can be put. It can be sold as individual
building lots for homes. It can have apartment buildings built on it, or
factories or warehouses. And it can house various commercial businesses
such as retail stores or office complexes. This is the kind of property you
should invest in. With this kind of land the factors of supply and demand
will be working in your favor.

For the beginning investor, the safest investment is in income property.
This may include rental homes, apartment buildings, office buildings,
shopping centers, retail and wholesale buildings, hotels, motels, rest
homes, warehouses, and industrial parks. Of the properties listed above,
rental homes and apartment buildings offer the least risk and require the
least amount of expertise.

A great deal of money can be made by finding older properties or
poorly maintained properties, adding a coat of cosmetic paint, giving the
property a general face lift, and reselling the property on the market for

a much higher price than you purchased it for. This type of investing is called the "fixer-upper." The quickest money is made in this kind of real estate, but it takes a dedicated individual who knows something about fixing up buildings. Personally, this is not my cup of tea. I can barely tell which is the right end of a hammer.

The type of investment that is universally beneficial—whether or not you have the special training and personality to fix up run-down real estate—is choosing well-constructed properties in a growing area. The long-run appreciation from such an investment will be steady and predictable. And it does not require a lot of supervision or work to bring such a building up to rentable standards. Don't be frightened away from investing in real estate because you don't understand a thing about repairs. Just buy solid property and hang on to it.

Several general principles will guide you as you invest in real estate. First, become very familiar with your own local real estate by studying properties on the market. Learn all about your particular city, its growth patterns, its depressed areas, where the path of growth is likely to extend. The more you know, the more prepared you will be to invest. And the more prepared you are to invest, the more confident you will become in your ability to spot a good opportunity. How do you find this information? Talk to realtors, pick an area of town and drive through the neighborhoods noting all of the "For Sale" signs . . . stop and ask questions. Check with your city or county planning departments who will be more than happy to sit down with you and tell an interested citizen about real estate areas. Use your common sense and always ask questions. Is this area growing or declining? How fast will our city grow and in which directions? Would I like to live here myself?

A good opportunity always goes to the investor who knows how to locate a good investment (something that only comes through practice) and who has the courage to act quickly.

Second, stay away from raw land—at least at first. This does not mean that land in predevelopment stages is a bad investment; it simply means that predeveloped land has some basic disadvantages that increase the risk for the beginning investor; it takes a greater degree of sophistication to invest in raw land. One big disadvantage: land does not generate a cash flow. Mortgage payments must be made out of the investor's pocket. That's why it's called an "alligator" investment—it eats up an investor's capital through monthly payments, but it does not produce any cash flow. The beginning investor soon runs out of money to feed his alligator a daily diet of principal, interest, and taxes. When you don't feed an alligator, it becomes very hungry and it eats you alive; many a property has been foreclosed because the owner couldn't keep the payments current.

Third, the safest kind of investment for the beginner is an income-producing property. Income-producing property is the kind of real estate that is rented out to a tenant: an apartment building, rental home, commercial retail space, office building, or industrial/warehouse building. The tenant pays rent that should be adequate to make your mortgage payment, pay operating expenses, and produce a small cash flow as a return on your investment. As a beginner you should concentrate on buying small houses (for rental) and small apartment buildings. Your first purchases of income-producing property will give you the knowledge, experience, and confidence you need to venture into other areas. However, I have found in my experience that the easiest and safest dollars can be made by concentrating one's efforts in homes and apartment buildings. I like to invest my money in a sure thing. I know that business and commercial properties are dependent upon a healthy economy and sound business management for success. This last requires sophisticated knowledge and experience. On the other hand, homes and apartment buildings will always be in demand, regardless of what the economy may do. People *must* live somewhere; they have no choice. Housing is a basic need. That's why I have most of my money invested in residential income property.

Besides, income-producing real estate is the most forgiving of all investments. Forgiving, because if you make a bad decision, more often than not, you can wait a year and values have increased enough to bail you out; your investment has the ability to carry itself through monthly flow from rents. It offers increased security.

Fourth, as often as you can, you should try to buy your properties with as much leverage as possible, in other words, with little or no money down. This book was written to tell you how.

Fifth, since well-selected real estate income properties are constantly increasing in value, the sooner you buy, the richer you will become.

It all sounds so easy, you say. If it is so easy to become wealthy through real estate investing, then why isn't everybody doing it? I think I would be safe in saying that most Americans now realize that real estate investment is one of the surest and safest ways to financial freedom. There is, therefore, only one explanation why so few Americans fail to reach financial independence. So few are willing to pay the price. So few are willing to take the risks. So few are willing to set their sights high and start climbing. Only a small number of those who read this book will actually buy any real estate, even though they may agree with the concept. And the difference between the failures and the successes is the subject of our next chapter. Goals.

CHAPTER THREE

"On My Thirtieth Birthday": Setting Financial Goals

W̶HAT IS your financial goal?

Think about what you just said to yourself. I can probably guess what it was:

"I'd like to be wealthy someday."

"I'd like to have enough money to retire within ten years."

"I'd like to be a millionaire."

"I'd like to be successful."

If you said that any of those was your goal—or anything like those statements—you might as well give up now. You'll never reach it.

Why?

Your goals are too vague.

It's a lot like going to a hardware store to buy a tool. In order to buy the tool—to accomplish your goal, your reason for going there—you have to know what you will be using the tool for. If you know that you need to cut some lumber, you'll look for a tool with a sharp edge that will make a quick and easy cut—probably a power saw. If you need to build a dog house, you'll buy only the tools you'll need: a hammer, a saw, some nails, maybe a tape measure.

Can you imagine how ridiculous it would be to go to a hardware store to buy tools without knowing what you wanted to do with the tools? None of the tools in the entire store would mean anything to you, because you wouldn't have a task to complete.

This book is like a hardware store stocked with tools. Read it, and you'll find the tools—the techniques—you need to reach your financial goal. But only if you know what that goal is. Specifically.

Have you written down your goals? If so, could you find your list right now? How long has it been since you looked at it? We're a nation of dreamers—we waste a lot of precious time dreaming about what we'd like the future to be like, and we do precious little to make our dreams come true.

It's not too late to start. You can do it right now. How? Follow some simple—but critical—steps.

1. *Determine where you are.* If you don't know where you are financially, how do you expect to get where you want to go?

Sit down. Prepare a realistic financial statement. You will find a copy of an excellent financial file that you should fill out on the next page.

I know you're tempted to skip over this step. *You can't.* It is essential to the goal-setting process.

As you prepare your statement, remember to list all those bad investments you still own—a dusty recreational lot in Nevada, an old car stored in a neighbor's garage. Because if you work things right, you might still be able to use them to your advantage. You'll need to know exactly what you've got.

2. *Set your financial goal.* Here's where your goal needs to differ drastically from the one you probably cited as you started to read this chapter.

Your financial goal shouldn't be, "I want to be wealthy someday."

There's nothing wrong with being wealthy. What's wrong is that you've skipped the details. You're trying to build a house with a blueprint that has only an outline and nothing filled in—no floor plan, no placing of doors, no dimensions. It's impossible.

Instead, your financial goal should sound something like this:

"On May 20, 1983 (my 30th, 40th or 50th birthday), I want to have a net worth of $800,000. This net worth will represent my equity in at least one hundred apartment units located in and around my home town. The annual cash flow—tax free—will be at least $75,000. On that day I will announce my retirement, quit my job, and devote my time fully to the things I enjoy."

You could get even more specific if you tried. Age is no barrier. Whether you're twenty or sixty, you can still set meaningful goals and make money in real estate.

Write your goal down. Put it somewhere where you can read it often—hopefully once a day. Then *do* read it once a day.

You might think this sounds silly, even fanatic. But it works. When

Confidential Check List and
Survey of Investment Objectives

PERSONAL AND FAMILY DATA

Name_____ Date_____

Mailing Address_____ Phone_____

Employer/Position_____ Phone_____

Spouse's Employer_____ Phone_____

	Age	Date of Birth	Health	Occupation	Social Security No.
Client					
Spouse					
Children					
Other Dependents					

	Firm	Phone
Attorney		
Banker		
C.P.A.		
Insurance Broker		
Property Manager		
Other Financial Adviser		

When was your present will executed?_____Spouse's?_____

Do you have a trust arrangement? ☐ Yes ☐ No   Type_____ Trustee _____

INCOME AND TAXATION

	Self	Spouse	Total
Current Annual Taxable Income			
From salary, fees, bonuses, etc.	$_____	$_____	$_____
From interest	$_____	$_____	$_____
From dividends	$_____	$_____	$_____
From real estate	$_____	$_____	$_____
From capital gains (½)	$_____	$_____	$_____
Other (trusts, etc.)	$_____	$_____	$_____
Total taxable income	$_____	$_____	$_____

Expected future income?_____ When? _____

What income increases or decreases do you expect?_____

Do you receive additional non-taxable income?_____

Do you have a regular savings or investment program now? ☐ Yes ☐ No

Present monthly savings $_____ Could comfortably save $_____ monthly.

1

TAX RETURN SUMMARY (LAST 4 YEARS)

	19____	19____	19____	19____
Adjusted gross income	$_____	$_____	$_____	$_____
Taxable income	$_____	$_____	$_____	$_____
Federal taxes paid	$_____	$_____	$_____	$_____
State ( ) taxes paid	$_____	$_____	$_____	$_____
Exemptions claimed	_____	_____	_____	_____

How many exemptions this year?_____ Estimated personal deductions $_____

Do you have any personal carry-over losses from last year?_____

Factors affecting future income _____

_____

_____

_____

_____

_____

_____

Comments _____

_____

_____

_____

_____

ASSETS AND LIABILITIES (EXCEPT INSURANCE)

Lender and Loan Number

REAL ESTATE

Type of Property and Location	How Acquired	Title Held In Name Of	Date Acquired	Adjusted Basis	Market Value	Amount of Mortgages	Present Equity	Monthly Cash Flow Before Taxes
				$	$	$	$	$
						TOTAL	$	$

SECURITIES (Listed and Unlisted)

Company and Type of Security	Registered In Name Of	Date Acquired	Cost Basis	Market Value	Margin or Loans	Present Equity	Annual Cash Flow Before Taxes
			$	$	$	$	$
					TOTAL	$	$

BUSINESS INTERESTS

Name of Company	Form of Organization	Date of Organization	Number of Employees	Percent Ownership	Client's Current Net Value	Client's Annual Net Income
					$	$
				TOTAL	$	$

2

EMPLOYEE BENEFITS

Type of Plan Company	Tax Qualified?	Retirement Age	Retirement Benefits	Voluntary Contributions	Current Value	Death Benefit Now
Pension			$	$	$	$
Profit Sharing						
Savings						
Tax Sheltered Annuity						

LIFE AND HEALTH INSURANCE

LIFE INSURANCE

Company	Type	Date Acquired	Insured	Owner	Beneficiary	Face Amount	Cash Value	Loans	Annual Premium
						$	$	$	$
					TOTAL	$	$	$	$

MEDICAL AND DISABILITY INSURANCE

Type	Cancelled? Yes No	Insurer	Insured	Periodic Benefit	Maximum Benefit	Exclusion	Annual Premium
Disability Income							$
Disability Income							
Hospitalization							
Major Medical							
Business Overhead							

FINANCIAL STATEMENT

ASSETS		LIABILITIES	
cash and checking	$_____		
savings accounts	_____		
real estate owned	_____	mortgages	$_____
securities	_____	notes payable	_____
notes receivable	_____	loans on life ins.	_____
bonds—face value	_____	debts, unsecured	_____
furniture & personal	_____	installment purchases	_____
automobiles	_____	property tax reserves	_____
life ins. cash value	_____	income tax reserves	_____
net worth business	_____	long-term leases	_____
net lease value	_____		_____
boats, trailers	_____		_____
alimony	_____		_____
deposits on real estate	_____		
pension & annuity value	_____		
other_____	_____		
	_____		
	_____		
	_____		
TOTAL ASSETS $_____		TOTAL LIABILITIES $_____	

NET WORTH $_____

3

INVESTMENT OBJECTIVES

What priority do you assign to the following investment objectives?
____ Additional current monthly income of $_____ .
____ Capital growth/Inflation hedge. ☐ Short Term ☐ Long Term
____ Tax shelter for ☐ Income ☐ Capital gain ☐ _____ .
____ Professional management for ☐ Property ☐ Securities ☐ Trust
____ Safety of investment.
____ Maintain minimum cash reserve of $_____ .
____ Diversification of investment program.
____ Provision for family in event of premature death or disability.
____ Other

At what age do you anticipate full retirement?_____
What do you consider to be a minimum retirement income (Today's dollars) $_____
What do you consider to be a comfortable retirement income (Today's dollars) $_____
Comments (Education funds, etc.): _____
_____
_____

COMMENTS

_____
_____
_____
_____
_____

BUDGETING - create your own wealth for pyramiding

Gross Income - including interest, dividends, rents $_____
      Less deductions - Federal _____ F.I.C.A. _____
                  State _____ Others _____   (_____)
                                                             $_____

Spendable Income

	BUDGET	SPENT
1. Savings for investment = at least 10% of gross income		
2. Committed expenses: a. Charitable		
b. Housing		
c. House maintenance		
d. Utilities		
e. Life insurance		
f. Automotive		
g. Medical		
h. Others:		
3. Manageable expenses: a. Food		
b. Clothing		
c. Personal expenses		
d. Appliances		
e. Furnishings		
f. Building and grounds		
g. Entertainment		
h. Others:		

                              Total Expenses $_____
                        Spendable less expenses $_____

If there is income remaining apply to your savings. If there is a deficiency of income find ways to alter your expenses or increase income. Do not decrease savings!

your mind becomes magnetized with a goal—when even your subconscious mind becomes magnetized, something that will happen if you read your goal every day—suddenly your mind begins to formulate solutions that will help you reach your goal.

I've seen it work in my own life. When I was twenty-six I decided to set a big goal and to write it down for daily reading. It went something like this:

"By my thirtieth birthday, May 20, 1978, I will have a net worth of at least $100,000." At the time, $100,000 was more money than I could have dared to dream for in an entire lifetime, and the pursuit of that goal has led me through several businesses—both good and bad. By the time I was twenty-eight I doubled the goal, so I set new sights: to retire by the time I was thirty with a net worth of at least $500,000. I just passed that birthday—and exceeded my goal.

Remember, whatever the mind of man can conceive and believe, man can achieve.

3. *Decide how you will reach your goal.* Some fundamental factors can contribute to your success:

GOALS. You've already set yours.

INVESTMENT VEHICLE. You've chosen real estate.

DESIRE. Indirectly or directly, it's what prompted you to buy this book. It's critical.

KNOWLEDGE. Keep reading. See the bibliography at the end of this chapter.

MONEY. Even if you're a beginner, you can learn to raise investment capital. You can learn how to purchase real estate with little or none of your own money.

TIME. Be patient. Work at it a little each day. Invest your time in finding right properties—a technique we'll discuss later.

Combined, those factors can spell success. And you've got another thing going for you: all real estate that is well selected and properly maintained will increase in value in time. We know that real estate property is currently appreciating at least 10 percent a year in most areas of the country. *At that rate of appreciation, any piece of property you buy will double in value in just over seven years!* This is an extremely important concept. If you think about it for a few minutes, you will see how exciting this can be. If any property you buy has the potential of doubling in value in seven years, then it is possible to set some very specific goals for how wealthy you would like to become.

For example, suppose you buy a $100,000 building today. Within seven years, if conditions have been favorable, that building will be worth approximately $200,000. Your profit will have been $100,000. If you think a doubling of real estate values is impossible, look back over the past seven years and ask yourself the question, "What factors will change in the future to prevent the same thing happening?"

Look at the following chart of the Gross Equity Appreciation Schedule.

Gross Equity Appreciation Schedule

$2,000,000	1.3	2.4	3.4	4.3	5.1	5.9	6.6	7.3	18.8
$1,750,000	1.4	2.7	3.8	4.8	5.7	6.5	7.3	8.0	20.0
$1,500,000	1.7	3.1	4.3	5.4	6.4	7.3	8.2	8.9	21.4
$1,250,000	2.0	3.6	5.0	6.2	7.3	8.3	9.2	10.1	23.1
$1,000,000	2.4	4.3	5.9	7.3	8.6	9.7	10.7	11.6	25.2
$ 750,000	3.1	5.4	7.3	8.9	10.3	11.6	12.7	13.7	28.0
$ 500,000	4.3	7.3	9.7	11.6	13.2	14.6	15.8	16.9	32.0
$ 250,000	7.3	11.6	14.6	16.9	18.8	20.5	21.9	23.1	39.0
	$250,000	500,000	750,000	1,000,000	1,250,000	1,500,000	1,750,000	2,000,000	10,000,000

Gross Value of Real Estate (vertical axis label)

Net Equity Columns

Assumptions:
  —Property values increase by 10 percent per year.
  —All of your purchases are nothing down.
  —Equity buildup is not counted in equity.
  —Figures are rounded to highest tenth.

This chart provides you with a quick and easy way to find out how much you can be worth in a prescribed time period. How does it work? Say that you want to have a net equity of $1,000,000 in 5½ years. Find $1,000,000 in the Net Equity column; now follow the column up until you find something close to 5½ years—5.4. Now go across to the Gross Value of Real Estate column; you'll have to buy $1,500,000 worth of property to reach your goal. What if you now have $250,000 worth of property? Find $1,000,000 in the Net Equity column and the $250,000 point in the Gross Value of Real Estate column. The point at which the two intersect is the number of years it will take your property to appreciate to a $1,000,000 net equity—16.9 years. Make sure you note the assumptions listed at the bottom of the chart.

This chart was created to teach you an important concept: the compounding effect of real estate price increases. You can see by playing with the numbers on the chart that there are infinite ways of creating a fortune. You just need to decide firmly how wealthy you want to become. However, there are drawbacks to the chart since an investor just doesn't walk into the market and buy a million dollars' worth of real estate at a time and wait for seven years to become wealthy. The normal process is to buy properties in increments—to eat the elephant bite by bite rather than at one sitting. This fact necessitates the use of another chart which I call the *gross equity accumulation schedule*. This more closely approaches the actual real life situation of the average investor, i.e., the purchase of individual properties slowly with building equities.

Gross Equity Accumulation Schedule

	$250,000	500,000	750,000	1,000,000	1,250,000	1,500,000	1,750,000	2,000,000
$300,000	3.5	5	6	7	8	8.5	9	9.5
$250,000	4	5.5	6.5	7.5	8.5	9	10	10.5
$200,000	4.5	6	7.5	8.5	9.5	10	11	11.5
$150,000	5	7	8.5	9.5	10.5	11.5	12.2	13
$100,000	6	8.5	10	11.5	12.5	13.5	14.5	15
$ 75,000	7	10	11.5	13	14	15	16	17
$ 50,000	8.5	11.5	13.5	15	16.5	17.5	18.5	19.5
$ 40,000	9.5	12.5	14.5	16.5	18	19	20	21

Annual Accumulation (left vertical label)

Net Equity Columns

Assumptions:
   —Property values increase by 10% per year
   —All of your purchases are nothing down
   —Equity build-up is not counted in equity
   —Figures are rounded to highest one half

Let me explain how this chart works. Let's assume that you have decided that you would like to retire in ten years with a steady yearly cash flow of $50,000 per year for the rest of your life. How can you relate this kind of goal to your real estate investment program? Easily. We will make the assumption that this $50,000 income represents a return on your investment in ten years from now. If you could conservatively invest your money to yield 10 percent, then your $50,000 income would represent your yield on a $500,000 net worth ($500,000 × .10 = $50,000). What you will need to have ten years from now, therefore, is a net worth of $500,000, which can be invested to yield you 10 percent on your investment. The next question is, "How can I attain a net worth of $500,000 in ten years?" This takes you to the gross equity accumulation schedule. Look for a net worth of $500,000 in the "Net Equity" columns in the table. Then, follow the column upward until you find the number of years until your intended retirement date—in this case ten years. Then, follow the column horizontally to the left to find the yearly purchase quota—in this case $75,000. This tells you that in order for you to accumulate a net worth of a half a million dollars within ten years, it will be necessary for you to purchase at least $75,000 worth of real estate each year for the next ten years. This should be held and not sold. If property values increase at an average rate of at least 10 percent per year for the next ten years the half-million dollar goal is feasible and realistic. If you want to get fancy in your goal-setting, you can use both the preceding charts to make predictions on your future net worth. The important concept to grasp here is that the building of a fortune is accomplished steadily, gradually, one step at a time. Many of us can get overwhelmed at the magnitude of our goals if we only focus on the end result without making the intermediate steps as palatable as possible. Surely you can bite off smaller chunks on your way to devouring the whole goal. To some of you, the purchase of even $75,000 worth of real estate each year for ten years seems as formidable as climbing Everest. You must realize that every little step counts: a small $45,000 home adds to your quota as does a large $200,000 apartment building. Some years you will not be able to find anything. And, the very next month, you could locate an excellent property to satisfy two or three years' quotas. I found that during a six-month period of 1978 I could not find anything that fit into my investment guidelines. Then, one week I located a "don't wanter" who had five smaller homes to sell in one transaction. And I was able to negotiate a *nothing down* purchase! It's either feast or famine.

As your confidence and your experience increase, you'll learn that you can pyramid your investments. Make sure that you buy solid real estate in good neighborhoods in growing areas. You should begin by purchasing small homes and apartment buildings until you get the hang of it (and so you don't get hung by risking your investment capital in unknown areas). You must choose each property carefully—with legal protection, assurance from professionals, and with some long-range objectives for creative appreciation. As you learn to master the techniques, you will eventually purchase larger apartment buildings, small office buildings, and land for subdivisions. Give yourself time: most of all, give yourself optimism.

Even the lofty million-dollar goal is not out of reach if you plan carefully and act according to the schedule. If you study the schedule, it shows you eight ways of becoming a millionaire. You can be ambitious and buy $300,000 worth of real estate each year for seven years—or you can take it a little easier and buy a small home each year (worth about $40,000) for the next 16.5 years. Either way is just as effective, provided the assumptions hold true. Whatever your financial dream is, take time to fill out the goal-commitment form on the next page. Don't pass up this opportunity to commit yourself in writing—and have your spouse

COMMITMENT:

I, _____, hereby

acknowledge that I have formally adopted the following financial goals:

On the _____ day of _____, 19____, my net worth

will be at least $ _____. This will generate a

yearly cash flow of approximately $_____. If I

so desire, I may announce my retirement from my job and devote time to do

the things which are important to me such as _____

_____

_____

In order to accomplish the above goals, I will have to purchase at least

$ _____ worth of real estate each

year for the next _____ years. My first purchase will be on or

before_____.

Signed this _____ day of ____

19_____

_____

_____

Witnessed by

_____

witness it with his or her signature so he or she can be a part of the process. This step could well be the most important thing you do to obtain financial independence.

Once again, don't be frightened by the magnitude of your goal. Start with one property at a time. Make me a promise that you will buy at least one piece of real estate each and every year. That's a challenge! You will be amazed at how fast your real estate garden will grow. And don't be worried by the fact that you don't have a lot of money to invest. You bought this book because you didn't have a lot of cash in the bank. Few people do. But you can still reach your investment goals; keep reading, and you'll learn how to do it with little or none of your own money.

Suggested Reading on Real Estate Investing

Bockl, George. *How Real Estate Fortunes Are Made.*
———. *How to Use Leverage to Make Money in Local Real Estate.*
de Benedictis, Daniel J. *The Complete Real Estate Advisor.*
Glubetich, Dave. *The Monopoly Game.*
Hill, Napoleon. *Think and Grow Rich.*
Lowry, Albert J. *How You Can Become Financially Independent by Investing in Real Estate.*
Nickerson, William. *How I Turned $1,000 into Three Million in Real Estate in My Spare Time.*
Ringer, Robert J. *Winning Through Intimidation.*

CHAPTER FOUR

Finding the Bargain: Once-in-a-Lifetime Deals Come Along Every Other Day If You Know What You're Looking For

FINDING THE right property for your limited investment dollars is like panning for gold: it takes a lot of sifting through gravel before any glitter is found.

And there are many properties that *appear*, like fool's gold, to be a rich find. Only close inspection will let you know for sure that you've located a real bargain. For this reason I try to maintain a very neutral, aloof attitude whenever I go looking for properties. If I get too emotionally involved in any investment decision, I may find myself swayed by too much non-financial detail.

The first assignment for students in my "Real Estate with Nothing Down" seminar is to find a property they think has potential, analyze it as best they can, and make an offer to the owner. They get excited about buying techniques. Within a few days, I invariably get a call, and the conversation might go something like this:

"Bob, I've really found a winner. The owner is willing to be flexible with his terms!"

Five questions I must ask of that student will give me a quick indication of whether or not the property could be the "gold" I am looking for—a one-in-ten chance.

"What is the address of the property?"

37

"Well, it's located in the northeast part of town approximately 150 Apartment Row East."

This is an area of town that has hundreds of apartment units. Rents are very competitive there because none of the apartment owners dares to raise his rents for fear that all of his tenants will move to other less expensive units in the same vicinity. This fact raises a red flag in my mind because there will be little opportunity to raise the rent and upgrade the property, and thereby raise the value of the building. If I get positive answers to my next four questions, I might still consider purchasing the property. If I don't get positive answers to the other questions, I'll counsel my student to keep looking.

"What is the owner asking for his units? And what is the capitalization rate?" (More on this later.)

"The owner told me that he wants to get $100,000, but he will settle for $95,000. The owner says the annual income is $12,000."

With my calculator in hand, I quickly determine what the price per unit is: $95,000 ÷ 4 = $23,750 per unit. Several units in that same location are advertised for $19,000 per unit, and a realtor friend told me several units have sold recently for $18,500 per unit, but all were cash prices. Again, I see a red flag. Maybe the owner can afford to be flexible because he is planning on taking a huge paper profit. What about income and expenses? The seller's projected annual income is $12,000. Divide this number by twelve to get the monthly income, and then divide the answer by four to get the monthly projected rent per apartment: $12,000 ÷ 12 = $1,000 ÷ 4 = $250 a month rent on each apartment. The vacancy rate in that area is at least five to ten percent, and rents in that area are barely $200 per month. More red flags. The owner is making an inaccurate projection.

"What about expenses?"

"He says they're $2,000 a year."

I can quickly calculate the ratio of expenses to income as $2,000 ÷ $12,000 = 17 percent. I know that can't be true, since the average in the area is at least 35 percent, perhaps higher. As a matter of habit I calculate the seller's capitalization rate by first determining the net operating income (NOI): $12,000 − $2,000 = $10,000 net operating income. I divide the NOI by the seller's price to get the cap rate: $10,000 ÷ $95,000 = 10.5. Then, I calculate my reconstructed capitalization rate based on the figures as I know them to be: rent for the year = $200 × 4 × 12 × .95 = $9,120; the expenses are 35 percent of that, or

$9,120 \times .35 = \$3,192$. That leaves a NOI of $\$9,120 - \$3,192 = \$5,928$, a far cry from the seller's projected $10,000 NOI. The reconstructed cap rate is $\$5,928 \div \$95,000$, or 6.2 percent. I won't buy a property that has a reconstructed cap rate of less than 7 percent, so I can eliminate this property at once. But I decide to see what else the seller has up his sleeve just for fun.

"What terms will the seller accept?"

"He is asking only $5,000 down, and he'll carry a contract for the $90,000 balance at 9.5 percent interest with monthly payments of $786. That's a twenty-five-year amortization!"

By asking a couple of other questions, I determine that the seller has an original loan of $70,000 with payments of $586 and interest of 9 percent. With monthly payments of $786 and income of only $5,928 (or $494 a month) there will be a monthly negative cash flow of $292 a month. That's almost *$300 a month*!

"Is the seller a don't wanter?"

A don't wanter is someone who, pardon the English, don't want his property. It's a term used among real estate exchangers to designate a desperate seller. We'll discuss this concept more later in the chapter. The important fact here is that this seller is *not* a don't wanter. Therefore, he is not flexible, and probably won't be amenable to the kinds of offers we'll be inclined to make.

"No! He says he knows that he can get his price and his terms if he just waits long enough."

That confirms my suspicion about the seller not being a don't wanter. Everything else pointed to my conclusion.

"Well," I summarized, "it seems like the price is too high. The terms aren't bad, but there will be a $300 monthly negative cash flow until the rents are raised, which is a slim possibility in the near future. The location is not so hot, and the seller is not a don't wanter. We've struck out on almost all of our most important criteria. (I'm not even going to care about the condition of the property since it's location is poor and the seller is not a don't wanter.) What is this joker's name, anyway?"

"Jerry Peterson."

"Now it's all clear to me," I chuckled. "Jerry is a former student of mine. He's just using one of the formulas that I taught him for developing a monthly cash flow."

Finding the right property to buy is not as easy as reading the real estate section of the newspaper's classified ads or cruising the streets. An

unwary buyer can find himself on the wrong end of an unhealthy negative cash flow and can unwittingly pay a price that the market will not
bear for at least another year or more. Five major elements need to be
considered before you can locate what you're looking for—a property
that's worth your gold: (1) location analysis; (2) market analysis; (3)
seller analysis (the don't-wanter seller); (4) financial analysis; (5) property analysis (condition of the property).

Location is the first critical element. The three cardinal rules in buying
real estate are: (1) Location. (2) Location. (3) Location. Don't be
blinded by attractive terms. If the property is in a bad location, no
amount of good terms are worth the price you'll eventually have to pay
in bad tenants, measly rents, and poor resale profits. You don't make
profit by throwing your precious money and time and effort down the
rathole of a poor location. I have owned property in a bad location
before, and it wasn't long before I became the biggest don't wanter in
town. My location attracted the worst tenants and commanded the lowest
rents. Expenses were higher because of these tenants, and added to the
expenses were my purchases of antacids for my unsettled stomach.

How do you analyze location?

Take a look around. Is the neighborhood deteriorating or upgrading?
A drive down the street should answer this question easily enough. You
don't have to be an expert to recognize slummy buildings, uncut lawns,
and debris in the street.

A cardinal rule in buying property is to buy the worst property in the
best neighborhood, *not* the best property in the worst neighborhood. If
you buy the worst property in the best neighborhood, at least you have
the chance to upgrade the property to match the standards of the
neighborhood, and your property value will increase.

In a bad area, your property will only decline in value along with the
rest of the neighborhood. Remember, you're buying a neighborhood, not
just a property. Choose carefully.

If you're still in doubt about the neighborhood, there are several
people who can give you some good insight about your prospective buy.
First, ask the city's planning department what is planned for the area
you're considering. They will be glad to answer any and all of your
questions; just let them know you want the answers to be blunt. Or call
a local property management firm, and ask one of their account managers
to discuss the pros and cons of the area.

Another source of help is a local realtor. And if you still don't think you know enough about the area, start knocking on doors in the neighborhood. Ask some of the apartment owners what they think about their investment. You might get some good insight. Or ask the tenants themselves. They know better than anyone what the neighborhood's really like.

Another way to analyze location is to size up the competition. If you are buying a home as an investment, determine whether the neighborhood rentals are high enough to support your mortgage payment. If you are considering buying an apartment or commercial building, do a thorough study of competitive rents in the area; determine if there is room for increase. You'll also learn from this how your location compares with others in town.

Nearby amenities are another clue to a good location. Apartments and homes need to be close to shopping centers, churches, schools, and other services. If you're considering a commercial building, determine if there is adequate traffic flow or proximity to working establishments.

Generally speaking, the value of properties conforms to what I call the concentric circle theory. For example, let's assume you're analyzing an apartment building that is rented to single students who are attending your local university. The closer the apartment to campus, the higher the rents and the higher sale prices. But by the same token, the vacancy rates will be lower, and you will probably have less tenant turnover. The same theory applies to homes. How close are they to places of employment, shopping centers, and churches?

This diagram illustrates the concentric circle theory. Section A buildings would command the highest rent, Section D the lowest.

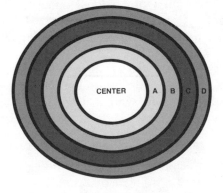

CONCENTRIC CIRCLE THEORY

Generally, I try to avoid properties in the D area unless it is for quick turnover. I try as much as possible to buy properties in A, close to the center of demand. Thus, my rents are higher and my property values increase faster.

The second major element to consider is the market. I usually don't start to get excited about any particular property until I determine that it can be purchased for below market price. *This implies that I first know what the market is!*

How can you know the market? First of all, keep track of every sale you hear about. Keep a record of the sale price and terms of the property; classify the information under type of unit, special amenities, price per unit, and available terms. Sometimes you'll get only sketchy information in a casual conversation; call the new owner and ask him what you need to know.

When you are in the market for single-family homes, you must know the approximate selling price of a 1,250-square-foot home with three bedrooms and one-and-a-half baths. The best source of this information is a local realtor. Ask him about his present listings and the listings he just sold. The form on page 43 should be of great value to you in compiling any comparable sales information you should happen to find.

If you want to know the market values of homes or buildings in a specific neighborhood, stop and ask a property owner. We all keep our ear to the ground and we have a fairly good idea what our own property is worth by comparing it to what our neighbors sold their property for. Just ask around. In a few short minutes you'll know approximate values.

If you still aren't sure what kind of a deal you're getting, hire an appraiser. He can give you a professional opinion. Use any information you have already gathered to help you judge the validity of the appraiser's estimate. In the end, you're responsible for your decision, and you should use all the input you can get.

Identifying the owner as a *don't wanter* is the third major element in finding a good buy. A don't wanter is a seller who is willing to be flexible in his price or terms. Someone who is desperate to sell his property is usually flexible and willing to negotiate. Consider this classic example:

INFORMATION SHEET ON EL DUMPO APARTMENTS

Property Description: Ten-unit apartment building located at _____ approximately 50 miles northwest of _____ and 250 miles southwest of _____. The property is fully furnished and totally vacant.

COMPARATIVE MARKET ANALYSIS FORM

Subject Property Address _____ Date _____

Information on other properties which are located in the same general area and have the same approximate value as the subject property:

FOR SALE NOW	Bed-rooms	Baths	Den	Sq.Ft.	Mtgs.	Price	Days on Mkt.	Terms

SOLD PAST 12 MONTHS

EXPIRED PAST 12 MONTHS

Realtors can be of great help in finding sold and expired information.

Financial Details: Price: $45,000
  Loans: $23,000, payable at $285.20 per month, including interest at
    8½ percent per annum. Can be assumed. No qualifying.
  Equity: $22,000
Special Information: This is a newly acquired property. While it was
  still in escrow, the owner received a job offer in another state that
  he couldn't refuse. He cannot manage the property because of
  the distance problem. This property is listed at 33 percent under
  market value due to the vacancy situation. This is a good opportunity
  for an individual with initiative and ability to solve problems. Local
  officials are expecting a construction boom and a massive housing
  shortage in the area in the near future due to extensive geothermal
  exploration and construction of an alunite processing plant near the
  city.
Will Take and Close: The owner will exchange his equity in this property
  for land, paper, construction equipment, or personal property. There
  are no geographic limitations. In other words, make me an offer. I won't
  refuse.
Sweeteners: In order to make a deal the seller will lease back the property
  at $285.20 per month until the occupancy reaches at least 60 percent or
  for one year, whichever comes first. And he will also provide for a
  resident manager on the property on or before the possession date.

Do you get the picture? This is an actual example. *This owner is a
don't wanter!* He can become one of your most valuable assets. Let's look
more closely at this fascinating creature.

CHAPTER FIVE

The Don't-Wanter Seller: You Pick the Price
and the Terms

WHAT IS a don't wanter?

A don't wanter is a person who will do anything to get rid of his property. Like the person in the previous example, he will take a personal note secured against nothing but your signature. He will take your stereo or your recreation lot in southern Nevada. He will take your Ford pickup. He will take anything, because he needs to act now. He wants out!

This is the kind of seller you need to do business with. He won't care if your Master Charge account is overdrawn, because he won't even check your credit. He's irrational. He is flexible. Don't wanters are on their knees every night praying for deliverance, and you could be the answer to their prayers.

How many don't wanters are there? Even in extremely tight sellers' markets there are still plenty of don't wanters. Perhaps 10 percent of all sellers are willing to be flexible enough to be called don't wanters. Most neophyte investors get discouraged early because they haven't learned that 90 percent of the sellers are not flexible. They need to be dealing with the 10 percent who are don't wanters.

One word of caution. Sometimes a don't wanter is a don't wanter for a very legitimate reason. Sometimes the problems that go with a property aren't easily solved. If you are not careful in analyzing what has made the seller a don't wanter, you could buy the property and end up being a don't wanter for the very same reasons!

But often a don't wanter's problems aren't as serious as he perceives them. They're only serious to the owner's situation, and you may be able to overcome them quite easily.

What makes someone a don't wanter?

Management problems lead the list of reasons why people want to sell their property. Some people cannot deal with tenants on a daily basis; they bought the property hoping to make a profit and didn't anticipate management problems.

The first multiple unit I purchased was a seven-unit building located in a fairly decent part of town on a busy street. The building was a converted home and had seven furnished apartments. Since the original structure was at least fifty years old, the plumbing was just beginning to cause weekly problems.

It took only a couple of months for me to realize that the good terms I'd received when I bought the building were the only good thing about the property. One morning at about 1:30 I was awakened by a telephone call from an upset tenant. She whispered, "Mr. Allen, I think you'd better get over here right away. The tenants in number seven are having an orgy." I rushed over immediately to find a drunken party in full progress. Since this was the third time this had happened, I called the police and went home.

All that summer I received similar complaints once or twice a week. "Mr. Allen, Ben in number three is running a heroin operation. He's smoking marijuana right now. I think that you should do something before he harms one of us."

"Mr. Allen, the unwed mother in number seven is having a brawl with her friends on the lawn."

"Mr. Allen, the girl in number six moved out in the middle of the night without paying her rent for the last two months."

"Mr. Allen, someone broke into our apartment last night and stole our television set." (As it turned out, Ben in number three, my resident manager, who *was* running a heroin operation, was arrested two days later with the television set in his possession. He was stealing from the tenants to help buy heroin.)

"Mr. Allen, I'm moving out of here unless you ask the people in number seven to leave immediately."

The last straw was when I cosigned with my trustworthy Ben of number three on a $200 loan to help him buy a pickup truck. Of course, I had no idea that he had been stealing things from other tenants. When the police caught him with the stolen TV set they gave him two alternatives: either he leave town before the sun set, or he go to jail. And so, he left town that night. In my truck! Every month when I made out that $22 check to pay for the small loan I had cosigned on, I remembered the seven-unit building, and I swore I would never get involved in another situation like that. I was a don't wanter.

Early that fall I put the building on the market for exactly the same price I had paid for it eighteen months earlier. I was suffering from a severe advanced case of don't wanteritis. I wanted to get rid of my property at all costs. Luckily I found someone to buy the building and cash out my equity.

But this decision was irrational. Rather than selling, I should have solved the real problem which was the management of the property. I did not know how to manage. I would have been much better off to keep the property and turn the management over to a professional management company. This same property which I so hastily sold for $69,000 three years ago, sold again, one year after I sold it, for $85,000. It then sold again for $106,000. And now, it is on the market again. What's the new asking price? $129,500! And someone will come along and pay it. A don't wanter is very often short-sighted and concentrates only on his immediate problem. If I had realized my problem and solved it without selling, I would have made $60,000!

Other management problems include:

—Vacancy problems (your tenants move into a competitor's apartment).

—Tenant problems (your tenants refuse to pay the rent).

—Anticipated future expenses (old water heaters need replacing).

—Distance factor (the owner is an absentee landlord living in a neighboring state; whenever there is a problem, he has to travel to solve it).

—Time problems (the owner is an extremely busy man; his wife tells him it is either his family or his apartment building).

There is a very simple solution to the management problem. Every city has access to professional management, and the services are listed in the Yellow Pages under professional property management. For a fee— usually 5 to 10 percent of the gross income—the professionals will take responsibility for the maintenance, collect the rents, handle minor and major problems, evict bad tenants, advertise the building, and handle bookkeeping. In short, they do everything. If you are short on time, the management company route may be just what you are looking for.

Financial headaches can turn any owner into a don't wanter. Maybe he's been hit with a tax bill he wasn't expecting, he has discovered another, better investment and needs cash to make the move, or maybe he's in trouble—needs to reduce indebtedness, pay a note that is coming due, or save himself from foreclosure. With experience you'll be able to recognize this symptom of "don't wanteritis." This kind of owner will usually negotiate willingly just to move his property quickly.

The first twelve-unit building I purchased was owned by an attorney. He had recently bought his other partners out by placing a heavy wrap-around mortgage on the building. The time required to manage the property, coupled with the unit's $300 monthly negative cash flow, made him a serious don't wanter. My required down payment was less than $4,500 with a $135,000 mortgage. I promptly raised the rents and did some minor repairs and cosmetic work with the paint. Now the building carries itself, and next year I hope to have a small positive cash flow. The reason I was able to get such a good deal was my understanding of the attorney's problem, which was largely financial. He simply couldn't continue to feed his monthly alligator and still make ends meet with his family obligations. He was a perfect example of a don't wanter.

A third reason an owner becomes a don't wanter is because his property is suffering from physical problems—the building doesn't meet fire codes, the plumbing is deteriorating, or the parking lot is too small. Other physical problems are:

—The competition next door (all the units next to yours have been installing new swimming pools to attract new tenants; it's working— they're attracting your tenants).

—Age of the building (structural elements or appliances may need replacing at great expense to the owner).

—Location (the neighborhood is going to the dogs, and you're the only turkey left).

—Functional obsolescence (appraisers use this term to describe the particular faults of a building that will not be easily corrected: high ceilings, lack of electrical outlets, or small units, for example).

Buyer beware. <u>Physical problems are the most serious that confront owners.</u> When you solve the problem of the don't wanter by buying his dilapidating building, you may end up making his incurable problem *your* incurable problem.

Individual owners have all sorts of personal problems, either real or imaginary, which cause them to want to sell their property. Foremost among these are:

—Retirement (the seller decides he has worked long enough: it's about time he sold his rental units and lived in the manner that he always wanted to get accustomed to).

—Health (some owners who have actively managed their own real estate portfolios may suddenly find that their health is so bad that they can't leave the house; one such owner refused to relinquish management of her lifetime investment, and she ran the business out of her home. Unfortunately, the units rapidly became the slum area of town due to lack of attention, and her children were forced to take over management themselves to avoid catastrophe. They became don't wanters when they saw the units' state of disrepair).

—Social activities and status improvement (some owners would rather have the money than the investments; they sell to buy a better lifestyle for themselves).

—Transfers (when a property owner is transferred to a new location, he must dispose of all his holdings unless he plans to manage them from a distance; this gives a buyer the opportunity to buy the property at distressed prices).

I have discovered more good buys as the result of dissatisfied partners in partnerships than as the result of any other kind of problem. In such a situation, the property isn't bad—the partnership is bad. The partners disagree about how funds should be spent or dispersed as dividends; one partner wants to sell, while the other partner can't because of tax problems. A don't-wanter partner will do almost anything to get out of a bad relationship.

Recently I was involved in the sale of a beautiful twelve-unit apartment building in an excellent location. The two partners had decided to sell; each of them wanted to keep the building, but neither could tolerate the other. Neither of them would allow the other partner to buy him out for fear of being cheated. They put the property on the market, and I was there immediately with an offer they accepted. They knew that the property was worth more than the price we agreed on, but each of them realized they could go on no longer. They sold for a price that was $30,000 under market, but they solved their problem.

Every fisherman has his "big fish that got away" story, and I have my "great deal that fell through" story. A partnership of seven brothers and sisters were left with a conglomeration of over forty apartment units in one small Utah town. They were living in different cities all over the West and had no way to manage the property effectively. They jointly decided that they would not sell the property to any family member for fear of what the future might bring. In addition, none of them wanted to be responsible for any litigation should anything happen to one of their tenants. They had sold the buildings once before, but the buyer had gone belly up in another enterprise and could not keep the units; the brothers and sisters reluctantly proceeded to try to sell the units again. They were serious don't wanters. The symptoms were all there: they were willing to sell for 30 percent below the appraised price, willing to subordinate their interest to a second trust deed secured by other property, willing to deliver free and clear title to their property, willing to close immediately, and willing to sell with 10 percent down and carry the rest on excellent terms with 7 percent interest. They were willing to do almost anything to get rid of the property. They knew that the property was worth more than the eventual sales price, but that was of little consequence—they were don't wanters; they didn't want the property.

Due to my heavy time commitments and due to a very conservative banker (who, by the way, is no longer my banker), I wasn't able to secure a loan for the down payment and the money necessary for repairs to bring the units up to rentable condition. I calculate that my banker cost me at least $35,000 in lost profit. (That is why he is no longer my banker.)

Another similar don't-wanter problem results when an owner dies and the property is divided among his heirs.

Heirs usually don't know the real value of the property they have inherited, and since it is just a gift anyway, they are sometimes inclined to give good prices for property they don't know what to do with. Many heirs also end up owning a piece of a larger property which, in order to simplify things, they sell at a reduced price for cash.

Keep your eye out for good property that is being sold because of partnership problems—a family that can't agree on terms, a group who have become heirs to an estate, or property splits caused by a divorce. It's probably not a good idea to go into partnership yourself in an already poor situation, but you can often make an offer and take the disputed property off their hands—at a good price!

Whenever you get involved with a don't wanter, you must be sure that the problems you are buying are solvable; otherwise, you'll end up being a don't wanter for the very same piece of property and the very same reason.

When you recognize why the owner is a don't wanter, ask yourself, "Is this problem real or imaginary?" If the problem is real, consider whether it can be solved by a new owner. Realize that certain problems are not solvable. Sometimes the neighborhood is bad, sometimes the building has deteriorated too far. Use your best judgment, and don't take on someone else's incurable problems.

Now you know how to *recognize* a bargain. How do you go about *finding* one?

The first source, of course, is a realtor. I consider realtors so important that I have discussed them in detail in Chapter Eight. But what are other sources?

The classified ad section of your local newspaper lists all of the don't wanters in town. *Isn't the newspaper just a collection of "cries for help"?* People are paying good money to let you know they want to sell. Most of the people advertising won't have what you need, but I can guarantee you that at least one out of ten has a good piece of property and wants to sell it badly enough that he will lower his price drastically for your all-cash offer! Try it. Respond to every ad in the paper one night, and make all-cash offers at least 20 percent below the advertised price on every property. Even if you have no cash, you will have satisfied yourself that such bargains do exist. You can then do some serious searching and secure enough money to take advantage of the best buys. *I guarantee you'll run out of cash before you run out of good properties to buy!*

The newspaper is your cheapest and most productive tool for finding properties for sale. Use it wisely and often. You might even consider running an ad yourself. Try something like this:

> I want to buy your house or investment property! Don't call unless you need to sell immediately and are willing to accept my small down payment. I can take possession immediately. Your investment will be secured by equities in other properties. Call Bob, daytime only, 555–1978.

You probably won't have a lot of response, but when someone *does* call, you'll know the caller is genuinely interested, and you'll be able to close if you want to. Run the ad in the *Real Estate Wanted* section of your newspaper. Yours won't be the only ad there, so write creative copy that will attract callers. It only takes one transaction to repay all of your advertising costs.

Pay attention to FOR SALE BY OWNER signs. When you see one, make a habit of stopping and asking the owner about the details of the sale. Don't be afraid to stop; the fact that the property has a sign on it is an indication that the owner welcomes passersby to stop and inquire. Walk in, inspect the property, and ask every question you can think of. It's the best free education available. When the property sells and the sign comes down, stop again and ask the new owner about the terms and conditions of the purchase. And, of course, if you should happen to find a bargain, buy it yourself!

Another good source is to establish a *listing farm.* Realtors choose one area of town they feel they can service well, and they contact every property owner in that area. They tell the owners that they are specializing in properties in that particular area, and they offer to help property owners either buy or sell property. The realtor will then visit each owner occasionally to learn about recent sales in the area and to discover any imminent plans to sell.

The listing farm is a very successful technique for the realtors, and it could be useful to the real estate buyer as well. You can call it your "buying farm." Find a neighborhood you're interested in, and circulate a flyer similar to this one:

> Property owners! I buy real estate. If you are planning to sell in the near future call me before you list with a realtor. I just might be able to save you a commission and the anxiety of waiting for the right buyer to come along. Call Bob at 555–1978.

You can find a wealth of information in your local county courthouse. Look at legal notices filed on the bulletin board. They will list individuals and companies who have had judgments rendered against them, who have had properties foreclosed, or who are behind on their payments. The same location should list individuals who are seriously delinquent in payment of property taxes. All of these people are don't wanters; most would welcome your help.

Another good source of don't wanters is the divorce file. Look for recent divorces. You can examine the complete files, which give information about property jointly owned (and probably available for sale).

Compile a list of recent divorce filings and addresses of the parties involved. Then try sending each individual a letter that reads something like this:

> Dear _____: I understand that you have had some recent changes in your life and that you may need to sell some of your

property. I buy real estate and will be more than happy to make an offer on your property. If you are interested, please call at your earliest convenience.

Sincerely, Bob Allen 555–1978

You will also be able to obtain at the courthouse the addresses of individuals who own property in your buying farm. You may want to send each of them a letter expressing your interest in buying their property. If you want to see what a property looks like on the official plats of the county, tell the county recorder. Be sure to ask questions; it's the only way you learn.

Still another good way to find bargains is to search the commercial record, a publication that lists all of the divorces, judgments, bankruptcies, foreclosures, deaths, and probates for the benefit of attorneys and title companies. The commercial record costs as little as $100 annually and can be a very valuable listing of don't wanters. Ask your attorney if he knows about such a publication. Check into the possibility of getting used copies from your attorney or title company. Most public libraries have copies for use.

Talk to as many attorneys and accountants as you can. The first person a seller talks to about selling his property is usually his accountant or lawyer. My accountant calls me regularly with news of good properties because I let him know that I was interested in buying real estate. And be sure to let all your friends and acquaintances know you're interested— one might give you a good lead. Some people distribute printed cards that say:

I BUY REAL ESTATE.
CALL BOB, 555–1978

If you are really creative, try T-shirts and bumper stickers. Or contact your local apartment owner's association for a list of all apartment owners in your city. Contact them all, one by one, and explore the possibilities. Some people even try billboards.

Those of you who have teenage children might try involving them in the search for your real estate. It's a great training for adulthood, and they could get really excited if you paid them a couple of hundred dollars for every super buy they located. I have used students between semesters or in the summer months to act as finders for me in locating real estate. These college students learn quickly and can make excellent money while they help you reach your financial goals. If you are extremely busy in your present job, this might be just what you need.

There are hundreds of ways to find out where property is for sale. Just remember that only a certain percentage of the property on the market will be right for you. Don't get discouraged; don't get overanxious; your money will run out before the opportunity does.

Keep looking. Keep prospecting. Spend a few minutes a day on a regular schedule, and you're bound to discover a vein of pure gold if you just keep at it!

CHAPTER SIX

Financial Analysis: The Numbers Tell an Important Story

Tʜᴇ ꜰᴏᴜʀᴛʜ major element in finding a good buy is financial analysis. Let's examine an income-producing piece of real estate to see how it operates. It's really not that difficult. The figures I use may not be representative of your particular area, but the principles I use should apply anywhere.

Our example, a five-unit apartment building, is well located in a growing city; the rental situation is excellent because the building is in good condition. Each has two bedrooms and one and three-quarter baths and is rented for $250 a month. The renter pays the electric and gas bills.

How do you determine if the investment is a good one? To help with our analysis, consult the *cash flow analysis* form on page 56. This shows the annual property operating data. The top one-third provides space for all of the important data you will need to learn about the property: the purchase price is $100,000; there is an existing loan of $60,000 with monthly payments of $504. (All figures are rounded to the nearest dollar.) The seller's equity (the difference between the sales price or value and the existing loan) is $40,000, but the seller has agreed to sell the building to us with a down payment of $10,000. This will result in a new loan of $90,000. Payments over a twenty-five-year period with an interest rate of 9.25 percent will be $771 a month. The seller's situation is illustrated at left; our new situation is on the right in the following illustration.

Annual Property Operating Data

Purpose _____   Date __August 18_____

Name __Ridgeview Apartments__

Location __1005 Apartment Row__   Price $ __100,000__

Type of Property __5 units__   Loans $ __60,000__

Assessed/Appraised Values   Equity $ __40,000__

Land	$ __4,000__	__20__ %		
Improvement	$ __16,000__	__80__ %		
Personal Property	$ _____	____ %		
Total	$ __20,000__	__100__ %		

FINANCING

	Balance	Payment	Period	Interest	Term
Existing $	60,000	504	mo.	9 %	20 yrs
1st $				%	
2nd $				%	
3rd $				%	
Potential					
1st $	90,000	771	mo.	9.25 %	25 yrs
2nd $				%	

Adjusted Basis as of _____ $ _____

		%	2	3	Comments
1	GROSS SCHEDULED RENTAL INCOME			15 000	5 x 250 x 12
2	Plus: Other Income			180	
3	TOTAL GROSS INCOME			15 180	
4	Less: Vacancy and Credit Losses	5%		750	
5	GROSS OPERATING INCOME			14 430	
6	Less: Operating Expenses				
7	Accounting and Legal		100		
8	Advertising, Licenses and Permits		150		
9	Property Insurance		200		
10	Property Management	5%	722		
11	Payroll - Resident Management		360		
12	Other				
13	Taxes-Workmen's Compensation				
14	Personal Property Taxes		1 000		
15	Real Estate Taxes				
16	Repairs and Maintenance	5%	750		
17	Services - Elevator				
18	Janitorial				
19	Lawn _mgt. firm and resident				
20	Pool mgr. do this				
21	Rubbish -tenant pays				
22	Other				
23	Supplies	1%	150		
24	Utilities - Electricity -tenant pays				
25	Gas and Oil " "				
26	Sewer and Water		1 200		
27	Telephone				
28	Other				
29	Miscellaneous		200		
30					
31	TOTAL OPERATING EXPENSES	34		4 832	
32	NET OPERATING INCOME			9 598	
33	Less: Total Annual Debt Service			9 252	771 x 12
34	CASH FLOW BEFORE TAXES			346	

The statements and figures presented herein, while not guaranteed, are secured from sources we believe authoritative.   Prepared by_____

$40,000 SELLERS EQUITY

$100,000 VALUE

$10,000 DOWN PAYMENT

$100,000 VALUE

$60,000 FIRST MORTGAGE

$90,000 CONTRACT OF SALE

$60,000 FIRST MORTGAGE

BEFORE   **AFTER**

5-UNIT APARTMENT BUILDING

This type of sale is referred to as a Uniform Real Estate Contract, a Land Sales Contract, a Wrap-Around Mortgage, or "Seller Carries the Financing" depending on which area of the country you are in. The seller receives monthly payments of $771 from us (the buyer) on the new loan; with this, he makes the monthly payment of $504 on the existing loan of $60,000. The difference of $267 a month belongs to the seller as a repayment of the $30,000 equity, which he does not receive in cash at the time of the sale. The seller has an advantage, because we make payments to him based on a 9.25 percent interest rate, while he only has to pay 9 percent on his loan. This spread in interest rate sometimes prompts a seller to accept a lower down payment with a contract sale, especially if the spread is great. Under certain circumstances he will also receive substantial tax benefits (installment sale) if he does not receive his equity in cash. These two benefits often help the buyer who doesn't have a lot of cash to invest.

Our seller has agreed to accept a small down payment (10 percent) and to have the rest of his equity paid to him over a twenty-five-year period.

We have also found out that the property has an assessed value for tax purposes as follows:

Land	$ 4,000	20 percent of value
Improvements	16,000	80 percent of value
Total	$20,000	100 percent of value

You can obtain this information, which is important for computing individual tax return consequences, by looking at the county tax notice the seller should have in his files. If the seller doesn't have the information, call the county tax assessor and ask for the assessed value of the property. He'll give you a projection for the coming year's taxes. You will notice that the assessed value is different from the actual value of the property. Each state has a different method of calculating property taxes, but generally the county assessor determines an assessed value for each property, which is sometimes four to five times less than the appraised market value. This assessed value is the figure that is used to calculate the county taxes.

After you have obtained from the seller the information for the first one-third of the form, gather information for the income and expense analysis (lines 1 through 34). This information is vital and *must* be verified whenever possible. The seller usually doesn't have readily available financial data on the operation of his building. He may estimate, projecting figures far from reality. He might not be lying (although this could be the case), but the tendency is to project high rents and low expenses, neither of which is accurate. After all, he wants to portray a positive situation to the buyer. Therefore, be wary of the seller's figures; double check *everything* yourself. If possible, try to obtain the seller's income tax records. The tax records will probably be closer to the truth; the seller will have the tendency to report the lowest income and the highest expenses. The seller may balk at showing you these records, but it doesn't hurt to ask.

Let's examine each of the items in the Annual Property Operating Data form on page 56 to see how each is calculated:

1. *Gross Scheduled Rental Income.* This is the amount of income the property would generate if the building were rented all year with no vacancies. In our example our five-unit building is rented for $250 per apartment.

$$\$250 \times 5 = \$1,250 \text{ monthly income}$$
$$\$1,250 \times 12 = \$15,000 \text{ yearly income}$$

If every apartment in the building was rented all year, you could expect to collect $15,000 in rents.

2. *Other Income.* This income may be vending machines (from soft drink, candy, or laundry machines), furniture rental, pet fees, rental of parking spaces (covered or uncovered), or forfeited deposits. In our example, the building has a small candy vending machine that generates about $15 a month net profit. Yearly income from this source is $180.

3. *Total Gross Income.* List here the total of all money collected from the operation of the building—add lines 1 and 2.

4. *Less Vacancy and Credit Losses.* Unless you are in an extremely tight rental market, your building will always have some vacancy. Even if the seller tells you that he hasn't had a vacancy in three years, you should impute a 3–5 percent vacancy rate on the gross scheduled income to account for lost days in rent between tenants or lost income when one of the tenants moves out in the middle of the night without paying the rent. It is almost impossible to have 100 percent rent collection, so plan accordingly.

There may be some markets where overbuilding of apartments has occurred. In this case, you should call up your local rental agency or several professional property management companies (listed in the Yellow Pages of the phone book under Real Estate Rental Services and Property Management Firms). These people are experts in the field and will be able to give you valuable and free information concerning current rental rates and current vacancy rates in various areas of your city. You can also do your own rental and vacancy study by asking other area resident managers some pertinent questions about their rental projects. But seek professional advice early so that you cut your risk and increase your safety.

5. *Gross Operating Income.* After vacancy and credit losses are subtracted from the gross income, you know the total amount of income this property should generate in a year's time.

6. *Operating Expenses.* Subtract all of the expenses you will incur during the year from the gross operating income. These operating expenses include:

Accounting and legal
Advertising, licenses, and permits
Property insurance
Property management

Payroll and resident management
Taxes
Repairs and maintenance
Services
Supplies
Utilities

7. *Accounting and Legal.* Make an estimate here based on your own situation. In our example, we have included $100 for an accountant to balance our books at the end of the year.

8. *Advertising, Licenses, and Permits.* This expense will vary from state to state and will depend on the various laws and rental markets. We have made provision here for 1 percent of the gross scheduled income to be used for these purposes.

9. *Property Insurance.* The seller may let you assume the existing insurance on the property. It would be wiser, however, to have your own insurance agent make a bid; the seller may have underinsured the property, and the building may not be fully protected. It pays to have several insurance bids; you will be amazed at the difference in rates. Bids are free, so you have nothing to lose.

10. *Property Management.* If you plan to manage the property yourself, you will not have to include any fee here for outside professional management services. Although fees for such service vary from state to state, they range from 5 to 10 percent of the gross operating income. If you own many units, your rates can be negotiated even lower.

As soon as you can afford it, I would recommend that you hire a professional management firm. Such a firm takes care of everything that has to do with operating the property, including the collection of rents, payments for expenses, and mortgage payments. If requested, the firm will send you a check each month with an accounting of all expenses and income. You never have to worry about plugged toilets or leaking roofs; your management company will take care of everything and will call you only for major decisions, if that's what you want. In addition, they have paid maintenance men on the staff or have connections for the lowest rates in town. They can even purchase supplies at wholesale prices.

For the first several months it's a good idea to manage your own property so that you can see the problems of managing an apartment building. One of the best books on the market about property management is Albert J. Lowry's book entitled *How to Manage Real Estate Successfully—in Your Spare Time* published by Simon and Schuster. If you plan on managing your own properties, reading this book is a *must!* As you grow, you can turn over all of the headaches (and believe me, there are headaches!) to a professional company. The professionals know their business, and you should begin to use them as soon as you have experience and can afford their services. They can save you precious time and money. In our example, I have included professional management at 5 percent.

11, 12, 13. *Payroll and Resident Management.* The larger the apartment building, the more people you will need on your staff. Up to about twenty-five apartment units, you can probably expect your resident manager to handle all minor repairs and problems. The resident manager should be trained to collect rents and handle minor problems without calling in outside help; it's important to find a handyman for this position. His salary should be enough to motivate him to do his job well. You may pay as little as $25 a month off the rent or as much as free rent plus a small salary. This will depend on your area. In our example, we have a resident manager who receives $30 off his rent for the services he provides. This amount is *not* paid by the management company—it is paid by you, although the management company handles the mechanical aspect of giving him the money and will train him.

14, 15. *Taxes.* Depending on your county, you will have to pay both personal property taxes and real estate taxes. You can determine what your current tax bill will be by calling the county assessor and asking for the tax assessment for the current year. Don't rely on your seller's past year's taxes. In many cases the taxes and insurance payments are paid monthly as a part of the mortgage payment; know what your mortgage payment includes, or you will be deducting these expenses twice.

16. *Repairs and Maintenance.* These expenses usually amount to between 5 and 10 percent of the gross operating income. On newer buildings the figure will be closer to 5 percent; it will be closer to 10 percent on older buildings. Try to obtain the seller's receipts for repairs during the past several years so you can see the trend. For our example, repairs were calculated at 5 percent.

17–22. *Services.* Each of these expenses should be verified as closely as possible. Calls to various experts can help immensely; check with the firms that are currently providing the service to the seller. In our example, the resident manager takes care of the lawn.

23. *Supplies.* There is always a need for small items such as tools, faucet rings, fertilizer, and so on. You should budget about 1 percent of your gross operating income for such expenditures. After a year's operation you can make a more accurate projection. You may give your resident manager a small petty cash fund so he can take care of these small items without having to bother you; if your property is professionally managed, all of these items will be handled through the management firm.

24–28. *Utilities.* Cost of each utility item should be verified by going to the local agency and asking for the past several years' utilities records for the building. In my area the gas company will give you (with the seller's permission) a computer printout of the past eighteen months' gas bills. This can reveal any trends and can help you make projections for the coming year. In our example, I have made an estimate for water and sewer expenses. The tenants pay for their own electricity, gas, and garbage collection.

29, 30. *Miscellaneous.* This is just an estimate of expenses which have not been included in other categories. It will amount to at least 1 percent of gross scheduled income.

31. *Total Operation Expenses.* A total of all expenses is made here. The ratio of expenses to total operating income is an important figure. Across the country this ratio varies from 30 to 50 percent. In other words, from 30 to 50 percent of your total collected income will eventually be paid out as operating expenses. If the seller gives you a projection for expenses that is lower than 30 percent, something is not right somewhere. It is possible to have expenses lower than 30 percent if the building is new and if the tenants pay all of their own utilities; such a situation is rare. If property taxes are high in your state, your expense ratio will be higher. I have used about 34 percent expense ratio in our example because of my own experience with my units. Check with your local management firm to determine what your local expense ratio will be.

32. *Net Operating Income.* Subtract all your expenses (line 31) from your gross operating income. What's left is called net operating income. If you have been conservative in your projection and have verified as many figures as possible, this net operating income will be the amount of money you should collect for a year's operation of the building—before paying the mortgage payment. This figure is a critical one in judging the value of the investment as you will see later.

33. *Total Annual Debt Service or Mortgage Payments.* Monthly mortgage payments multiplied by twelve will total the debt service figure.

34. *Cash Flow Before Taxes.* After all expenses and mortgage payments have been figured, you should have a small cash flow.

By filling out the Annual Property Operating Data form on our subject property, we have learned some of the valuable information needed to make a good investment. Your projection should be conservative, based on conservative information. First of all, we have collected *all* of the necessary information needed to enable us to make a wise decision based on costs. The figures have all been verified and are conservative. This one sheet is all that any investor needs to do a preliminary investment analysis. Blank copies of this form are available through the National Association of Realtors, 430 North Michigan Avenue, Chicago, Illinois, 60611. Ask for a pad of APOD forms.

Second, we have been able to determine if there is a positive or a negative cash flow on this property. Just like in a land investment, it is possible to have a negative cash flow—an alligator—in an income property. If the mortgage payments are too high because of small down payments or if the expenses are inordinately high because the building is an older one (or income is very low due to low rents), there could be a negative cash flow. The only way to eliminate a negative cash flow is to restructure the mortgage payments, pay less for the property, increase the rents, or lower the expenses. More on this later.

If you determine after your analysis that the property has a heavy negative cash flow, and it will not be possible to raise rents in the immediate future, you will have to be prepared to subsidize your investment on a monthly basis until the cash flow can be improved. If you are not prepared to subsidize the investment, then don't buy the property. It is better not to buy something than to lose it to foreclosure for failure to make the payments.

The bottom line of the analysis form tells how much debt you can amortize without going in the hole.

In short, make sure you do your homework at this stage of your investment planning. You will avoid costly mistakes later.

CHAPTER SEVEN

It's Fun Figuring Out How Much Money
You're Going to Make

Now THAT you've determined what kind of a cash flow will exist, find out what return you'll receive on your investment (ROI). Let's use the same example: we have invested $10,000 as a down payment toward the purchase price of the five-unit building. If we had taken the same $10,000 and invested it in a savings account at a local bank, we may have earned up to 8 percent on the $10,000 for one year. How well does real estate compare to a savings account's guaranteed return of 8 percent?

There are four kinds of return from a normal income property investment:

1. Cash flow is money left over after all expenses and mortgage payments have been made.

2. Equity buildup results as mortgage payments gradually reduce the loan—a return on invested dollars.

3. Tax savings come from the favorable tax advantages of owning real estate.

4. Appreciation develops as the property (if well selected) increases in value over time.

If we analyze the five-unit building with respect to these four kinds of investment return, we discover some interesting figures that will answer our questions about real estate versus savings accounts.

1. *Cash Flow.*

$$\frac{\text{Annual Net Cash Flow}}{\text{Down Payment}} = \frac{\$346}{\$10,000} = 3.5 \text{ percent}$$

This kind of cash on cash return seems extremely low. After all, you can go to the bank and get 8 percent without any trouble at all. But let's keep going.

2. *Equity Buildup.* As the mortgage payments of $771 are made each month, a portion applies toward the reduction of the $90,000 loan. Using a calculator with special functions (Hewlett Packard and Texas Instruments both make excellent calculators for real estate math), it is possible to determine that at the end of the first year of ownership and after paying the interest, the loan balance will be $89,036. If you then sold the building you would collect the $964 in principal reduction that took place during your ownership of the property. This is a return on investment that amounts to 9.6 percent. That's a little better. Keep going.

$$\frac{\text{Loan Principal Reduction}}{\text{Down Payment}} = \frac{\$964}{\$10,000} = 9.6 \text{ percent}$$

3. *Tax Savings.* Real estate is one of the few remaining tax shelters in the United States. The 1976 tax reform act slashed all other tax shelters but left real estate relatively untouched. Consequently, there has been an increased demand for real estate investments in the past few years. The government has encouraged taxpayers to invest in buildings for business purposes such as offices, apartments, and commercial stores. Then Uncle Sam lets the real estate investor pretend that the building he buys (not the land, though) actually wears out over the life of the ownership and therefore loses value from year to year. This "wearing out" process is called depreciation.

In our example, the value of the total investment was $100,000, but only a certain percentage of this total cost can be attributed to the building. The rest must be allocated to the land on which the building stands. In our example, the county tax assessment reveals that 80 percent of the value for county tax purposes is attributed to the building and 20 percent is attributed to the land. Using this same proportion, we can determine that the building has an assessed value of $80,000 ($100,000 × .80) and the land is worth $20,000. The Internal Revenue Service has a schedule detailing useful lives for different types of buildings. A well-constructed commercial or apartment building has a useful life of forty years. Since this building is an apartment building that is about fifteen years old, the Internal Revenue Service would probably allow a twenty-five year remaining life to the building. The $80,000 building will then lose value each year as far as the IRS is concerned until at the end of twenty-five years it will have a value (only to the IRS) of zero. If we divide twenty-five years into $80,000, we see that each year the apartment building will lose $3,200 in depreciation; the IRS lets the investor deduct this depreciation as a loss from the income generated from operation of the apartment building.

The IRS also permits the investor to deduct the amount of interest paid on the mortgage loan, but not the principal.

To arrive at the total loss allowable by the IRS, calculate the following:

Cash Flow	$346
Plus: Equity Buildup	$964
Less: Depreciation	($3,200)
TOTAL LOSS	($1,890)

Therefore, even though you put $346 cash flow into your pocket and the loan went down by $964, you do not have to pay any income tax. What's more, the IRS assumes that the $1,890 loss from the building can be applied against your other income; this will reduce your tax on income derived from other sources. If you owned enough real estate that had substantial depreciation losses each year, you could write off almost all of your salary income and end up paying no income taxes at all!

This is the beauty of real estate: the more you own, the lower your income taxes can be. The benefit of depreciation and tax shelter comes when you file your yearly income tax return. If you pay 30 percent of your taxable income to the government as taxes, then for each dollar of depreciation loss you apply against your income, you will save $.30. In our example there was an $1,890 tax loss from the apartment building. Multiply $1,890 by 30 percent: you'll save $567 in income taxes. Since this is a return on (a benefit from) your investment, include it in your return on investment:

$$\frac{\text{Tax Savings}}{\text{Down Payment}} = \frac{\$567}{\$10,000} = 5.8 \text{ percent}$$

This still doesn't seem like much of a return. Keep going.

4. *Appreciation.* Appreciation is where the real money is made in real estate investing. It is not possible to accurately project the increase in property values, since the increase depends on inflation, investor demand, and supply of available units. But with inflation of at least 6 percent for the next few years, a 10 percent rate of increase in value is completely

reasonable. Actually, many of my units have increased at 20 to 30 percent annually. If appreciation rates change, so will your rate of return. But let's conservatively figure an appreciation rate of 10 percent. Our investment return is 100 percent!

$$\frac{\text{Rate of Increase in Value} \times \text{Purchase Price}}{\text{Down Payment}} = \frac{10\% \times \$100,000}{\$10,000} = 100 \text{ percent}$$

When all of the above rates of return are combined, your total rate of return from this real estate investment looks like this:

Cash Flow	3.5 percent
Equity Buildup	9.6 percent
Tax Savings	5.8 percent
Appreciation	100.0 percent
TOTAL RETURN	118.9 percent

That's right! ONE HUNDRED AND EIGHTEEN PERCENT. Compared to your 8 percent return at the bank, 118 percent looks rather exciting. This is, of course, your return on investment in the first year of ownership. The ROI will decline each year thereafter, although slowly.

If you had invested your dollars at the bank, you would have $10,800 at the end of the year. By investing the same amount of money in an apartment building, your $10,000 has grown into $21,877. Of course, the 8 percent in the bank is guaranteed and is paid without management hassle: you know—without fail—that your money will be there at the end of the year. You won't have to lift a finger to earn it. But you can put up with an awful lot of hassle to get the returns that real estate can earn.

Safe as it may be, there is no profit in keeping your money in a savings account (unless you are waiting for the right real estate investment), because inflation and taxes render your investment useless. You must take the risk that real estate investment requires: you must cope with management problems (or give them to a management company for a fee); you must learn that your financial independence comes at a price, but the price is well worth it. Nothing worth anything is free.

Two final elements need to be considered in an analysis of a real estate investment: the power of leverage and the determination of value.

Leverage makes real estate advantageous. Think of using a small lever to move a large boulder. You could never move the boulder by yourself;

use a lever, and the job's easy. Leverage in real estate is the ability to control a large number of investment dollars with a small amount of money. Without leverage the $100,000 investment in our example would not have been nearly as exciting.

In the example, you could control $100,000 worth of real estate with only $10,000. You borrowed the other $90,000 from other people or you used other people's money. If you had purchased the building with your own money—$100,000 cash—then your return on your investment would have been very different.

Cash Flow without mortgage payments:

$$\frac{\$9,598}{\$100,000} = 9.6 \text{ percent}$$

Equity Buildup: Since there is no mortgage, there is no equity buildup.

Tax Savings:	$9,598	cash flow less depreciation of $3,200 =
	$6,398	taxable income × 30 percent tax bracket =
	$1,919	taxes owed, or a negative 1.9 percent

$$\frac{(\$1,919)}{\$100,000} = -1.9 \text{ percent}$$

Appreciation: $$\frac{\$10,000}{\$100,000} = 10 \text{ percent}$$

TOTAL RETURN: 17.7 percent

With leverage your return is 118.9 percent; without leverage, 17.7 percent. That is the power of leverage: the more you can buy with the least amount of money, the greater your rate of return. The more leverage, too, the greater the risk—an element that must be overcome. Real estate is one of the few areas where an average investor with average knowledge can borrow other people's money to use leverage in investing and, by doing so, can increase his own return. That's what the "nothing down" concept is all about.

The final area of analysis is determination of value. After all, who is to say the building you buy today for $100,000 on fairly good terms isn't really an $80,000 building? How do you make sure you're not being swindled out of $20,000? Real estate land schemes have been notorious for selling property on good terms at prices much higher than market value. One of my clients insisted on purchasing sixty acres of desert property for $20,000, a price that is still too high ten years later. How can you avoid making the same mistake?

Determination of value is accomplished through three processes known as appraisal of value. The easiest way to determine a building's accurate value is to hire a professional real estate appraiser; you will find them listed in the Yellow Pages, or you can write to the American Society of Appraisers, Dulles International Airport, P.O. Box 17265, Washington, D.C. 20041. Appraisal costs will vary from fifty to several thousand dollars, depending on the size of the property. A less expensive—and probably free—way to determine value is to ask a local realtor to do a comparative market analysis. You can do your own estimate of value by employing the same process as a professional appraiser.

Cost Approach—determine what it would cost at present rates to replace the building by talking with local building contractors.

Income Approach—determine value by analyzing the income the building generates.

Market Approach—determine what other, similar properties have sold for recently, which will give an indication what the investor in the marketplace will pay for a similar unit.

Of these three approaches, the market approach or determining the market value is the most effective method of determining value. The prize for investing in real estate goes to the investor who *knows*—not who guesses—the current market price of similar units. The more time you spend studying the market, the more you will know about market prices and the more prepared you will be to judge them. This must be a continual process; with real estate values skyrocketing in some areas of the country, you need to analyze the market every month.

Until recently, sophisticated investors usually arrived at a determination of value through the process of capitalization of the future stream of cash flow from an investment. They used this formula:

$$\text{Value} = \frac{\text{Income (Net Operating Income)}}{\text{Capitalization Rate}} \text{ or } V = \frac{I}{CR}$$

Most investors wouldn't invest in a piece of real estate unless there was at least a 10 percent capitalization rate on the investment. If a property had a net operating income of $10,000, then its value would have to be at least $100,000—or the investor wouldn't invest. This position has changed radically in the past several years. In our example, the value was $100,000 and the net operating income was only $9,598. The formula reveals a lower capitalization rate:

$$\$100,000 = \frac{\text{Rate}}{\$9,598} \quad \text{or} \quad \text{Rate} = \frac{\$9,598}{\$100,000} = 9.6 \text{ percent}$$

Therefore, the formula for determining the capitalization rate of any property is:

$$\text{Capitalization (Cap Rate)} = \frac{\text{Net Operating Income (NOI)}}{\text{Price}}$$

In some areas of the country the capitalization rates are as low as 5 percent.

So what's the trend now?

Investors are looking less to the income from a building and more toward its appreciation potential as they calculate what will provide the greatest return on their investment. In other words, many investors have begun to speculate on the increased appreciation of the properties they buy. Obviously, this trend has caused real estate prices to jump drastically. As people have expected prices automatically to increase, they have sacrificed cash flow return in anticipation of high appreciation profits. Since rents haven't kept pace with property values, cash flows from real estate are low, and can even be negative, depending on financing.

What you must remember is not to get caught up in the feverish purchase of highly overpriced properties just for the sake of investing. Each property must be carefully analyzed on its financial merits before an offer is presented or accepted. Follow the steps outlined below:

1. Determine the gross operating income of the property you are considering buying (gross yearly rents less vacancy estimate).

2. As a rough guess, estimate what percentage of your gross rents above which will be spent on expenses. As you learned earlier, this may be as low as 30 percent or as high as 50 percent. As you gain experience in your particular area you will learn how to estimate accurately. For the time being, use 40 percent until you learn if your area has a higher or lower average expense ratio. Of course, as soon as possible your estimate of annual expenses (ratio used here of 40 percent) should be replaced with the actual expense projection obtained by going into a more detailed analysis of the property operating expenses.

3. Subtract the expenses (2) from the gross operating income (1) to come up with Net Operating Income. Once you have this all-important figure, you are ready to use the capitalization formula to determine the property value.

4. Using the formula, determine the property capitalization rate. This is done as follows:

$$\frac{\text{Net Operating Income}}{\text{Seller Asking Price}} = \text{Capitalization Rate}$$

For example, if your property has a net operating income of $6,300 and the seller wants a price of $97,000 for his property, then the cap rate (shortened in real estate lingo) is:

$$\frac{\$6,300}{\$97,000} = .065 \text{ or } 6.5 \text{ percent}$$

As a general rule, in most areas of the country, the higher the cap rate the better the price of the property. If the property has a cap rate of ten or higher, you had better act fast. That property can't last long at such a price. On the other end of the scale, if a property has a cap rate of five or less, you can be sure that one of three things is wrong:
—The rents are too low.
—The expenses are too high.
—The price of the property is out of line.
You may still be safe in buying the property with a low cap rate if you are certain that you can immediately raise rents or lower expenses significantly, and therefore raise the cap rate.

Generally, however, a property with a low cap rate is being sold by an individual who is trying to make a killing in the real estate market. Make sure you don't become his victim.

The higher the cap rate, the greater the possibility of a positive cash flow even with small down payments. As the cap rate approaches 7 percent or less, the greater the possibility that you will have an alligator on your hands. Since the price of real estate is going up continually (and thereby causing lower cap rates), it is easy to see why it is more and more difficult these days to find a property with a positive cash flow. In some areas of California, some properties show a negative cash flow even after the buyer places a substantial down payment to buy the building. I am of the opinion that a once in a lifetime buy comes on the market about every seven days. I would rather be investing my time finding the best buys than spending my money feeding an alligator property which is overpriced. As a general rule then, buy if the cap rate is close to 10 percent. Be careful, if it is below 7 percent.

One last word about using the cap rate formula. It is generally very difficult to find a home, duplex or four-unit apartment building which has an adequate capitalization rate. This is not because the smaller property is not a good buy—it is because the smaller property has an additional reason for being built. The rationale for the smaller unit is to provide the owner with a way to live in his property and have renters pay enough to make the owner's mortgage payment. As a rule, it is better to rely on the market sales approach when purchasing smaller units. What have similar properties sold for recently? On properties over four units, the capitalization rate formula will begin to be more accurate.

This is a rather simplistic view of an extremely complicated subject. If you are a beginner and don't quite understand the valuation process, hire a professional appraiser, or use a realtor who knows his investment market well. The best realtor to deal with will have a CCIM designation (Certified Commercial Investment Member). This is a strenuous program of certification which is granted by the Realtors' National Marketing Institute. For a listing of all CCIM realtors in your area write RNMI, 430 North Michigan Avenue, Chicago, Illinois 60611, or call (312) 440–8000. Through practice your confidence will grow, and you will be able to make accurate market value estimates yourself.

Now a word about rules of thumb.

Each area of the country has its own special rule of thumb. For example, California uses the Gross Rent Multiplier rule of thumb quite extensively. In other words, properties are valued by multiplying the property's gross scheduled rent by a figure which is average for the area. This figure might be anywhere from five to ten or more. The gross rent multiplier for our book example is found by dividing the sales price by the gross rents: $100,000 ÷ $15,000 = 6.67. The lower the multiplier, the better the price. If the multiplier is ten or above, the price is very high.

What is important to understand about any rule of thumb that is indicative of your area of the country is this: it cannot be as accurate as the valuation process that I have outlined in this book. The capitalization rate technique is what all real estate professionals use all across the country. Do the same.

The fifth major area of analysis is the condition of the property: It goes without saying that the location should be good, the price in line with the market, the seller anxious to sell, and flexible, and the financial details favorable. However, if each of the previous four major areas gives us a green light and the property condition gives us a red light, then we should not buy. The condition of the property is extremely important. What you should be looking for as you inspect the property are areas of structural problems. Is the roof sound? Is the foundation solid? Is the plumbing and heating system adequate and in good condition? Is the electrical system working? Does the property meet current building codes? (a call to the city might help here). Are there adequate parking spaces? What about termites? In many major cities an inspection company will come in and check each of these areas for you and give you an estimate of cost to repair deficient areas. I highly recommend such an inspection. It's cheap insurance. You should not be too concerned with *cosmetic* problems. These things include: landscaping, painting, draperies, small appliances, carpets and minor repairs. The cost of these items is small in comparison to the increase in value resulting from a minor fix-up (or touch-up). Al Lowry's book, *How You Can Become Financially Independent by Investing in Real Estate* goes into more detail in this area.

With this in mind, how do you proceed? How do you gain confidence? Look at several properties each month and take note of their net operating incomes, their prices, and their other amenities. I use a comparative market analysis form whenever I do market research (see page 43). Whenever I hear of a new building that has sold I try to find out what the sale price was and what the special terms of sale were. This gives me ammunition against sellers whose prices may be out of line with the current market value. There is another benefit: if I know that two-bedroom four-unit buildings are selling for $90,000 (or $22,500 per unit) in a certain area of town, I can be on the lookout for anything priced lower. If I happen to find a seller who hasn't kept abreast of the market and has priced his building at $75,000 for a quick sale, I know I am looking at an immediate profit of $15,000—and that I had better act quickly before someone else comes along with the same intent.

I can't stress enough the importance of learning the market. Go out and compare prices. This one simple exercise will prepare you for wise investments better than any other thing you can do.

Choose several pieces of property from the classified ads. Call the owners; visit the properties. Stop whenever you see a "For Sale" sign posted on a lawn. Ask the owner questions; record the answers on your comparative analysis form. Get a feeling for which areas of town have the best and the worst properties. Always be on the lookout for a don't wanter.

In the process, you'll get the best education in the nation.

Remember: you don't need to have a lot of cash in the bank before you start your search for the right investment. Practice first: Practice makes perfect.

CHAPTER EIGHT

Help! It's Too Complicated for Me
(Putting the Professionals on Your Side)

Y OU'RE CONVINCED. Income-producing property is the wisest way to invest your money. So you venture into the marketplace and make a few feeble attempts at investment. But you encounter a problem you hadn't anticipated: you can't understand what they're all talking about.

What's a trust deed? A warrantee deed? A title policy? A legal description? A contract of sale? A land contract? A wrap-around mortgage?

Your head is swimming. A seemingly sane thought crosses your mind: maybe you'd better go back to the savings and loan or the stock market, where at least you understand the jargon.

Stop! Don't do anything foolish. There is a simple solution.

There are hundreds of experts in your area who spend their entire lives answering the kinds of questions that you need answered. And in many cases, these services are—or with ingenuity can be obtained—free of charge. You are literally surrounded by your own private team of consultants. Let's see how they can help you.

The *realtor* is one of the most important consultants on your team. This man is a wealth of information because he understands something about every phase of the real estate business. He has walked through the entire purchasing (or selling) process dozens of times. He understands the vocabulary thoroughly. He can answer any questions you have, or he can tell you where to get help.

The best service a realtor provides is market analysis. His job is to take the pulse rate of the market. He knows what properties are selling for, how fast they sell, and for what terms, and where the hottest areas are. He has access to the local board of realtors file, where he can check information on any sales made during the last two or three months.

Many real estate offices provide free appraisal services for sellers. Your realtor, then, could help you appraise properties you want to buy and could give you an estimate of market value.

A realtor is a watchdog on the lookout for bargain properties that come on the market. One of my seminar graduates recently bought a run-down one-bedroom home for $8,000 (you don't find too many like this!) because he had learned about it through his realtor and had made an offer to buy it within hours after it was placed on the market for sale. The property was thousands of dollars underpriced.

In addition to market knowledge, the realtor has information from contacts about the financial details of the purchase. He knows which banks are easiest to deal with and which loan officers most readily lend money for real estate mortgages. This information could save you hours of research and leg work.

As a source of help, a realtor is a great benefit. But don't let that blind you to some of the disadvantages of working with realtors. A realtor's services are not free. He charges a commission, so you need to be prepared to pay him if you intend to use his services. Generally, the seller pays the real estate commission, but the cash to pay the fee comes out of the buyer's down payment.

There are other drawbacks to using a realtor: According to the law of agency, the realtor is legally and morally obligated to act for and in behalf of the person with whom he has signed a contractual agreement. This person is usually the seller, who has signed a binding listing agreement usually lasting from three to six months. In exchange for his services, the real estate agent is paid a commission in cash ranging from 3 to 10 percent of the sales value. He is paid by the seller. He is working for the seller. He is under signed agreement to represent *only* the seller.

This means that a real estate agent doesn't look out for your best interests first; he represents the seller, because the seller pays him. Generally it is illegal for him even to tell you if a seller is considering lowering the price or changing the terms. He must relate to you only what has been put down in writing, only what is already in the signed listing agreement. Anything else is taboo. (Just because he is not supposed to tell you a lot of these details does not mean that he will not. Each realtor is individually responsible for upholding professional standards. Some simply do not.)

Worst of all, because the realtor is supposed to represent the seller, he is going to be reluctant to present the seller with the kinds of creative transactions you want to offer.

So what can you do? Try something very few people think of: offer a realtor a buyer's broker agreement. In simple terms, this is an agreement signed between the *buyer* and the agent. You, as buyer, agree in advance to pay the realtor a specific fee if he is able to locate for you the kind of property that you are looking for. I have included an example of a completed buyer's broker agreement for your examination on page 81; it is much like an attorney's retainer agreement.

Questions and Answers on Employing a "Buyer's Broker"

Q. Who really pays the brokerage fee in a real estate transaction?

A. While the fee or commission may be deducted from the seller's proceeds, it is really "built-in" the price and therefore is paid by the buyer. Most sellers think in terms of "net" to themselves and add on commission to their listing price or sales price.

Q. Who really receives the representation?

A. The seller, provided of course, that the broker is living up to his employment agreement (listing) as the seller's agent.

Q. Can't I (as a buyer) get representation by dealing with a broker other than the listing broker?

A. If the co-broker will receive compensation from the seller then he is legally a sub-agent of the seller and owes his allegiance to that seller. Suggesting prices below the asking price would be a violation of the Agency relationship for either broker.

Q. For which client is a broker going to devote his time, effort, ability and overhead?

A. In representing sellers, the broker spends most of his time on exclusively listed properties and little or no time on open listings or uncontrolled situations. The broker who has been employed (under contract) by a buyer to locate a specific or non specific property will concentrate his time to fulfill this obligation. A good broker will spend little time and effort with uncontrolled buyers who are shopping with every other broker and "for sale by owner" in town. In this latter case he will only try to sell his own exclusive listings.

Q. Under a "Buyer's Broker" contract, can my agent collect two fees?

A. No! The contract precludes the broker from accepting a fee from anyone other than his client. The transaction is on a "net" basis to the seller with the "Buyer's Broker" negotiating the best possible price. The buyer then evaluates the benefits to be obtained in view of the combined "net" price and his broker's fee. If the seller pays a fee to another broker he does so out of the "net" price.

Q. What if the broker I employ as "Buyer's Broker" turns out to be unproductive?

A. The contract can provide for cancellation on reasonable notice with protection for the broker on any properties previously submitted to the buyer.

Q. Will the "Buyer's Broker" arrangement save me any time?

A. Yes. Since the buyer's objectives and capabilities need only be explained to one broker, this saves time. It also keeps the buyer's affairs more confidential. Because of the closer broker/client relationship the broker can eliminate many weak possibilities and wasted hours and the buyer need inspect only properties with the "right benefits."

Q. What can I (as a buyer) expect from my "Buyer's Broker"?

A. 1. More conscientious representation.
    2. A more thorough job;
        a. A seller's broker is interested in a ready, willing and able buyer
        —no questions asked.

    b. A "Buyer's Broker" has a greater responsibility. Since his fee is protected he seeks the best property in the best location, with minimum problems and maximum benefits to accomplish his buyer's objective.

3. A better negotiated transaction.

Dealing direct with the owner or listing broker may put you at a competitive disadvantage. A "Buyer's Broker" becomes YOUR negotiator. He can often negotiate a price down to the "real world" and save you more than his fee!

4. Preliminary negotiations.

If you wish, the "Buyer's Broker" may submit preliminary offers on your behalf subject to your inspection and final written approval.

5. Anonymity!

Selling prices tend to become very firm where the buyer is a well known real estate investor, wealthy individual or large corporation. The "Buyer's Broker" can now act as agent for an undisclosed principal.

6. After a successful transaction the "Buyer's Broker" becomes an important contributor to the buyer's continuing program.

Q. Can compensation to the "Buyer's Broker" be based on something other than a percentage of the purchase price?

A. Yes. Frequently "Buyer's Brokers" work on a flat fee! In some cases they can be employed on an hourly basis but in these cases their fee is usually not contingent on the outcome of the transaction.

Q. Will I get maximum exposure to suitable properties using this "Buyer's Broker" approach?

A. ABSOLUTELY, AND THIS IS THE BIGGEST BENEFIT OF ALL. Normally a good broker will show a buyer only listed properties in order to protect his commission and avoid having "customers" go around him.

Since the "Buyer's Broker" is contractually protected on his fee he can contact owners of any and all properties that will benefit his client, even those "not on the market." A buying broker who doesn't have to cloud up his approach to an owner by asking for a commission usually has a better psychological relationship with the owner. It is amazing how some owners who have not publicly expressed any interest in selling suddenly come to life if they think they can "save a commission." Some brokers who have exclusive listings on excellent, desirable properties frequently try to avoid dealing with other brokers because they want to keep the entire commission for themselves. The buyer knows what he is willing to pay for the property including his broker's fee, and the benefits to be derived from the acquisition. If the benefits are there, why should the buyer concern himself with what the seller does with his money?

Q. How do I select the right broker to represent me in the capacity of a "Buyer's Broker"?

A. Ask people in related fields, Attorneys, C.P.A.s, Bankers, Title Insurance people, as to who are the most knowledgeable and experienced investment real estate brokers in the community. After a few inquiries several names will be repeated over and over. Concentrate further inquiries on these individuals and learn of their specialties, methods of operation and expertise. Select the one who seems to be the best qualified for your purposes, and make an appointment to discuss your situation. If the two of you decide not to work together make an appointment with the remaining one and counsel with him or her. Usually, one or the other will be just who you need to help you. When you feel you have found the right broker to represent you, then stop searching, place your trust and confidence in that person just as you do with your doctor, attorney and C.P.A., and work with him to accomplish your objective.*

By using the agreement on page 81 you accomplish two very important things: First, you put the realtor on your side legally and morally. Now the realtor can be aggressive with any seller that he meets, even if the seller has already signed a listing agreement with another broker! If that is the case, your broker will receive his buying commission directly from you, and the seller's listing broker will receive his normal percentage of listing commission from the seller.

Second, a buyer's broker agreement gives you and your realtor greater flexibility and enables him to help find you good properties. Since you're not obligated to buy anything, you only have to sit back and wait until the realtor brings you a piece of property you think is valuable enough to invest in. This puts you in the driver's seat all the way. It also puts him in a stronger negotiating position with sellers who have not listed their property. He doesn't have to beg for a listing but can negotiate on your behalf, knowing that if you buy the property he will get paid.

One weakness with most realtor/buyer relationships is the realtor's lack of understanding concerning the many kinds of creative transactions you will need to make. Since the realtor has worked so much with sellers,

---

* Questions and Answers material on pages 77–80 are © 1974—Arnett & Broadbent Inc. All rights reserved.

EXCLUSIVE RETAINER AGREEMENT TO LOCATE REAL PROPERTY

RETAINER AGREEMENT: The undersigned Client hereby retains the undersigned Broker, for a period commencing this date and terminating at midnight of _____ Jan. 1 _____, 19 79 for the purpose of locating real property of a nature outlined below and to negotiate terms and conditions for the purpose thereof, or for obtaining an option thereon, acceptable to Client.

BROKERAGE FEE: Client agrees to pay Broker as compensation for locating and negotiating the purchase of a property acceptable to Client a fee of ___ 3 ___ % of the purchase price; Client agrees further to pay Broker as compensation for obtaining an option on a property acceptable to Client a fee of $ _____ N/A _____ and agrees further to pay Broker the balance of a fee of ___ N/A ___ % of the purchase price in the event the option is exercised or assigned prior to the expiration of the option; Client agrees to pay Broker as compensation for locating a property acceptable to Client and negotiating a lease thereon a fee of _____ Not Applicable _____ ; IF:

(1) Client or any other person acting for Client or in Client's behalf, purchases, obtains an option for, or leases any real property of the nature described herein during the term hereof, through the services of Broker in the state of Utah.

(2) Client, or any person acting for Client or in Client's behalf, purchases, obtains an option for, or leases any real property within one year after termination of this retainer, which property Broker presented or submitted to Client during the term hereof and the description of which Broker shall have submitted in writing to Client, either in person or by mail, within ten days after termination of this retainer agreement.

Broker agrees that he will act for Client only and will not accept a fee from the seller, optionor or lessor unless full disclosure thereof is made to Client prior to the execution of an offer to purchase, option or lease.

CREDIT: In the event that the seller, optionor or lessor has agreed to pay a fee, and Broker, with the consent of Client, is entitled to receive any portion thereof, the full amount of the fee payable by seller, including any portion paid to cooperating brokers, shall be credited against the obligations of Client hereunder.

BROKER'S OBLIGATIONS: In consideration of Client's agreement set forth above, Broker agrees to use diligence in locating a property acceptable to Client and to negotiate terms and conditions for the purchase or lease of said property or for obtaining an option on said property, acceptable to Client.

ADDITIONAL TERMS AND CONDITIONS:
If client or agent of client locates a piece of real estate in Utah without the aid of Broker the 3% fee will be waived.

It is brokers responsibility to analyze and do research and act as an investment counselor with the objective of determining the long term value of the property as compared to other available properties.

A $500.00 retainer will be paid by client as credit for a $50.00 per hour fee that Broker will charge for all time spent in locating, organizing and closing the purchase of property.

The Rider attached hereto is an integral part of this Agreement.

GENERAL NATURE OF PROPERTY:
Apartment units and commercial building located in Utah preferably Provo or Orem but not excluding Salt Lake, Ogden, or other cities depending upon the particular investment.
Size: N/A up to 36 units
Location: Located in Utah preferably Provo or Orem, but not excluding Salt Lake, Ogden, or other cities depending upon the particular investment.

Price Range/Rental Anything up to $75,000 down payment with maximum leverage for tax
Terms: purposes
Special Requirements: _____

RECEIPT OF A COPY OF THIS AGREEMENT IS HEREBY ACKNOWLEDGED.

DATED _John Drake_

Robert G. Allen _____ Broker
1325 South 800 East
Temple View Terrace, Suite #300 _____ Address
Orem, Utah 84057
Telephone: 224-1978 _____ Phone

John Drake _____ Client
_____ Client
_____ Address
_____ Phone

By _____

he is accustomed only to the normal transactions: Seller has property. Buyer has lots of cash. Buyer gives seller lots of cash in exchange for the property. Realtor gets cash commission from seller. All live happily ever after.

Most inexperienced buyers become discouraged when they first approach a realtor about finding property for them with no down payment; the realtor usually listens to their story and then tells them that it can't be done.

I'm telling you that it *can* be done.

Picture how difficult it must be to have an unbelieving realtor present a creative offer to purchase to a seller who is not desperate. The realtor is flustered—perhaps even embarrassed—to have to present such an unconventional offer to the seller. The seller is equally upset, because the realtor virtually promised the seller a cash customer. The seller counters with an angry full-cash, full-price deal. The realtor just looks at you hopelessly and says, "See, I told you so!"

There *are* ways to work with a realtor creatively, ways to overcome any lack of understanding. Use these guidelines:

Give the realtor specifics. For example, whenever I work with a realtor (which is almost always), I give him the following restrictions: I tell him I will buy any property he brings me when the seller will

—sell for 10 percent down payment or less;

—carry back at least a 25 percent second mortgage subordinated to new financing;

—sell his property for 15 to 20 percent below the market value for a quick cash-out.

Now, my realtor has something concrete to use. Whenever he finds a suitable property he calls me up, and I inspect the property exterior within twenty-four hours. I reject most because of location or physical appearance. But if I'm interested I have him arrange for an interior inspection of the building. The realtors I work closely with will usually give me a list of properties to inspect at one time. I drive by and do the exterior inspection by myself without the realtor present. He doesn't have to give me a tour of the town or spend his valuable time giving me a sales pitch. I let my realtors know that when I find a property that interests me, I will act immediately to prepare a written offer through the realtor. I let them know I appreciate their efforts and that I will be fair with them.

If you have the time, always do your own negotiating. If the realtor is not familiar with your *modus operandi,* he will try to convince you that he must act as a go-between, and he will try to present your earnest money agreement to the seller himself. This is *not* always the best approach. When you talk to the seller face to face you can determine for yourself what kinds of things the seller wants and needs without trying to interpret these needs and wants through the eyes of a third party.

Work with at least five good realtors simultaneously. To give yourself the maximum exposure to the marketplace, you should have good relationships with several realtors, and the only way to establish them is to talk to several realtors every week. Explain your guidelines and let them know you will not give them a run-around. If you talk to twenty-five or thirty realtors, you will probably only have two or three who will eventually begin bringing you properties because of your strict guidelines and because many realtors are looking for the same kinds of properties to buy themselves.

Don't get discouraged.

The last major problem in dealing with a realtor is the fact that the realtor makes his living from selling properties. Since your criteria for buying property are rather unusual and strict, he will cut down his chances of making a sale by working with you. What's more, he needs to be paid in cash for his services. Therefore, if you want to get into a property with little or nothing down, you are obviously not thinking in terms of his best interests.

I find that the only kinds of properties I can work with a realtor on are those that require some kind of cash down payment and those that are too good to pass up. Since I am always buying properties with the same realtors, they know they can make money serving my account. Once I have established that, I can ask my realtor to let me give him a short-term note for his commission, which I can pay off as soon as I can find the partners.

And now a few words to those realtors who may find themselves reading this chapter: you are in the best position of all to find the kind of properties I have been discussing. You have first access to the multiple listing books, to the new listings in your office, to well-known investors who may want to become partners with you, and so on. To top it all off, you can use your commissions as part of the down payment on any property listed. This puts you a jump ahead of the rest of the world.

But having a license has its drawbacks. When I had my license I found that my liability was greater. Whenever I bought a property from a client and thereby received a commission, the seller had more grounds to sue me by maintaining that I acted with superior knowledge, took advantage of the seller, and was even paid for it. I also found that fellow realtors would not deal with me as eagerly because I wanted a piece of the action for myself. And finally, I found that sellers who had not listed their properties would always want to know if I was a realtor; when they found out that I was, they were always more reluctant to deal with me.

Because of all these disadvantages, I decided I'd be better off surrendering my license and working as an investor on a full-time basis. You might consider doing the same, especially if your current broker frowns on your investment practices.

The realtor is only one member of your private team of consultants. Let's look at what the rest of them can do to help you:

Accountants. Don't undertake any major real estate venture without establishing a relationship with a good real estate-oriented tax accountant; he will keep you from paying all of your income to the government as taxes. It doesn't *cost* to have help from an accountant—it *pays!*

If you run in to a property owner who doesn't want to sell his property because of the tax ramifications, you should find out as much as you can about the details and discuss them with your accountant. He may give you a new idea that might not have crossed your mind about how the seller could sell his property without major tax consequences.

I consult with my accountant constantly, and I have never regretted it. Don't be shy.

Attorneys. Attorneys are oriented to finding out what could possibly go wrong with any given real estate transaction or agreement and to preparing ways to avoid adverse consequences. Because of their cautious stance, they are known among real estate investors as "deal killers." But you *need* to know what could go wrong and how to avoid it. You need to know how the deal should be written up to offer you the greatest possible protection.

Not all real estate transactions require the help of an attorney, but it is worth the extra money in most cases. It may cost you $50 for an hour's worth of specialized help, but that amount is minuscule compared to a default costing thousands of dollars due to a faulty closing document.

If you have any doubt about what is taking place, get an attorney to review your problem with you. Young attorneys just establishing themselves might offer you a free hour of counseling in the hopes you will become a permanent client. If you have never visited an attorney because of the cost involved, you should seek out one that has reasonable rates and that offers a free first visit so that you can get acquainted and comfortable. If you can trust him, then stick with that attorney throughout the rest of your real estate lifetime.

Title Companies. Title companies provide you with insurance that the person who is selling you his property has been proven to legally own the property and has the right to transfer title of his property to you. The title company prepares a title policy that indicates all of the liens, mortgages, and encumbrances on the legal record against the property.

Can you imagine the catastrophe that would result without title companies? You would never know if a person was the legal owner of a piece of real estate. I heard of one instance where a con-artist sold one piece of property several times to different individuals—each time collecting a down payment. Then the thief left town, leaving no forwarding address. There were several angry investors when they found out they had been swindled—and that none of them owned the property, because the seller didn't either!

Even though title insurance is expensive, it is obviously critical. You *must* get title insurance for every property you buy. In most states the responsibility for paying the costs of title insurance is borne by the seller. If this is true in your state, you shouldn't hesitate to require that the seller purchase title insurance.

Title companies offer many services besides title insurance. In many states title insurance companies offer what they call a "listing package." If you promise to purchase title insurance through their company, they will research out the title to any property you are considering and will provide you with information such as current taxes, legal descriptions, a copy of the property and its boundary lines as they appear on the county records, and the names and addresses of current owners. Some even find out what the property originally sold for and on what terms. Such information is helpful to you in preparing an analysis of a potential investment.

The competition among title companies can be very fierce. A progressive company will put you on their mailing list, and you will receive from local lending institutions monthly quotes on their interest rates and loan fees. These fees are called "points" and can be from 1 percent to 10 percent of the face value of the loan—e.g., 3 points is equal to 3 percent of the amount borrowed. I have had title officers accompany me to the courthouse and teach me how to locate divorce files, files on properties that are going into foreclosure, and other important information. Ask and ye shall receive.

Title companies also usually act as escrow agents and closing officers.

In other words, if you have a complicated transaction, a title officer will give you information you need to complete the transaction. If you have questions about trust deeds or warrantee deeds, your first source of free information is a title company officer. He will be glad to help you with any real estate problem.

Appraisers. Simply put, a professional appraiser can give you an accurate (and legally recognized) figure detailing a property's value. The appraiser can let you know whether the property is overpriced or underpriced, and you can use the appraiser's estimate as the basis to obtain funding.

Management Companies. These can be your most valuable asset.

Let me give you a short course on managing your own properties: Don't!

Don't, that is, unless you enjoy being awakened in the middle of the night by a frantic renter who is telling you grim tales of a backed-up toilet. Management companies handle _all_ maintenance details. They're professional. They have staff members (or contacts) who can do repair work at the lowest possible prices. They have connections, too, so that they can often purchase supplies at wholesale prices—all of which means lower cost for you.

In addition to handling maintenance, management companies also collect rents, pay all utility bills (with collected rent money), and pay mortgage payments (with collected rent money). In short, they will handle all aspects of the operation of your building. They'll even provide you with a monthly financial statement including bills and a cash flow check. All you have to do is receive a rent check and spend it as you wish.

Best of all, you can wash your hands of the whole matter and concentrate your energy and creativity on your next investment.

What's the price? It will cost you about 5 to 10 percent of the property's gross income. The more units you have the lower the fee; fees can go as low as 3 percent. The cost for the services is well worth it.

Managing your own properties for a while can be a very good experience, though—you can get a feel for the problems that can arise and can understand better the process of property management. If you choose to keep at it, fine. Some properties involve very little hassle and would be a good management experience.

For those properties that involve a great deal of management, however, you should hire a management company as soon as possible. You probably won't be able to afford one right away, so make sure your cash flow is adequate before you take the step.

Property Rental Firms. Every town has small companies that charge potential renters a fee for the privilege of examining their listings of vacant rental properties. If you are trying to rent some of your properties, contact one of these rental agencies. They are listed in the Yellow Pages of your phone directory, their services are free to property owners, and they usually refer good tenants (those who are willing to pay money to find a good place to live).

Bankers. The role of bankers is so important and so involved that several chapters are dedicated to a discussion of their services and methods of working with them.

If you feel overwhelmed with the detail of the real estate business, you are only normal. Go to the professionals in the business and ask their advice. They are ready with answers. A confused mind always says No; don't let your confused mind tell you No simply because of a lack of confidence on your part. There are people who are ready to help. Use them.

CHAPTER NINE

Negotiations: The First Person to Mention a Number Loses

ALL RIGHT. You've found a property with promise. Now what do you do?

Hang on. Here comes the fun—and critical—part of investing in real estate: negotiating with the seller.

Negotiating is an art that becomes easier the more highly motivated the seller becomes to sell his property. In other words, it's necessary to find a don't wanter if you want to have a successful negotiating experience.

It's possible to turn a seller into a don't wanter just by the way you conduct your negotiation. Let's look at the rules that, if followed, will lead to a successful negotiation experience.

1. *If a seller is firm on his price, you must be able to negotiate flexible terms! If a seller is firm on his terms (usually meaning all cash), then you must be able to choose the price (usually lower). Whenever possible, try to choose both the price and terms.*

If you can't obtain either your price or your terms, move on. The only way you should deal with an inflexible seller is if his original price and terms are already good enough to get excited about. You can't afford to waste precious time dealing with a seller who might not budge. Move on to the next deal.

2. *Destroy all expectations of high profit in the seller's mind!*

There are some very effective ways of doing this. If you are inspecting the property with the seller, ask him a series of questions something like these:

89

"Does the roof leak?"

"Are you behind on your mortgage payments?"

"How long have you been trying to sell?" (Ask this one as you examine the dilapidated For Sale sign.)

"Is the builder of this property still in business?" (This implies that the construction is so lousy that the contractor must have been forced to go out of business.)

"Does everything work properly?" (Ask this as you examine a broken refrigerator door.)

Sniffing at a pungent odor, you might say, "Do you have animals?"

Pointing at a leaky faucet, exclaim, "It looks like this will be a very high maintenance unit!"

Looking at the surrounding mountains out the window, you might ask, "Is this property on a fault line?"

Try to point out every small detail that needs attention, every fault. Go over the property with a finetoothed comb and point out every single negative thing you can. You do this for two reasons. First, you may not really want the property after all. It may be just too much of a hassle; you may decide against it. Second, you want to show the seller that his property has flaws and problems that need correcting. Almost every property owner (except the don't wanter) has learned to ignore the flaws in his property and has learned to overemphasize the good aspects. Bring the seller back to reality. You might be able to bring his price back into the real world, too.

You must destroy all of the seller's expectations of high profit! Don't let the seller blind you with all of his fancy reasons why his property is worth a fortune. Most importantly, require the seller to correct all of the faults you found in your examination before you buy his property if you decide to invest. And if you sincerely follow my advice to notice all the flaws in the property, you may do yourself a big favor—you may destroy your *own* expectations of high profit. Don't buy a property if you can see all your profit going into deferred maintenance.

There are other ways of destroying the seller's expectations of high profit:

Act disinterested in the seller's property. Let the seller know directly or indirectly that his property is only one of several you will be visiting that day. Let him know, too, that there are competitive properties on the market every bit as attractive as his property. You might say to the realtor who is with you, "What time is our appointment to visit that ten-unit building on Charles Avenue?" Or "The bedrooms in this unit are not as big as the bedrooms in the Terrace Apartments." Or "This house is priced $4,000 more than the identical one on Seventh Street." Do your homework and let the seller know in no uncertain terms that the market-place does not command a price as high as he is asking. Show him comparable figures on comparable units. If your figures are accurate and your analysis is convincing, you may cut thousands of dollars off the price the seller wants.

Teach the seller whose property has been on the market for some time a lesson that neither he nor you should ever forget: *The only reason that a property doesn't sell is that the price is too high.* Any property in the world will sell immediately if it is put on the market at the right price. If a property has been on the market for more than three months, the property is not worth what the seller is asking, no matter what the terms are. Before I negotiate any transaction I always ask,

"How long has this property been listed or been offered for sale?"

"Before you listed this property did you try to sell it by yourself? At what price?"

"How many offers have you had for your property? Why didn't you accept them?"

Don't be shy about asking questions like these. It's your right to have them answered before you buy the property. Don't stay silent out of a fear of offending the seller—as long as the questions are questions you wouldn't hesitate to ask in any normal, casual conversation. You must be bold. Remember, *your money* is at stake here. You need answers.

Other questions might affect your purchase decision; make a list of the questions before you meet with the seller. Some that might help are:

When did you buy the property and from whom?

What did you pay for the property? Even though this is a very personal question, more often than not, the seller will answer you without hesitation.

How much did you spend on repairs and capital improvements during your ownership? What structural changes did you make?

Why did you list your property for sale with XYZ Realty?

What is the worst thing you can think of about your ownership of these apartments?

Are there any major improvements that will have to be made shortly?

The seller will more than likely answer all of your questions without hesitation because you asked in a straightforward manner. If he balks at any of these questions, ask him, "Is there any reason why I shouldn't know that information? Would the answer to that question keep me from buying your property?" If he says no, repeat the question and wait for his answer.

Success during this questioning phase requires that you visit the seller personally. A realtor—or any other third party—will reduce the effectiveness of the technique and will probably affect the honesty of the seller's answers.

3. *Interpret and relieve the seller's fears.*

In essence, try to understand why the seller is selling his property. The answers you get will probably surprise both you and the seller. The seller probably hasn't really been asked these kinds of questions before. As you probe deep into the seller's motivations and show an interest in his needs, he will become more confident in your ability to solve his problems.

You need to ask and understand the answers to questions like these: What would happen if you didn't sell for six months? This will help you determine just how much the seller wants to sell. If he says he can wait as long as necessary, he's probably just speculating and hoping someone will come along and pay his price. If he says he must sell before the first of the month, your seller might consider creative terms. The closer you are to the deadline the seller sets, the more anxious the seller will become.

Do you have other property for sale? This might lead you to a property that isn't listed that might better suit your needs.

What are you going to do with the cash proceeds of this sale? The seller may say that he intends to pay off some nagging debts. Offer to pay the debts for him; you might be able to prolong the payment of these debts, requiring you to come up with less cash at the closing. If the seller says that he plans to buy a plane ticket to Rome, offer to buy it for him as part of the down payment. Then buy the ticket with your Master Charge card—another way to defer the payment of cash at the closing. Do you get the point? Try to find ways of solving the seller's dilemma without investing any of your precious cash. Probe deeply. It can probably be done.

What is the lowest cash price that you will accept if I give you all of your equity within forty-eight hours? This is a critical question; it reveals the rock bottom price. Sometimes you should look for a way to raise the cash quickly instead of pressing for terms. Your profit potential may be much greater this way. Don't avoid the question. You might make a lot of money as a result.

What is the real reason that you want to sell? Now you'll really find out if you have a don't wanter. He'll tell you he has management headaches, financial headaches, physical plant problems, personal problems, or partnership problems. You solve his problem. But don't oversolve! Remember the last time you had an itch? You could scratch all around the itch, but until you scratched the itch itself you still had that nagging itch. The don't wanter has the same problem: an itch of sorts. And all you have to do is listen, determine where the itch is, and scratch *only* the itch—no more. Whatever he says, solve his exact problem. If the management is too much for him, stress your management skills. If he has a deadline to meet, stress your ability to close now, today. If he is afraid to sell with a low down payment, offer him security on other property you own. If he is concerned about closing costs, you sell him on the fact that he will pay no closing costs whatsoever (of course you lower the price to compensate you for having to pay the seller's closing costs). If he is afraid of tax consequences take him to your accountant; let your accountant show the seller the many avenues open for him to reduce his tax liability. Whatever his problem or fear, come up with a solution. This technique will be your strongest selling point.

Once you understand the seller's position, you will be in a better position yourself to proceed with negotiation. Remember these rules for the buyer:

1. *Decide beforehand the benefits you want for yourself. Pick a price and terms beyond which you will not bend. Get up and walk out graciously when you can see that you are not getting what you had hoped to gain.* The seller may realize that you are not bluffing and back down on his terms so he won't lose a good prospect.

2. *The first person to mention a number loses.* If you wait long enough, the seller will tell you exactly where he will go. You don't need to mention any numbers; if you do you may weaken your position. An anxious seller becomes even more anxious in the presence of a silent negotiator. Your conversation might go something like this: "I've got to have $50,000 or I won't sell." Silence. "Why?" "Because that's the figure that I said I needed." Silence. "Well, I guess I could settle for $45,000 if you pay all the closing costs." Silence. "I won't go a penny below $41,000." Let the seller do the talking. Silence is devastating if used in the right places.

3. *Keep it simple.* Don't say, "We'll have to draw up a wrap-around mortgage with a substitution of collateral agreement and we'll place them

in escrow." Using the vernacular of real estate with a novice seller will just confuse him; and remember that a confused mind always says No. Keep it simple. Say, "We'll have everything done legally so that you won't have anything to worry about."

4. *Make sure the seller is well aware of the problems you will be saving him from.*

5. *Try the would-you-take technique.* Once you have listened to the seller's reasons, test your own ability to listen by using the would-you-take technique (Pronounced "woodjatake"—a term used frequently by real estate exchangers). Would-you-take questions expose the flexibility of a don't wanter. For example:

Would-you-take a duplex equity for your fourplex equity?

Would-you-take some raw ground instead of cash?

Would-you-take a new car in exchange for your equity in your home?

Would-you-take a note due in one year for part of your equity?

Try to give the seller dozens of alternatives to choose from. This will prepare him for your final offer, which will probably incorporate some of the successful would-you-takes. The seller needs to be reminded that cash is only one form of payment for equity. Point out that there may be other more suitable solutions short of a large cash down payment. Use the would-you-take technique to give you a little advantage in the final round of negotiations.

6. *As soon as you have as much information as you need, leave the seller, go somewhere where you can analyze all of the data that you have collected and prepare a formal offer to purchase.*

CHAPTER TEN

The Final Round of Negotiations: The Effective Non-use of Cash

Y OU'VE HAD some time alone to consider your investment, and you've decided to go ahead. Even though you've negotiated verbally, nothing's legal yet. You still need to make final negotiations.

In most states of the union negotiations become legally binding when both the seller and the buyer have affixed their signatures to a written agreement called an Earnest Money Receipt (also referred to as an Offer to Purchase, a Purchase Money Receipt, or a Deposit Receipt). Any realtor in your city can show you one of the state-approved forms, or you can obtain one at any stationery or office supply store.

Even if a particular form is not legally required in your state, the law still requires that you show your earnestness to buy the property by giving the seller a cash deposit; the seller or the seller's agent will hold the deposit, and the seller will keep your deposit as liquidated damages if the buyer defaults.

Three rules will serve as guidelines as you fill out an offer to purchase. First, try to negotiate price. Get it as low as you can before you do anything else. Second, start to think of your cash as a precious commodity—a disappearing species, so to speak. One millionaire referred to his tight-fisted policy as the Effective Non-use of Cash. Many of us, on the other hand, spend our cash as if our policy was the Non-effective Use of Cash. Guard your investment capital with your life. Negotiate for low down or nothing down deals. Set this goal now. You'll be more successful. Third, you need to be aware of a hierarchy of negotiation. What does it mean? Examine the chart below:

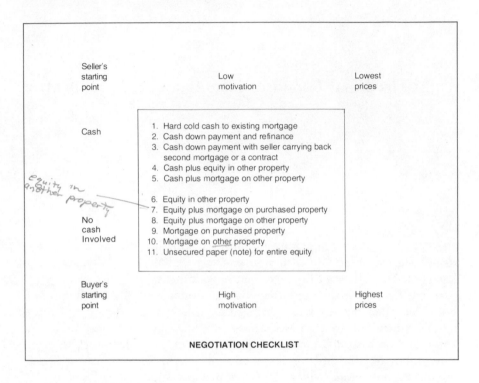

| Seller's starting point | Low motivation | Lowest prices |

Cash

1. Hard cold cash to existing mortgage
2. Cash down payment and refinance
3. Cash down payment with seller carrying back second mortgage or a contract
4. Cash plus equity in other property
5. Cash plus mortgage on other property

6. Equity in other property
7. Equity plus mortgage on purchased property
8. Equity plus mortgage on other property
9. Mortgage on purchased property
10. Mortgage on other property
11. Unsecured paper (note) for entire equity

No cash Involved

Buyer's starting point   High motivation   Highest prices

NEGOTIATION CHECKLIST

(handwritten note: equity in another property)

You can see this checklist has eleven basic alternatives for you and the seller to choose from as you arrive at a price and terms for the final purchase.

At the top of the list is the seller's first choice: the buyer pays all cash. The buyer, of course, wants to start at the bottom of the list at number eleven: the seller accepts an unsecured note for his equity with no cash changing hands. You will learn soon enough that neither the buyer nor the seller ever get exactly what they want.

In between the top and the bottom are nine other choices. As you conduct your negotiation, always begin at the bottom, and don't get too close to the top! Stick to your guns. If your seller is a don't wanter, he'll come down to meet you closer to the bottom of the chart.

You will see why the chart is organized the way it is as you read further in this book. Items 6 through 11 do not involve cash at all. For example, if you were to make an offer using number seven, you would offer equity you have in another property (perhaps a motorcycle or another piece of real estate) plus a note for the rest of the seller's equity. With number ten, the seller may agree to accept a second mortgage on another piece of property you own as full equity in his property. The point is, avoid using cash if at all possible.

Once your negotiations have been completed and price and terms agreed upon, you need to fill out the Offer to Purchase form. At this stage in the game, you may involve the real estate agent as a third party negotiator between yourself and the seller. I always recommend that you speak with the seller first, to determine his flexibility, then use a realtor if there is one involved, to complete the negotiation. Follow these guidelines to insure that you are covered in all cases:

1. *Name of purchaser.* This should always read "John Doe (your name) or his assigns." This phrasing should appear anywhere on the form where your name needs to be listed. Where the name to be used on the closing document is to be listed, write "To Be Designated at Closing." Why? You might decide before closing that you want to sell the property and make a profit. You don't want the offer to purchase to limit your flexibility. Your new buyer can legally qualify as your "assigns."

2. *Amount of earnest money or deposit.* I always use $100. Why? First, the law says that $1 is legal and binding, so I give 100 times what is legal and binding. Second, I like to limit my liability; if for some reason I am forced to default, I want to suffer as small a loss as possible. Early in my career I put up $1,000 with a partner as earnest money and committed to coming up with financing for a duplex in one week. It was sheer stupidity on my part—I ended up paying back the $500 I borrowed from the bank to make up for not coming through with the money. Third, you might be making offers on several properties at the same time—as I often do—and you certainly don't want several thousand-dollar checks in circulation.

If the seller demands more earnest money, tell the realtor that the seller can request this in a written counter-offer. Stress that you have good reasons for the small amount. Let the seller give you a good reason that justifies coming up with more money. If you do come up with more, designate it as "additional deposit, not to be called earnest money." Then if you default you'll forfeit only your original $100—depending on the laws in your state, of course.

If you are working through a real estate agency, it will collect the earnest money from you and will hold it in a trust account until fulfillment of the terms and conditions on the offer to purchase is completed. If you are dealing directly with a seller, you can either give the funds to the seller or to a third party. I feel more comfortable giving the money to my title company, which acts as an escrow agent between me and the seller; I know that my money is safe with an independent third party. I have been known to give a $500 check to a seller with instructions not to cash the check until the closing. This way I could use the funds until closing, but I also had to trust that the seller wouldn't cash my check and disappear. It's a risky proposition at best.

3. *The closing date.* Sometimes it is best to prolong the closing as long as possible; this gives you the flexibility to raise the needed capital for the down payment, to search for a partner, or to sell the property to another individual for a higher price. If, however, you can sense that the seller will not last long in an extended closing situation, negotiate a short closing. Use your judgment. I generally allow myself at least four weeks to close, and longer if I have to get conventional financing.

Engineer the closing to fall on the day the rents are due if you are buying a rental property. You are normally not required to make your first mortgage payment for thirty days after closing, but you are allowed to collect all of the rents on the first day of ownership. In some cases you will have thousands of dollars worth of rents and tenant deposits, and no obligation to make a first mortgage payment for thirty days. You could even use the money as part of your down payment!

4. *The "subject-to" clauses.* (Better known as "weasel clauses.") These are clauses that you insert into the offer to purchase (wherever indicated on your form) that limit your liability even further. Here you state that the offer is *subject to* certain limitations and conditions that must be fulfilled before the offer is valid, such as:

—Subject to the inspection of my partner, whoever he may be, within three days of the seller's acceptance of this offer. (If you decide within three days that you don't want the property after all, just have your partner write a letter saying that he does not give approval to the purchase. Your partner can be anyone—your wife, your doctor, your next-door neighbor, a friend.)

—Subject to all appliances, heaters, refrigerators, stoves, air conditioners and all other equipment pertaining to the operation of the property being in good working order as of the day of the closing. (Then, if anything goes wrong before the closing day, the seller has to pay for repairs or replacement—not you!)

—Subject to the seller obtaining a termite inspection of the property. (This applies equally to a building code inspection, a roofing inspection, or any other kind of inspection you want conducted.)

—Subject to having all the things done to the property that need to be done to bring it up to standard. (Be specific—list repair to cracked foundation, front porch painted, grounds cleanup, and so on. Make the seller bring the property up to your standard.)

—Subject to obtaining suitable and adequate financing (specify the amount and interest rate) on or before the day of closing. (If you can't obtain financing, you can get your earnest money back.)

—Subject to the seller providing clear and marketable title to his property. (You might request a survey to verify the title search.)

Your possibilities are limitless.

Of course, the realtor will try to get you to eliminate most of these "subject tos" because they stand in the way of an easy closing. The realtor wants to take his money and run. But be sure that you include enough of the clauses to limit your liability. Make sure that if anything goes wrong, you've got something to fall back on.

And refuse to let the seller list *any* subject-to clauses on his side of the negotiation!

One last negotiation technique: the Front Porch offer. If there is something in the offer that you don't want the seller to notice, throw in something outlandish to draw his attention away. For instance, if you don't want him to notice that the price you've offered is ridiculously low, list as a condition that he must paint the front porch. The seller's usual reaction? "Paint your own darn porch!" He'll spend his time in the counter-offer refusing your decoy and not paying attention to your real area of concern.

Some common front porch clauses are:

—Seller must pay all closing costs.

—Seller must relinquish all of his tax and insurance impounds.

—Seller must paint the property inside and out.

—Seller must pay any FHA or VA points.

If the seller accepts your front porch offer without any changes, then you just got a free paint job for the front porch. If he refuses your offer, it's no skin off your teeth.

Visit your local office supply store and ask to see their supply of legal forms. Buy a large supply of Offers to Purchase real estate forms and put them in your car, in your briefcase or purse; in short, have one with you at all times. You never can tell when you'll need one. Look at as many properties that are for sale as time permits.

Make offers on everything. Even if you don't have the time to go through the long process of formal negotiation, at least get in the habit of making acceptable offers. Set a goal to write a certain number of offers each week. Be specific. This is a numbers game: the more offers you write, the greater your chances of buying property will be. Make as many offers as you can, and don't be afraid to offer low. You might find a taker. One realtor I know wrote offers to over 1,700 properties in a California listing book, offering all cash down to the existing mortgage with a price 20 percent below the listed price. Forty of his offers were ultimately accepted!

What about a counter-offer? Suppose the seller doesn't like your offer —which is not uncommon. What do you do next? The seller will inform you, usually in writing, that your offer is unacceptable, and he will usually propose a counter-offer. This process of offer/counter-offer is a critical one, as both you and the seller are jockeying for position, seeing just how far the other party will bend. If you have had previous discussions with the seller personally, you will have a fairly good idea of how flexible he will be. Just remember not to bend yourself beyond your limits to pay. If you can't see the light at the end of the tunnel, you may decide to back out of the negotiations quickly and move on to your next project. You can't afford to waste time and mental energy with an inflexible seller. If the property is an excellent buy, then I would suggest moving rapidly. I have known properties to be sold out from underneath a negotiating buyer because he persisted in demanding minor concessions. Remember, you don't steal in slow motion! If you find a seller who completely refuses to negotiate because he is offended by your first "creative" offer, you should respond in this manner:

"I have taken the time and spent precious money analyzing your property. I have even been courteous enough to put my offer in writing. Please be courteous enough to give me a written counter-offer if my original offer is not acceptable to you. Don't tell me what you won't do; tell me what you will do."

Practice making your offers. Your chances of being able to negotiate and close properly when you do find a good buy will be greatly increased.

Now get ready to buy your property!

CHAPTER ELEVEN

Paper: The Difference Between Success and Failure

Before you proceed with your investment plans, you need to familiarize yourself with a term commonly used in the real estate business: "paper." Paper refers to mortgages or notes either secured or unsecured by real estate or other collateral. *Hard paper* comes from a bank or lending institution. *Soft paper* is a note with lenient, flexible terms.

A typical first mortgage held by the bank that financed your house is called *paper.*

When you buy your first investment property with nothing down, the seller will take back 100 percent *paper.* (Maybe it is a $30,000 first mortgage on the property, with monthly payments of $250 over the next thirty years.)

When you borrowed $2,000 on your signature from your bank, you filled out a personal note that said you owed the bank $2,000; that note is *paper.* (The note would still be *paper* even if it was secured against other property.)

Whenever you buy real estate with little down payment there will be paper involved. The creative use of paper makes the difference between success and failure in those investments.

How can you make the best use of paper? Let's start with notes. The obligation to pay a note (1) should be unsecured by collateral if possible, (2) should be negotiated at the lowest possible interest rate, (3) should be negotiated with the longest term acceptable to the seller, and (4) should not require monthly payments or should require only low monthly payments. These conditions are critical to success.

The key to borrowing money and making good use of paper is to incur

101

debt by deferring the obligation to repay as far into the future as possible. This concept is against the seller's goals, which more often than not include the repayment of loans as soon as possible. The more the seller is a don't wanter—and the more serious a don't wanter he becomes as the negotiations proceed—the better your chances of working paper to your advantage.

The hierarchy of paper is clearly illustrated below:

High interest rate	Short term payoff	High monthly payments
.	.	.
.	.	.
.	.	.
.	.	.
Low interest rate	Long term payoff	Low monthly payments or no monthly payments

Always start at the bottom of each column in your negotiating. Avoid the top like the plague. High monthly payments can kill you.

Using paper to your benefit is *critical* to the success of any investment you make. Let's look at an investor who ignored the conditions that would have ensured his success:

John is just beginning to invest in real estate and wants to build up a portfolio for future retirement. He has little money saved, and has about $100 extra cash flow a month to invest.

John locates a fairly sound five-unit apartment building selling for $80,000. The seller is a don't wanter, but he needs $5,000 in cash. The seller's existing first mortgage of $60,000 is payable at $524.22 a month; the seller wants to receive the balance of his $15,000 equity over a seven-year period at 10 percent interest, secured by a second trust deed (mortgage) on the property. Monthly payments would be $249.02.

John is so excited about what seems to be a great deal that he ceases to negotiate and hurriedly signs the earnest money receipt. He arranges for a personal loan of $5,000 from his credit union, due and payable in six months with an interest rate of 11 percent.

The closing date arrives; John becomes the proud owner of an "alligator"; John hadn't done his homework. The seller had told him rents were $200 per unit and that monthly expenses were about $200. But the first few months are a real revelation: three of the units are rented out for $190; the other two are rented for $195. Expenses during the summer months *do* run about $200 a month, but during the winter, when gas bills are higher, monthly expenses go as high as $400.

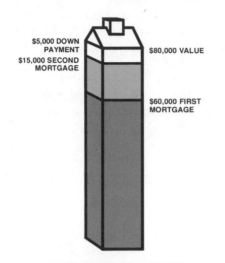

$5,000 DOWN PAYMENT

$15,000 SECOND MORTGAGE

$80,000 VALUE

$60,000 FIRST MORTGAGE

5-UNIT APARTMENT BUILDING

John took possession in December. Financial details were:

Monthly gross rents	$960
January expenses	($400)
First mortgage payment	($524.22)
Second mortgage paid to seller	($249.02)
Monthly negative cash flow	($213.24)

Things are all right for the first six months. Even though John really only has $100 to spare each month for negative cash flows, he manages to come up with the extra $113.24 to feed his alligator. (And John is lucky; if a major repair had been needed or a unit went vacant, he really would have been in trouble.)

Suddenly the six months are up. John's note is due.

John has learned the hard way what happens with a "short fuse" note: it explodes. He doesn't want to sell the building, so what are his alternatives? He'll need to earn the money, collect the money from another investment, or convert the note to a monthly payment. That monthly payment will be about $125 over a five-year period with 11 percent interest.

John obviously can't handle an additional $125 each month. His alternatives, then, are rather limited.

John ends up selling the building. He suddenly becomes a serious don't wanter. John has learned that when you don't feed your alligator, it eats you! And a person who is being eaten alive by an alligator is the most desperate don't wanter of all.

Today's real estate investor must be on the lookout for alligators every time he negotiates to buy a piece of real estate. The lower the down payment the more probable the creation of an alligator. You must learn how to cage the alligator from the very start. See the illustration below:

ALLIGATOR CAGES

Strategies for caging the alligator
(negative cash flow):

Cut the seller's price
Ask for more rent
Give more toward down payment
Eliminate more expenses
Structure the mortgage payments

There are five surefire ways to avoid negative cash flow properties. The first and most effective is to cut the seller's price. If this is not possible, then you should analyze the rents and expenses to see if there is room for improvement. How long will it take to increase rents to a level whereby there will be no negative cash flow? Can I afford to feed this property until the rents break even? If the answers to these questions are not satisfactory, then you may consider giving a larger down payment, thus lowering the mortgage payment. If none of the above solutions seems to solve the problem, then you have only one avenue left to you: structuring the mortgage payments to meet your cash flow needs. This must be done in your negotiating with the seller from the very beginning. That's why it is so important to know as much as you can about the property you are trying to buy before you enter formal negotiations. Once you have bought the property it is impossible to go back and ask the seller to accept a different payout schedule.

Let's rework John's situation so there is some comfortable leeway. Consider these solutions:

PAPER FORMULA #1. *Structure the seller's note to seasonal demands.*

In John's situation summer monthly expenses were $200 for six months; winter monthly expenses were $400 for six months. Yearly total was $3,600. If the seller is really anxious to sell, he should agree to receive payments on his note that coincide with your payment schedule. Suggest that during the summer months he will receive $349.02 ($100 a month more than originally negotiated) and during the six lean months of winter his monthly payment will be only $149.02 ($100 less than normal). Such a payment plan will give you extra money when you need it and structure extra payments when you have extra money to spend.

Remember: note payments are not sacred. Play with the numbers so that they come out to your advantage.

PAPER FORMULA #2. *Structure a balloon mortgage.*

Rather than giving the seller monthly payments, throw a balloon mortgage at him. A balloon mortgage is any type of note that has lump sum payments during the life of the note.

If John had wanted to apply a balloon payment in his situation, he would have offered the seller a $15,000 mortgage secured against his property with no monthly or yearly payments. The interest on the note would accrue from year to year, and the entire balance would be due in one lump sum or "balloon" at the end of seven years. (If a seller balks at this solution, calculate for him what his balloon payment will be in seven years: the $15,000 will have grown to $29,230.76. The figure may have some influence on the seller who is considering retirement and who will need something to live on.)

Having no monthly payments relieves you of an additional burden, and the obligation to pay is deferred. But don't forget that you *do* have an obligation to pay. Your extra cash flow should be reinvested into something else that will be used to help defray the large future obligation. The property itself will be one of the best sources for repaying this obligation. If the building is worth $80,000 when you buy it, it will be worth almost $156,000 at the end of seven years if it appreciates at the rate of 10 percent per year. You could then refinance the building and come up with the necessary money.

This method sounds easy. But there are cautions. It is always a good idea to protect yourself against the future possibility that it will be impossible to refinance the property. What if mortgage money is tight and you can't find a lender who will make you a loan? Ask the holder of the note for a grace period if mortgage money is impossible to find. Perhaps you could make a token payment of $5,000 every six months until you find a willing bank. And let the holder of the note do his own checking; he might be able to find a source of financing *for* you.

PAPER FORMULA #3. *Try reverse paper.*

This is sometimes called walking the paper backwards. Rather than agreeing to such a high monthly figure to the seller ($249.02), John could have agreed to make only a $100 monthly payment. Although this amount is not enough to cover the interest charges (thus the name "reverse"), it will at least help the seller in his cash flow situation and will reduce the final amount owing. Of course the note will still continue to grow, but not at as great a rate.

PAPER FORMULA #4. *Increase the length of the amortization with a lump sum payment (or balloon payment).*

This formula is successful because sellers usually like to receive a monthly payment on their notes but would like to receive their cash as soon as possible. Have the seller accept the monthly payment of his note *as if* the note were going to be paid over a period of twenty-five or thirty years. At the end of seven years, balloon the remaining balance to the seller. For example, if you owed $15,000 and it was set up on a thirty-year amortization, the monthly payments would be only $131.64. That's less than $249.02 and might give you some breathing room. In seven years the remaining balance on the note will be $14,196.89, and you will have to pay it in one lump sum. Again, consider cashing in on the increased property value.

The following chart shows some different amortization schedules:

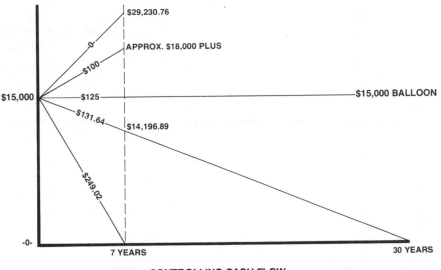

CONTROLLING CASH FLOW

The longer the amortization without a balloon payment, the better. Balloon payments are *not* good except when the property they are used on has such a negative cash flow that they cannot carry themselves (assuming the property's price is not out of line)—then use a balloon if you feel confident that you will be able to obtain the money at the end of the period.

PAPER FORMULA #5. *Increase the interest rate.*

Depending on his motivation, you may be able to convince the seller that you will have a rough time making payments under the stringent terms he demands. You may ask that the interest on the $15,000 note be 6 percent for the first year, and that it increase a percentage point each year until you are paying 10 percent on the remaining balance. With this formula your payments at first would be lower, escalating in line with your increasing ability to pay.

PAPER FORMULA #6. *Pay interest only.*

Rather than amortizing the loan, negotiate a semiannual or annual interest-only payment. In John's situation he would make a $750 payment twice a year or a $1,500 payment once a year. This solution relieves the constant monthly burden of a fully amortized loan over a short period of time and allows you a full year (or half a year) to obtain the needed money.

Again, there are some cautions. Many a poor soul has hung himself out to dry with such short-term payments. This formula breeds potential don't wanters—those who are unprepared on the due date. You must have the discipline to save for the payment date or to be ready for it when it comes.

PAPER FORMULA #7. *Moratorium on interest payments until cash flow increases.*

If John had done his homework, he would have realized that he would be experiencing a substantial negative cash flow during part of the year. Until he had a chance to raise the rents to a level that would cover all of his expenses, he should have negotiated a note with the seller that did not have any payments for the first twenty-four months but that converted to an amortizing loan at that time with monthly payments of $249.02 or higher.

PAPER FORMULA #8. *Convert any balloon notes to amortizing notes when they are due.*

Whenever possible, defer payments until you have a chance to become comfortable with your situation. John should have negotiated with the bank on his due date to have the $5,000 balloon note converted into a monthly amortizing loan; in fact, he should have written that into the note at the beginning of the arrangement. If the banker balked, John could have offered him a higher interest rate on the unpaid balance of the loan; a loan of $5,000 fully amortized over a five-year period with 12 percent interest would have monthly payments of only $111.22. John could have raised rents enough in a six month period to cover most of the added cash flow needed to amortize the new monthly payment (an increase of $10 an apartment would have raised the needed money).

These first eight formulas work well to increase your flexibility when you've written a note.

But what about mortgages?

Most people mistakenly believe that once a mortgage is placed on a property it cannot be removed unless it is paid off in cash. While banks and lending institutions are rather rigid about creative maneuvers with mortgages, you *can* be creative with mortgages assumed from private persons.

Mortgages are not riveted to a property once a property is mortgaged.
A mortgage is nothing more or less than a note for the repayment of a
debt and a collateral agreement in case the note is not repaid. If you
understand that, you can work all kinds of creative twists in your
purchases.

PAPER FORMULA #9. *Move the mortgage.*

If you are buying a piece of property from a seller who is going to
carry back a second mortgage (or trust deed) for part of his equity, tell
the seller you want to move the mortgage to your home (or some other
piece of property you own). He might question you. Explain that his
mortgage will be just as secure against your own home as against the
purchased property—in fact, it will be more secure because you are not
going to lose your own home to foreclosure. Since a mortgage is simply
a security agreement anyway, he should feel secure enough with what you
are offering.

Moving a mortgage has several advantages. If you don't want to sell
your home, another mortgage on it shouldn't bother you. Chances are,
there's not enough equity in your home to profitably borrow against for
a bank loan. Transferring the loan to your own home frees you to sell (or
trade) the newly purchased property at any time and to collect all of the
equity instead of paying part of it to the previous owner. It leaves you
with greater flexibility.

I recently counseled with a client who had a four-unit apartment
building; he wanted to trade up to a twelve-unit building I had found
for him. He began to arrange for a sale of his four-unit building that
would give him $25,000 in cash for his equity, but he still lacked enough
for the necessary down payment of $50,000. He approached the holder
of a $25,000 note against his four-unit building and asked if the note
could be secured instead against a twelve-unit building. The note holder
gave the go-ahead. When the sale of the fourplex was finally completed,
my client collected the $50,000 in cash for the fourplex and used it as a
down payment on the twelve-unit building. The holder of the note
transferred his note to the new property. Everyone was satisfied. Without
this technique my client would have had to seek a $25,000 loan from a
conventional source, and he might have been denied. The transaction
could not have taken place. The diagram on page 110 tells how it worked.

How can you convince a holder of a second mortgage to move it to
another piece of collateral? Following a few guidelines will help you
convince him that he will be protected.

Give him the right to refuse the move if he feels his security is in-

MOVING THE MORTGAGE

adequate. Let him inspect the new building and feel comfortable about the move.

As an inducement to move, offer the seller one of the following alternatives: (1) an increase in position from a third to a second mortgage or from a second to a first (use only as a last resort); (2) an increase in interest rate after the move (a good way to give him something without giving up much yourself); (3) improve the value of the collateral with more equity or a larger building; (4) pay off a portion of the note in the move, a technique that will give him some cash and shorten the length of your obligation to him; or (5) agree to increase the monthly payment without paying any immediate cash (with this offer he will have more cash to spend monthly).

Try to include the "move of mortgage" concept in all notes secured by your property, because you will need greater flexibility as you progress into your investment program.

The legal terminology of moving the mortgage is called "the substitution of collateral." In other words, the seller agrees to accept a different form of collateral for security on the note you owe him. In the note, you will want your title company to include a clause such as:

"The seller agrees to accept a substitution of collateral for this note at any time in the future as long as the seller has the opportunity to inspect the new property and can feel comfortable that his note is adequately secured. Of course, this approval will not be unreasonably withheld by the seller."

As another example, I have title to a sixty-acre piece of property in a sparsely inhabited Utah region. There is a $12,000 note against the property. There is virtually no way I will be able to sell or exchange the property unless I can move the mortgage off the property and offer it free and clear as an exchange equity. The holder of the note is flexible and willing to remove the mortgage any time I want to sell the land. So whenever I make an offer on a building I always include a sixty-acre tract of *free and clear* property as part of the equity. If a seller accepts my offer, all I have to do is to transfer the note onto my new property.

This kind of transaction is also referred to as *definancing*: the process of either paying off an existing indebtedness or moving the indebtedness to another collateral location. With this technique, your possibilities are endless!

—Allows you to borrow against unborrowable assets.

—Gives you flexibility to fix up new property and sell for cash to raise cash for buying program.

—Provides a pyramiding potential.

—Allows you to borrow cash without having to sell your property.

PAPER FORMULA #10. *Use the security blanket.*

The security blanket is used very successfully when a seller balks at one of your creative paper formulas. Consider, for example, 100 percent financing. The seller's first concern is, "Where is my security for the note you owe me? How do I know that you won't trick me out of my money?" The seller is obviously insecure. Play on that insecurity—give him more security than he bargained for. For example, if the seller of a five-unit building was concerned about a $15,000 note against the five-unit building (since you will be highly leveraged and might not be able to make your payments), offer him a "blanket mortgage" that not only gives him a mortgage of $15,000 on his own property, but also gives him additional collateral in the form of other equities in other properties you own and don't intend to sell in the near future. You can also use the blanket mortgage technique simultaneously with the "moving the mortgage" technique to placate a dubious note holder. Don't make the blanket mortgage permanent—you don't want to tie yourself up for the length of the note—but make it long enough to satisfy the seller that you will make your payments and that they'll be made on time. Then renegotiate the mortgage and free up your properties. Use a blanket mortgage as a last resort. But remember that it is extremely effective. More than 90 percent of the sellers who are initially reluctant to accept your original offer will be agreeable to a blanket mortgage.

If the seller is still concerned about his security, buy a life insurance policy (term, of course) with a face value equivalent to the mortgage, in this case $15,000. If you die, the policy will be paid to the holder of the note (since he is the beneficiary on the life insurance policy), and the mortgages will be removed. A term life insurance policy for $15,000 will cost about $80 a year—a small price to pay for something that might ensure your long-range success. (There's an additional benefit in this technique: if you do die, your family will be better off financially to be clear of the mortgage in question.)

PAPER FORMULA #11. *The creation of paper.*

As long as you own property, you can create paper against it to use as down payments on other property. Consider this example:

Suppose you find a don't wanter who is extremely flexible. Offer to buy his $100,000 apartment building; give him a $15,000 note for his equity and assume his $85,000 loan. You'll need to offer him collateral for his note so suggest he take a $15,000 mortgage on your home. The monthly payments would be $125 until the mortgage is paid in full.

You just created a note out of thin air and attached it to a property you already owned. You could do it forever! Now you can create a note against the equity in the $100,000 building and use it to buy another building. Whenever a bank turns you down, use this technique to finance your down payments.

THE CREATION OF PAPER

In essence, the power of the creation of paper technique lies in allowing an investor to borrow out 150 percent of his equity in his real estate holdings. He can structure the repayment schedule on the "created" note to fit his personal situation. All it takes is to find a don't wanter seller who would rather have a note than his property. For the nothing-down investor, the benefits are multiplied: no qualifying for bank loans, no complicated loan papers to fill out, no high interest charges, no high monthly payments, no credit checks.

Take this technique a step further: "create" an unsecured note against your future earnings. Write out a note on a standard promissory note form obtainable at any stationery store. A don't wanter would be happier with a note secured against your future earnings than he would be with his property. Very few buyers will accept a proposal like this, but you'll never know unless you ask. I've found several. Remember that it's worth a try.

PAPER FORMULA #12. *Use trade discounted paper for the down payment.*

Try buying an existing second mortgage at a substantial discount from someone who wants cash now. Then trade off the note at full face value and pick up your profit going in. In our five-unit building example, the seller was expecting a $15,000 note secured by his own building. If he is a real don't wanter he won't care if the note is secured by another piece of property. Your seller doesn't have to know that you paid $8,000 cash for the $15,000 note only two weeks earlier. Just sit back and enjoy your $7,000 profit!

PAPER FORMULA #13. *Use subordination.*

The technique of subordination is widely used in land development, but it has application in any field of real estate. Don't use the actual word *subordination*. Attorneys cringe when they hear it. Why? To subordinate means to allow someone to put a new loan on the property and to have the seller's equity subordinated to the first mortgage loan. In other words, if something goes wrong, the first mortgage holder is paid off first from the foreclosure sale. Whatever is left over is paid to the person who subordinated the interest. Sometimes there is not enough money to pay all the lien holders.

While subordination is used widely in the land development business, it can also be used in transactions involving already-developed property. One of my students was approached by a property owner (we'll call him Mr. Jones) who lived next door to one of his eight-unit apartment buildings. Mr. Jones wanted to sell my student a piece of ground suitable for construction of a four-unit apartment building. Mr. Jones didn't want much cash for his $12,000 equity in the land, so my student offered him a cash down payment of $2,000 if he would accept a third mortgage against the eight-unit apartment building with monthly payments of $100 until the balance was paid in full. Mr. Jones accepted. My student accepted the building lot free and clear of mortgages, and Mr. Jones got $2,000 in cash plus a third mortgage on another piece of property. With the free and clear lot, my student was able to obtain adequate financing to build a new four-unit building without investing additional funds.

SUBORDINATION

The second mortgage crank technique (see Chapter Sixteen) is another method of using subordination.

PAPER FORMULA #14. *Keep the payment constant, lower interest rate, increase principal amount.*

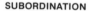

If you have a $15,000 note payable at 10 percent interest over a fifteen year period of time, the monthly payments are $161.19. By keeping the payment at $161.19 and lowering the interest rate from 10 percent to 6 percent, it is possible to amortize a much larger loan—$19,101.58, to be exact. In other words, by lowering the interest rate you can increase the amount of loan you can pay back.

Perhaps you can even pay more for a property than what it is listed for by negotiating for a lower interest rate on the mortgage. A greedy seller may agree to accept a larger purchase price and let you have a lower down payment.

By creating this situation you will make your real estate more attractive to future buyers because of the low interest rate.

PAPER FORMULA #15. *Reduce your mortgage payment period by half.*

For those readers who are chicken-hearted and can't imagine using any of the previous paper techniques, there is a technique that any home-owner can use to pay off a mortgage sooner. Did you know that the mortgage payment you make on your home is not fixed? You probably can't make a smaller than normal payment, but you *can* make a larger one. The results of a small increase in your monthly mortgage payment can make a drastic effect on your mortgage balance.

Let me illustrate: Suppose you just received a mortgage of $35,000 with monthly payments (for principal and interest only) of $281.62; interest is 9 percent over a thirty year period of time. By increasing your mortgage payment by only $50 a month, you will pay off your mortgage in seventeen years and six months instead of thirty years. That meager $50 a month was an extra $10,000 outlay over the seventeen year period, but you saved $42,243 that you would have had to make over the last twelve and a half years of the loan.

If you were to make an extra $100 payment on the same loan, your total loan payout time would be cut to thirteen years. It's a fast way to build up equity.

Make sure you check with your mortgage company to verify that the extra payment is being applied to the principal each month. Each company has different rules about extra payments.

Study these paper formulas. Apply them when you invest in real estate. There are limitless combinations and variations; tailor them to meet your specific needs. You'll find they can bring success and enhance the final negotiation process.

CHAPTER TWELVE

Running Out of Cash Before You Run Out of Good Buys: Creative Solutions to the Money Problem

Wഀ HY WOULD anyone want to buy real estate with little or no money down?

First, the smaller the investment in terms of down payment, the larger the rate of return due to the power of leverage.

Second, most of us don't have much money, if any money at all, for investment purposes.

This second reason is the most compelling reason behind the nothing down philosophy: we have no other choice.

So you're a cash-poor novice investor. The real estate investment world is still open to you if you understand money and if you know how to make money (or the lack of it) work for you.

Consider a building that is selling for $100,000. The seller wants $10,000 down.

The property is a great investment as it stands, but there is one glaring problem: who has $10,000 sitting around in a bank account waiting for the right deal to come along? The majority of us barely have enough money in savings (if we have any savings at all) to buy a new lawn mower. Obviously, we'll have to come up with some rather creative solutions.

There are eight major sources of creative down payments:

1. Cash saved by living the guns and butter theory (heaven forbid).
2. Soft paper notes used with all parties involved—including the seller.

117

$10,000 SELLERS EQUITY $100,000 VALUE

$90,000 FIRST MORTGAGE

3. The use of rent and deposits, or creative splits involving the subject property.
4. Short-term borrowings from hard-money lenders.
5. Long-term borrowings from hard-money lenders.
6. Exchanging and the use of other equities.
7. Partnerships.
8. Options.

The first source is up to you. You must begin to save money. Limit your current consumption of butter items in favor of future, long-term gun items. A savings account isn't the best solution. Even if you were able to put $200 a month into a 6 percent interest savings account, it would take you almost four years to raise the $10,000 needed for the down payment in our example. By that time the $100,000 building would be worth about $146,000, much beyond your reach with your $10,000. You will obviously have to turn to other sources to obtain that $10,000. We will now examine all of the areas open to you.

Meanwhile, you must realize that the nothing-down concept involves the use of borrowed money. This money may come from the seller himself, or from banks, or from partners—just as long as it does *not* come from your own pocket. This process requires a creative mind, one that is willing to try any solution. Basically, it is a process of borrowing yourself to wealth using other people's money.

The process of creativity is a mysterious and interesting one. It is brilliantly described in the following story. A student refused to parrot back what he had been taught in class. When the student protested, Mr. Calandra was asked to act as arbiter between the student and his professor.

"I went to my colleague's office and read the examination question: 'Show how it is possible to determine the height of a tall building with the aid of a barometer.'

"The student had answered: 'Take the barometer to the top of the building, attach a long rope to it, lower the barometer to the street and then bring it up, measuring the length of the rope. The length of the rope is the height of the building.'

"A high grade is supposed to certify competence in physics, but the answer did not confirm this. I suggested that the student have another try at answering the question. I gave the student six minutes, with the warning that his answer should show some knowledge of physics. In the next minute he dashed off his answer, which read:

" 'Take the barometer to the top of the building and lean over the edge of the roof. Drop the barometer, timing its fall with a stopwatch. Then, using the formula $S = \frac{1}{2}at^2$, calculate the height of the building.'

"At this point, I asked my colleague if he would give up. He conceded, and I gave the student almost full credit.

"In leaving my colleague's office, I recalled that the student had said he had other answers to the problem, so I asked him what they were.

" 'Oh, yes,' said the student. 'There are many ways of getting the height of a tall building with the aid of a barometer. For example, you could take the barometer out on a sunny day and measure the height of the barometer, the length of its shadow, and the length of the shadow of the building, and by the use of a simple proportion, determine the height of the building.'

" 'Fine,' I said. 'And the others?'

" 'Yes,' said the student. 'Take the barometer and begin to walk up the stairs. As you climb the stairs, you mark off the length of the barometer along the wall. You then count the number of marks, and this will give you the height of the building in barometer units. A very direct method.

" 'Finally,' he concluded, 'there are many other ways of solving the problem. Probably the best,' he said, 'is to take the barometer to the basement and knock on the superintendent's door. When the superintendent answers, you speak to him as follows: "Mr. Superintendent, here

I have a fine barometer. If you will tell me the height of this building, I will give you this barometer." ' " (Alexander Calandra, *The Teaching of Elementary Science and Mathematics.*)

Creativity is born when you have a problem to solve. And as you can see from the above story, there are many ways of solving a problem. Creativity is the art of looking for solutions that are out of the ordinary, different, unorthodox.

Most of us spend countless hours trying to solve ordinary problems in the same old ways. We enter school at age six and exit about fifteen years later with hardly the bare essentials we need to solve problems. We have usually been drilled to see only the *obvious* solutions; we haven't learned to dig just a little bit deeper for fresh ideas. We haven't learned to devise creative solutions to both ordinary and complex problems.

Consider, for instance, the most common problem of every real estate investor: Lack of investment capital. Some of us don't even have enough cash to make an initial investment. To make matters worse, most of us have been trained to believe that it is impossible to buy real estate unless we have cash down payments bursting our bank accounts wide open. So most of us—lacking that kind of bank account—never even *try* to invest.

There are other solutions to the cash problem. Those solutions require creative thinking. Some of the solutions presented in this book will appear ridiculously contrived. That kind of thinking, though, is a trap. Don't let it muddle your creativity. Be concerned only with whether or not the solution will work.

Stretch your mind to new dimensions. Begin to be creative. To do these things, you will have to make a firm commitment to the following:

Positive Thinking. Positive solutions require positive thoughts. If you continually tell yourself, "It can't be done," you will find exactly that. It can't be done. Creativity is born and nurtured in an environment of "can do" thoughts. It *is* possible for you to buy hundreds of thousands of dollars worth of real estate in your own area. I have done it with little or none of my own money. Over 75 percent of those who have taken my seminar have done the same. You can, too.

Broadmindedness. Regard the obvious real estate solutions, such as large cash down payments, as only a small percentage of the solutions that will ultimately work. Look for these solutions like a prospector looks for gold. They are just as precious as gold to you, because they will enable you to buy real estate without having to invest the cash you either don't have or don't want to spend. Whenever someone says, "I must have cash," dig deeper for a better solution.

Disdain of the Ordinary Solution. Develop a healthy disdain for the ordinary solution. Try your hardest to practice creative solutions whenever possible. Deal with buyers and sellers who are creative. You can learn from them.

Brainstorming. Discuss your problem. The realtor, the seller, the seller's attorney, and anyone else who could have an impact on the decision to sell or buy should be involved. Search for solutions other than cash. Ask probing questions. Forget that cash is even a solution.

Deep Thinking. Ponder. Don't give up. You'll learn the excitement of flashes of creative genius.

Cultivate a creative mind. Treasure it. Some will tell you that the only avenue that leads to successful real estate investment is paved with cash. Don't believe it. You will eventually run out of cash—probably very soon. You'll never run out of creativity. Plunderers can rob you of your cash. No one can steal your creativity. Cash loses value. Creativity never will.

It is your most vital asset.

Commit to it now.

CHAPTER THIRTEEN

Nothing Down: Five Success Stratagems

Y**OUR GOAL** is to buy real estate with nothing down. "Nothing down" does not mean that the seller receives no down payment. It means that the down payment comes from somewhere. It means that *the down payment never comes out of your pocket*.

You've learned to incorporate creativity in your life. Now use it. Study the sample solutions I've listed in this chapter. Use one alone, or combine them to increase your effectiveness.

Let me involve you in an actual example of the nothing-down concept.

One evening I received a call from a man who had been attending my investment seminar. He described a fourteen-unit building located in a small town; it had been advertised for several months in our local newspaper, and I had checked it out with the realtor when it first appeared on the market. I had not been impressed. The seller required too much down payment. The units were too small. The rent was too low.

My student had gone a step further. After the unit had been on the market for several months, the seller had become a serious don't wanter. My student realized that the seller would be willing to be a little creative in the terms of the sale.

Here are the facts pertaining to the property. Let's see if you can be as creative as my student was:

> Description of property: 14 one-bedroom units (a converted home and motel).
>
> Listed price: $180,000.

Mortgage information: $155,000 contract with payments of $1,250 @ 9 percent interest.

Down payment: seller would like $25,000.

Average monthly rent collection: 13 units @ $150 + 1 unit @ $200 = $1,875. (Rents were all too low.)

Tenants' deposits: $100 per unit = $1,400.

Realtor's commission: 6 percent of sales price = $10,500 (based on final $175,000 price).

Reason seller needed to sell: a don't wanter.

Seller's outstanding obligations: $7,000 small incidental debts at hardware stores, lumber yards and so on.

Make a guess! How much cash out of your own pocket will you need to buy this property? How will you come up with it?

The first thing my student (we'll call him Harold) did was to offer less—$175,000. Now he had to solve the problem of the $20,000 down payment. As it eventually turned out, Harold only had to come up with $2,000 in cash—for closing costs; to get the cash, he formed a partnership with his father, and his father funded the venture. In addition to forming a partnership, Harold used five fundamental creative ways to lower the amount of the down payment. Let's look at them one by one:

1. *Rents and deposits.* Harold learned early in the negotiation process that rents were due on the first of each month. Because of this, he knew that barring any major vacancies before the closing, there would be $1,875 in rents and $1,400 in total renter cleaning or security deposits that would become the property of the buyer on the closing day. He also knew that the first mortgage payment would not be due for thirty days following the closing date, so, he negotiated the closing date to coincide with the day the rents were due. He also made sure that his first regular mortgage payment to the seller would fall due thirty days after the apartment building had been purchased. Harold ended up collecting over $1,800 in rent at the closing; after taking care of some minor operational expenses, Harold could apply what remained to the down payment. When the thirty days were up, Harold just collected the next month's rent and applied it to the mortgage payment.

Harold also used security deposits (amounting to $1,400) toward the down payment. But don't deposits belong to the tenants, and don't they have to be returned to the tenant when he moves out? Yes. But when one tenant moves out, another moves in—and the deposit from the new tenant can be given as a refund to the old tenant. In Utah deposits can be held (co-mingled) in the bank account of the building owner; in some other states the law requires the funds to be held in a separate escrow account which cannot be touched. Make sure you know the law and obey it; if you are allowed to hold the money in your account, you can apply it to down payments instead of taking money out of your own pocket.

2. *The realtor's commission.* One of the seller's first obligations at completion of the sale is to pay the realtor his commission. In our example, the realtor's fee was 6 percent ($175,000 $\times$ .06 = $10,500). That $10,500 amounts to a large share of the required down payment. Harold approached the realtor about lending him some of the commission; in return, Harold gave the realtor a personal note guaranteeing to pay the money in two payments: $2,000 in cash and the balance—$8,500 —on a note due in three years. The seller wasn't involved in the transaction or the negotiation—he doesn't need to know what happens to the commission.

Not all realtors will agree to loan you part of the commission, but the ones who do will probably not charge you a high interest rate, will not require credit checks or extensive paper work, and will not ask you to secure the note against any property. You should be able to negotiate some excellent terms. One way to convince the realtor to take a note is to tell him that if he doesn't help you out, you can't buy the property— then there will be no sale and no commission at all. If necessary and if you can handle it, give him a small monthly payment.

It will be much more difficult for you to arrange this kind of loan if the realtor is not his own broker. If the realtor works for another broker, he must share any commissions he earns—sometimes up to 50 percent of the commission will go to the broker. This leaves a realtor little to live on, let alone to loan out. Try to deal with the listing agents or brokers if you plan on borrowing commissions. The more people involved in the commission split, the less you will be able to borrow. Try always to deal with the listing agent on a large piece of property. If he can list and sell a property at the same time, he earns so much that he thinks he can afford to lend you some of it. In Harold's case, the listing, selling, and broker were the same person. This situation is ideal.

3. *Assume the seller's obligations.* The seller's major reason for dumping his property was to relieve himself of some financial obligations. Harold sensed the seller's motivation and agreed to transfer part of the seller's obligations to his own name. This offer appealed to the seller, so Harold contacted all of the seller's creditors to explain that he, not the seller, was

going to pay the notes off. Harold was able to extend the notes' due dates and in some cases he was able to get a discount by paying cash. Harold then subtracted the amount of the obligations he assumed from the down payment. Harold assumed obligations totalling $7,000, so he subtracted that amount from the down payment he owed the seller.

You could arrange something like this in several ways. One seller had not paid his bills for several months. An astute buyer entered the picture and visited each of the seller's creditors (who had understandably become quite anxious) and negotiated to pay them off in cash if they would accept $.50 on the dollar for their outstanding notes. Many took him up on his offer, and he was able to lower both the price of the property and the amount of required down payment substantially.

4. *Prepaid rent as part of the down payment.* Harold discovered early in the negotiation period that the seller and his family—who lived in the apartment building Harold was buying—would have to find somewhere to live while looking for a house to buy. Harold offered to let the seller and his family live in his apartment until he found a new home or for at least six months. The rent of $250 a month would be applied toward Harold's down payment. In this case, the six months' rent prepaid was $1,500, which reduced the amount of down payment Harold had to take out of his own pocket.

5. *Supply the seller what he needs.* Harold learned from spending some time with the seller that the seller needed to buy some appliances and furniture for a home he was building. He bought $2,000 worth of needed items using credit cards and stores' credit. He then offered the package to the seller for $2,000 as part of the down payment, substantially reducing the amount of cash required for the down payment.

Look at Harold's final negotiation on the building:

He was able to receive credits totalling $22,000.

Realtor's fees borrowed	$ 8,500
Rents and deposits	3,000
Seller's obligations assumed	7,000
Seller's furniture bought on credit	2,000
Prepaid rents to seller	1,500
Total credits	$22,000

Of course, there were some cash items needed to be paid out of the closing:

Realtor's cash	$ 2,000
Closing costs	2,000
Seller's down payment	20,000
Total debits	$24,000

The total amount of extra cash needed to close this transaction was only $2,000 (the difference between the debits and the credits). Harold borrowed that from his father. Harold took *nothing* out of his own pocket toward the down payment; he virtually purchased the building for *nothing down*.

Two things will make you successful in efforts to reduce a down payment. First, talk to the seller. Find out his needs, his obligations; try to determine why he is selling. Such information can give you clues to a workable approach. Second, use the techniques listed simultaneously in creative combinations. Look at what Harold did with all five.

And there are more. Keep reading!

CHAPTER FOURTEEN

Seven More Nothing-Down Techniques

B EFORE YOU learn other techniques to reduce down payment, understand that as far as a down payment is concerned, the seller is your best friend. Talk to him. Learn what you can about his situation. Let him tell you (without knowing it) which of these techniques will bring a favorable response:

1. *The ultimate paper-out.* I was once working with a very close friend (we'll call him Louis) as a partner on a subdivision. He wanted to invest in more real estate as a way of bettering his tax position, but he didn't have any cash to use for an investment.

I had recently been talking to another friend of mine who owned a four-unit apartment building; his time was spread so thin that he couldn't handle the management, and he desperately mentioned that he would gladly sell his building for nothing down. *He was a serious don't wanter.* He had all the symptoms: a rational decision to sell with totally irrational terms, the motivation to act immediately, and the willingness to be as flexible as necessary.

I considered buying the property myself, but my time was spread too thin, and I soon would have been a don't wanter for the same reason my friend was. But the property was perfect for Louis. Within one week we had the property signed over into his name. Here are some of the financial details:

Sale price	$70,000
First mortgage	55,000
Second mortgage	12,000
Third mortgage	3,000
Seller's required down	—0—

The seller arranged for a second mortgage of $12,000 through a lending institution that charged 10 percent. He paid the loan fees and interest fees to set up the new loan. Louis assumed both the first and second mortgage loans. The remaining $3,000 of the seller's equity was put in the form of a note secured by a third trust deed against the property; 12 percent interest accrued on the note for the first three years, but there were *no monthly payments*! At the end of the three years the note would begin a monthly schedule for a payout over a ten-year period.

A quick look at the cash flow situation revealed that the income from the rents was not enough to cover expenses and mortgage payments on both the first and second mortgages. Louis would have to come up with an additional $80–100 a month!

Wasn't it a crazy move to make? Shouldn't income from rental properties cover mortgage payments? Isn't it wrong to invest in something like this?

In Louis's case, no. Remember—he wanted to improve his tax situation. Paying out the extra $100 a month did just that—and didn't alter his lifestyle because of an adequate cash flow from other sources.

About two months before he'd owned the property for a year, Louis placed the following ad in the local newspaper:

Fourplex for sale by owner
$78,000
Call Louis, 555–1234

Three days later he sold the property for $78,000 cash. The original owner received his $3,000 from the sale, and Louis received $8,000 in cash.

Louis's down payment was nothing at the time of the purchase, but he had to make a "deferred down payment" of $100 negative cash flow each month. His total down payment amounted to about $1,000 during the ten months he owned the building. His net proceeds for his ten months ownership was $7,000 in cash.

Louis is not an isolated example. This kind of transaction happens every day in every major city of our country. It might as well start happening to you. The technique is called the paper-out formula because the seller actually takes his equity in the form of paper or mortgages. No cash is transferred. The buyer gives his promise to pay the seller's equity over a specified period of time. The buyer has 100 percent leverage. Total leverage almost always results in a negative cash flow.

What about negative cash flows? Don't be scared of a negative cash flow *if* you have the money to cover it, *if* you can eventually raise the rents to cover it, or *if* you plan on keeping the property only a short while and expect to sell it for a substantial profit.

One word of caution: be deadly accurate in your projection of the expenses. Most owners with negative cash flow end up in trouble because they didn't project accurately enough what the expenses would be, and the negative cash flow gets greater and greater. Do your homework carefully before you buy something that appears to be a marginal property.

2. *The balloon down payment.* In this transaction the buyer gives the seller part of the down payment in cash and then negotiates to pay the rest in several "balloon payments"—for instance, on a down payment of $3,000 the buyer might pay $600 at the time of the sale, $1,200 six months later, and $1,200 a year after the sale.

This approach is really quite logical. The seller who must have a majority of his equity in cash—and who therefore requires a cash down payment—may be persuaded to sell his property if he receives a portion of the down payment immediately and the rest in a relatively short period of time. You can take possession of the property with a relatively small down payment and a promise to pay the rest.

This is a gutsy technique, but it allows you to have some breathing room, some time in which to search for the remaining down payment. You may just want to fix the property up and put it back on the market for a quick profit. Your new buyer would provide you with the money to cover the balloon payment. A word of caution: have other sources to bail you out in case you can't sell quickly enough.

It is common practice for a seller to accept part of a down payment in cash and the rest in the form of a second or third mortgage.

"Taking out a second mortgage" does *not* mean that you go to the bank and borrow the money secured on a second mortgage. Banks are not involved in any way in the process; it's a transaction you work out with the seller.

Let's look at an example.

Upon graduating from college I began looking for properties to invest in. The first newspaper I picked up ran an ad in the income property section of the classified ads that read something like this:

> Income property, duplex close to campus, reasonable down payment.
> Seller anxious. Call Terry at 555–4321.

I called immediately and got an appointment to visit the property that afternoon.

The property was rather run down in appearance but was well built, and the location was excellent. The sellers, a mother-and-son partnership, had been trying to sell for some time. They were serious don't wanters. A real estate firm had tried for months with no success to sell the property at $26,500. In desperation the mother and son had cancelled the listing and had begun to advertise the property themselves for $25,500. Their loan was $19,000, and they wanted to cash out.

After examining the property "thoroughly" (at the time I didn't really know what to look for), I called up the least expensive appraiser in the Yellow Pages and had him do a quick appraisal. He estimated that the duplex was worth $22,500 without the furniture, which was probably worth $1,000.

That wasn't much consolation; I went to visit the seller at his apartment so I could assess the situation. The son was attending school and was in the middle of a master's degree program. He didn't have time to manage the duplex, and he needed the money.

After several hours of talking, we reached a solution. He would accept a price of $25,000. I would assume his loan of $19,000 at the bank. The remaining $6,000 equity would be paid as follows: (1) $1,500 upon closing, (2) $1,000 in two months, (3) an additional $1,000 in another two months, and (4) the remaining $2,500 in equal monthly installments of $75 until paid in full (about four years). The $75-a-month payment was secured by a second mortgage on the duplex.

Four days after I bought this property for $25,000 with a $1,500 down payment, a neighbor approached me and offered me $28,000 for the property. He agreed to continue to pay the balloon payments as I had negotiated with the seller. And he paid me back my original $1,500 down payment plus the $3,000 profit.

3. *Use talent, not cash.* Depending on who your seller is, you may be

able to trade the seller some of your valuable services as part of the down payment. If you are an accountant or an attorney, you could give your seller credits toward the use of your services—for instance, offer to do his taxes for the next ten years. I recently offered the foreman in my subdivision a partial equity in a building lot I owned in exchange for the use of his labor on my own personal residence. He will do all the carpentry work on my home for free and I will give him my equity in a $14,000 building lot so he can build himself a home. We both came out ahead— and happy.

Take advantage of any services you have that can be traded in part for real estate equities. One of my students was in the business of selling home food storage. He could buy the merchandise at dealer's cost and trade it for full retail value as equity in a piece of property. Let your imagination run wild.

4. *High monthly down payments.* If you are blessed with a high monthly surplus cash flow but don't want to wait to save for the down payment, consider offering the seller his equity in the form of a very high monthly payment. For example, suppose a seller wanted to sell, but he needed some cash for his $50,000 home with a $6,000 equity. Offer to buy his home with no down payment, assume his existing loan of $44,000, and make him a $500 monthly payment at 9 percent interest on his remaining equity. An anxious seller may bite because he knows that he can get his full price this way rather than a lesser price and an all-cash offer.

This technique offers you the flexibility of having at least thirty days to find another buyer if you are going to sell the property for quick profit. It also acts as a forced savings plan: at the end of twelve months you will have been forced to pay over $6,000 cash to buy the property, but the property will also have appreciated at least ten percent during that period of time. Compare the return to that of a savings account:

Real Estate Purchase		Savings Account	
$500/month in $50,000 home appreciating @ 10 percent annually		$500/month in savings account earning 6 percent interest	
One-year principal	$ 6,000	One-year principal	$6,000
Equity build-up	250 (approx.)	Interest earned at bank	168
Appreciation	5,000	Taxes paid @ 20 percent bracket	(34)
Tax savings	250 (approx.)		
Interest paid to seller	(254)		
Net position	$11,246	Net position	$6,134

The obvious winner is the real estate purchase.

5. *Raise the price, lower the terms.* If you determine that the seller is more concerned about his price than about what he receives in the form of cash, appeal to his sense of greed. Using the numbers from the previous example, offer him a price of $52,000 if he will sell the building to you with no down or low down terms. Tell him he can choose: $47,000 all cash or $52,000 with no cash down. The real estate industry operates on a universal rule: the more cash involved in the sale, the lower the price. The converse is also true: the lower the cash, the higher the price and profit to the seller. *It may be to your advantage to offer a higher price for a lower down payment.*

6. *Split the property.* I once bought a twelve-unit apartment building from an attorney who had purchased it less than eighteen months before. When he bought the building there was a small two-bedroom home on the same piece of property included in the deal. Since the property was commercially zoned and located near the city's downtown section, he simply split the home out of the legal description of the original property.

He paid $140,000 for the property. He sold me the twelve-unit building for $141,000, and he sold the small home to a title company for $19,500. His profit for an eighteen-month holding period was about $20,000.

One of my students came across the same sort of a situation not long ago. He and his wife had been looking for property ever since they had mortgaged their home to buy a fifteen-unit building. The wife made an offer on three duplexes; they asked me if there was a way for them to buy all three units without using any of their own cash. We decided they should sell two of the units for a higher price; the profit they earned would give them some cash to pay the owner of the three units. They had negotiated a three month closing date. The properties were substantially underpriced, so they went looking for someone who would pay a higher price on two of the units before the closing date arrived. Then they would have sold the two units to the new buyer in a simultaneous closing that would have given them enough profit to be able to buy the third unit without investing any of their own cash. This technique is discussed in more detail in the chapter on options. As it turned out, my students located a man who was willing to lend them the money for the down payments on the three units and they decided to buy the properties and keep them.

Another example clearly shows the splitting technique. A friend purchased an older thirty-unit apartment building which had a large amount of antique furniture in it. He removed the furniture and sold it to an antique dealer for $20,000. This helped him with the down payment he had negotiated, since he had given himself ample time to sell the furniture for cash.

Other splits? I recently bought a house that had a very deep, weed-covered back lot. The neighbor around the corner approached me before I closed on the sale and asked if I was interested in selling the back lot to him. I agreed to sell it for $2,900. Since my down payment to buy the home was only $2,000, I was able to take $2,000 of the money from the sale of the back lot to apply toward the down payment on the house. I put about $900 in my pocket. Of course, to accomplish the sale of the back lot I had to have it released from the mortgage with a lending institution. This required a new survey, a new appraisal, a new title policy, and some paper work. But it was well worth it!

7. *Defer down payment with no mortgage payments.* My students are always teaching me new techniques. At one of my seminars one of my repeat students related this story to me. I thought it was creative enough to include as one of the arsenal of nothing-down techniques.

After having taken the Nothing Down Seminar this student went out into the marketplace to find some property to buy. He located an older six-unit building which the seller owned free and clear of any mortgages. The property was in an excellent location and was priced right. There was only one problem. The seller wanted a $10,000 down payment, which my student did not have at the time. He began to use his head instead of his pocketbook and came up with the following solution. He reasoned that the seller had no mortgage payments to make each month and that he was wealthy enough so that the lack of monthly income for a few months would not be a burden to him. So my student proposed that the seller turn over the property to him with no down payment and *no mortgage payments* for six months. Interest would accrue on the mortgage for six months; at the end of this period, normal monthly payments would commence and continue for the next twenty-five years until paid in full. The seller reluctantly agreed, since he was able to obtain his full asking price and terms with the small exception of the six-month's delay in the down payment. As soon as the buyer took over the property, he was able to collect the rents and the security deposits and to put them in his bank account. And as each month rolled around he collected the rents and let them accrue in his bank account. He paid out only necessary expenses and did all of the maintenance work himself to save money. As you can guess by now, since he did not have a mortgage payment to make, the majority of the income he collected went right into savings, and during the next six months he was able to save enough money to come up with almost all the required $10,000 down payment. (E.g., six units renting at $275 per month gives a gross monthly income of $1,650. In six months' time, over $9,900 has been collected from rents not counting the tenant security deposits. If he can be frugal with his expense money, the $10,000 down payment is generated from the property rents.) In effect, the buyer borrowed the down payment from the seller, who let him repay it over the next twenty-five years. Not bad.

So far we've discussed twelve creative ways to come up with part or all of a down payment. There are times, though, when you will be forced to come up with cash. To do that, you might have to turn to banks and other lending institutions. Let's examine the best ways to use those sources.

CHAPTER FIFTEEN

Funds from the Philistines: Short-term Loans from Hard-money Lenders

S**o you've** located the perfect deal, a real bargain! How are you going to get your name on the deed if you don't have something put aside for a rainy day?

You'll need to borrow the money, probably from someone I call a "hard-money lender." Hard-money lenders offer you hard terms: the loan has a high interest rate, short-term payback period, and, as a consequence, high monthly payments. In addition, hard-money lenders always try to secure the loan by using another piece of property as collateral. There's another good reason for calling them "hard-money lenders"—the loans are hard to get! If your income is low, your monthly obligations are high, or you are self-employed, watch out. Hard-money lenders are wary of a borrower like you, especially if you are planning on investing the borrowed funds in real estate. For some reason most hard-money lenders haven't realized the potential such investments have. There is a saying in the banking business: "We don't give unsecured lines of credit to bullfighters, parachutists, and real estate investors."

Of course, you should turn to hard-money lenders only after you have exhausted all other sources of income and only if you are sure you can make a good profit. Under those circumstances and equipped with a little know-how, you can make banks and other lending institutions work for you.

There are five kinds of hard-money lenders: commercial banks; thrift institutions and finance companies; credit unions; money brokers; and

137

cash-by-mail companies. Each has its peculiar lending guidelines, and each has different goals and objectives.

As you gain experience you will find out which lender to contact first for the best terms; I've found that my own banker has given me the best service at the lowest interest rates. When I began investing in real estate, my strategy was to establish a strong credit rating so I could borrow large amounts of money quickly on an unsecured basis. I approached the banker who handled my checking account and explained my objective. I then began to borrow small amounts of money so I could establish a history of prompt repayment. My first loan was for $500; I worked my way up to a credit limit of $5,000 unsecured.

That's when I ran into trouble. As soon as I reached $5,000, the loan committee was reluctant to loan me any more money on an unsecured basis. As a result, I promptly moved all of my accounts to another more flexible bank that was confident in my abilities to repay large amounts of money.

Since then I have deposited my money in several banks so that my borrowing power could multiply. I currently have the capacity to borrow thousands of dollars from each of four or five banks. Even though this relationship was a long and tedious one to establish, it has proved worthwhile and necessary.

If you don't already have a good credit rating, open checking accounts at as many banks as you can. Find those whose loan officers are friendly and interested in helping you establish a credit rating through borrowing small amounts of money. There will be plenty of banks in your area to deal with, and banks are in a keenly competitive business, so don't be afraid to get up and walk out of a bank that is not responsive to your needs and wishes. Write letters to the officers of banks where you are treated poorly; let them know how you feel.

Constantly cultivate your sources for short-term funds by visiting with lenders weekly. Learn how their business operates and get to know the managers in each office. You will soon realize that bank officers and lending institution personnel are ordinary human beings, not fiery dragons. The more you know about borrowing, the more confident you will become about your ability to borrow money.

It is simultaneously amusing and exasperating to realize that the person most concerned about security usually finds himself employed at a bank, where there is a lot of money in the vault. The banker's salary is notoriously low, but he has all the security in the world. And he holds the purse-strings to your financial future. It's ironic that a man so security-conscious stands in the way of the enterprising investor who dares risk everything to make his dream come true. An odd couple, indeed.

So before you begin to borrow money, try to understand your banker's goals and objectives. They're probably in conflict with your investment goals and objectives: he is concerned about high security, while you are trying to negotiate the highest possible leverage. He wants collateral; you would rather have an unsecured loan. He needs appraisals, credit checks, approval from loan committees, title policies, and a pile of other paper work; you want to borrow money in the most simple and straight-forward manner. Whenever possible, try to supply what your banker wants, but explain that once you have proved your prompt repayment ability you would like to start doing business your way.

If you recognize that your personalities clash, go to another bank. Life is too short to waste your time dealing with someone who questions your integrity, points out all of the weak spots in your financial situation, reduces you to begging in order to get the loan, and then makes you pay for the "privilege" of doing business with him. There are plenty of good bankers in your area. Go to them.

There's a good analogy that describes the banker-borrower relationship. When you go to the doctor for a checkup, he asks you to strip to your shorts, stick your tongue out, and cough at the appropriate time. A banker interviewing you for a loan asks you to "strip to the shorts" financially. That's where the similarity ends, though. The banker is concerned with *his* security, not yours. Don't be fooled by all the advertising that portrays the friendly banker who is anxious to lend you money. Just remember: the people who are writing the ads aren't making the loans!

Try to locate a young, nonconservative, aggressive banker who has enough experience to understand your request but who has not been around long enough to be influenced by the "lifers" on his loan committee. Ask your loan officer if he owns any real estate besides his own home. If he does, your chances of getting a loan for real estate ventures will be increased, because the loan officer will understand your goals.

Let a banker know that he is competing for your dollars. There are plenty of banks, and he should be trying to attract you to his bank. Remember—*your* business is important to the bank, not the other way around. Adopt that attitude, and you will begin to win.

Try to help your banker—and yourself. Be prepared with typed financial statements, income tax statements for the last two years, pictures of some of your properties, and other supporting documents. Try to present as stable a picture to your banker as you possibly can. You might consider putting all of your highly leveraged properties in your spouse's name to reduce the loan-to-debt ratio.

Be as realistic with your financial statement as possible. If you want your banker to believe your statement, be sure that you enter the value of your car below the car's current market value; your banker can check values very easily with his used-car books. If he can see that you are realistic on the things he does understand, he will trust your values on the things (such as real estate holdings) he may not understand.

Critical questions that a banker will want answered are: How much money do you want or need? Why do you need to borrow it from me? Where is your bank account now? Why don't you borrow the money from your own bank? What are you going to use the money for? How will you pay the loan back? If you can't pay the loan back within the specified time limit, how can I be sure that I will be able to collect the money from you? Be prepared with answers to all of these questions. Keep your requests simple, and don't go into full detail about your creative trans-actions. *A confused mind always says no.* Don't confuse your banker with complicated real estate deals. Simply tell him how much money you need and how you intend to pay it back.

A banker's chance for promotion comes with his capacity to make good loans. That's why he's concerned about your highly leveraged position. Convince him that you are not a threat to his security and his chance to get ahead. From time to time drop in to discuss your progress with him. Let him know that you are successful and that you are a man of your word.

When you find a good banker, let everyone know about him. When your banker finds out that you have been favorably advertising him and his bank, he will appreciate it.

Once you've begun to establish good relationships with bankers, jump at the chance to borrow money. By borrowing money and repaying it on schedule, you can establish a credit history that could be worth hundreds of thousands of dollars later. Do what you can now. You might borrow $500 from one bank and deposit it in a savings account at another bank. When the note comes due, you can pay it off by withdrawing the money from the savings account. The interest charges on the loan will be largely offset by the amount of interest accrued from the savings account.

Or you could deposit $500 in your savings account and then ask the same bank for a $500 loan secured by your savings account deposit. You could then deposit the $500 loan in a savings account at another bank, where you would request another $500 loan. You could do this in four or five different banks simultaneously, proving to several bankers that you are able to both borrow money and have a savings account. This method requires $500 initial capital plus accrued interest for the term of the loan, but even if interest is $100 during a six-month period, the stronger financial position you will gain will be well worth the price.

Why use so many banks? First, when you can borrow funds from one of several sources, you have increased your flexibility and your capacity to buy larger properties. Second, if you have a short-term loan of $5,000 due at one bank, you can always go to another bank in your system and borrow the $5,000 to repay the first bank. This way you could keep a $5,000 note floating forever, and the only cost would be the interest. All the time you would be improving your credit rating through prompt loan repayment.

1. It is feasible for a person with good credit history to be able to borrow up to $50,000 on an unsecured basis from one bank. If you were able to borrow this amount from five banks, you could secure up to $250,000 in cash in less than a week. Of course, it would take you five or ten years to attain this level of borrowing, but you will make the most money when you are able to use other people's money to buy properties at good prices.

In the initial stages of your borrowing program, the banks may wish to secure your small loan on a piece of property you own. This is a normal procedure. But you should request that your loans be moved to an unsecured basis as soon as possible so you do not encumber properties you might want to keep free for trading purposes.

2. In addition to *commercial banks*, there are a host of financial institutions that specialize in making loans for buying cars, boats, trailers, and other "butter" items. These *thrift institutions* borrow funds from customers and loan it out at higher rates: up to 18 percent in many cases, and sometimes as high as 36 percent. Thrift institutions usually require a monthly repayment plan, while banks are equipped to lend money on a balloon basis for three to six months or up to a year. These thrift institutions charge higher interest rates and are not prone to lend money on an unsecured basis. They should be avoided; if you *do* use this kind of financial institution, settle only for the best terms you can find. Several

loan companies allow you to miss up to two payments per year on your loan without penalty; search for the terms that will give you the most flexibility.

3. If you belong to a *credit union*, your chance of obtaining a loan at reasonable rates is good. One of my former seminar graduates who did not have a high-salaried job applied for a $20,000 loan from his credit union to use as a down payment on a fifteen-unit apartment building. His loan was approved, and he was able to arrange for repayment terms that did not strap him with negative monthly payments. It's a good idea to join a credit union and to establish a good business relationship with one of the loan officers.

4. *Money brokers* make their living by introducing individuals who have money to lend to people who need to borrow money. The brokers charge a fee ranging from 1 to 10 percent of the loan they arrange. You can locate a money broker by checking the classified section of your local newspaper under "Loans" (or some similar heading). You may also find brokers listed in the Yellow Pages along with other financial institutions under "loans."

Money brokers primarily locate long-term loans for real estate, but some money brokers also find short-term second mortgage money. Their rates will be comparable to those of loan companies, but brokerage fees may be higher, so use these kinds of short-term monies only if you are certain you can make a healthy profit on your real estate investment after all interest charges are paid and only after you have exhausted all other sources.

5. Some loan companies offer a *loan-by-mail service*, often advertised in airline and executive magazines. These loans are unsecured, but the rates and monthly payments are high. To qualify you must have a substantial income and you must not be self-employed.

Whichever type of institution you decide to borrow from, search for the lowest rates available and, if possible, do not get locked into inflexible monthly payments. If such payments are required, always negotiate for the longest possible payback period, since this will lower your monthly payments. Commercial banks may have three-, six-, or nine-month commercial notes that do not carry monthly payment obligations, but you should *always* be prepared to come up with the lump sum when the loan comes due either by taking out another loan or by converting the balloon payment to a monthly payment until you are able to pay the loan in full.

There *are* some borrowing options open if you are unable to obtain an unsecured or a conventional loan. First, consider a second mortgage on your home. If you own your own home, you've probably built up a rather large equity because of the increase in the value of real estate over the years, and you might be able to borrow the down payment for your investment program by taking out a second mortgage on your house. Your spouse may disapprove of a second mortgage because it exposes the family's financial situation to risk. But if the real estate purchased with the borrowed funds is well-selected and underpriced in relation to the market value, the risk is minimal, and at best, it increases the family's long-range financial situation. Sometimes you need to take a risk to improve your position.

As an example, consider a family that owns a home valued at $50,000; they have a loan of $30,000. After checking with several financial institutions to find one with low interest and a long repayment period, the husband locates a company that will loan funds for a second mortgage with a fifteen-year term and 14 percent interest with no closing costs. The monthly payments on the $10,000 loan will be only $133.17.

The family has decided to invest in a duplex. The duplex is selling for $50,000 with a down payment of $10,000 cash; the seller agrees to carry the balance of the $40,000 with monthly payments of $335.68 for the next twenty-five years. This payment will be covered by rent paid by tenants of the duplex, and will leave up to $50 per month cash flow after the payment of all expenses (since the husband will make all minor repairs himself). The extra cash flow helps defray the second mortgage payment, and the family will have a net monthly payment of $133.17 — $50 = $83.17, not too burdensome a commitment.

What will the long-run picture look like? Suppose both the house and the duplex will appreciate at the rate of 10 percent annually for the next five years. At the end of five years, the home will have appreciated to $80,525 and the duplex will have appreciated to the same value. Taking into consideration the loan the family had to obtain on the home to buy the duplex, the family's risk of using a second mortgage has paid off to the tune of about $30,000.

Using a second mortgage is an excellent technique to raise capital for an investment program. Yes, it takes some fortitude to overcome the security complex, but the results only add to your family's security if the funds are well spent. Under *no* circumstances should any of the funds from a second mortgage be spent on butter items. Leave your house equity alone unless you plan to use it on a solid investment.

6. If your banker doesn't like the idea of lending you money on a

second mortgage for investment purposes, apply for a home improvement loan (which can usually be easily arranged). Who says that after you paint one room in your home, you can't change your mind about your home improvement plans and decide to invest the funds elsewhere? Maybe you could use the money to improve another home you buy.

7. If you can't use the second mortgage technique because you lack equity, try refinancing your car, boat, or trailer or try using your furniture, stereo, or some other valuable item as collateral for a loan. The monthly payments may by higher using this approach, but it provides a ready source of cash if the need arises.

8. While you are establishing a credit history, don't overlook the use of credit cards. Apply for as many credit cards as you can, especially those without a monthly surcharge. Use one of the cards for yourself, but reserve the others for investment purposes. How? Use your imagination. For example, one young investor found a homesick European couple who desperately wanted to return to Germany. The home they owned here had an equity of about $8,000. The investor recognized their situation and immediately bought two one-way tickets to Germany with his Master Charge card. He offered the couple the two tickets in exchange for the equity in their home. They gladly accepted: it was what they wanted more than anything. The investor paid for the tickets at $50 a month over the next year, and the home was his. Some sellers might accept a number of brand new items you could buy with a credit card.

Don't get caught in the thinking that you can only possess one Master Charge card and one Visa card at one time. Each different bank has the ability to qualify you for a separate credit card, regardless of how many cards you might have acquired through other banks. For example, in my area at least five different banks offer the Master Charge card to their customers. In fact, I could easily apply for a separate Master Charge card from each of the banks and not be stepping out of the bounds of the law. If each bank allowed me a credit limit of $1,000 on each of the cards, I could borrow $5,000 quickly and easily just on my signature alone. If the opportunity arose to put $5,000 to use quickly I would have the money ready and available. For this reason, I suggest that you have several cards in your possession for use in an emergency.

As a summary to this chapter, look at the following program of building your credit. Begin now to establish your credit and borrowing ability in as many places as possible. I offer you a challenge that you build up your borrowing ability so that you will be able to borrow $5,000 on your signature from at least five separate banks in your area. Armed with short-term money in the amount of at least $25,000 you are much better prepared.

Remember that whatever route you take to finance your real estate investment, you need to be flexible; settle only for terms you are comfortable with, and don't get trapped into a bad situation. The money is there for the borrowing; take what steps you can to get established so that the money will be there for you.

Short-term Funds from Hard-money Lenders

How to build your credit:

A. Choose five banks in your area immediately.
B. Pick a loan officer you can relate to.
C. Go to another bank if you feel you are not welcome.
D. Ask your loan officer if he owns real estate.
E. Determine what the loan officer's credit limit is.
F. Ask him if it is possible to establish an unsecured line of credit. If so, how long does it take?
G. Borrow as much as you can either secured or unsecured as soon as possible.
H. Repay your loans early, but not too early.
I. Repeat the loaning process with a larger amount.
J. GOAL: TO BE ABLE TO BORROW $5,000 FROM AT LEAST FIVE SEPARATE BANKS SIMULTANEOUSLY WITHIN TWO YEARS.

CHAPTER SIXTEEN

From Bankers to Crankers: Working for Long-term Loans

Mastering techniques for borrowing short-term funds will help you establish a credit rating and a good working relationship with several cooperative bankers. Sometimes long-term loans are more difficult to obtain; bankers may want you to have a good credit rating that has built up over several years. So if you establish the groundwork through short-term loan processes, your credit will help you get started.

There are two kinds of institutions that lend mortgage money. Banks are more difficult to deal with than savings and loan associations because most of the funds that banks have to lend originate from government-sponsored loans such as GI veteran loans and FHA loans. These loans usually call for lower down payments (GI loans require nothing down to qualified veterans) and lower interest over the life of the loan, and they are always available. But they are also more difficult to get because of endless government paperwork involved. In addition, appraisals are generally below the market. If you are buying a home to live in and you have a good credit rating, the FHA offers the lowest down payments and interest rates available.

Savings and loan associations are independent savings banks that borrow money from their depositors and lend it out for mortgages that eventually finance most of the homes in the country. Loans for houses are easier to get from savings and loan associations, but they require a minimum of 10 percent down—and usually more!

If you're borrowing money to buy property you won't be living in, watch out. It's a whole different story. Interest rates on loans for purchase of nonowner-occupied buildings are much higher, and the down payments required are sometimes higher than 25 percent.

Be prepared to answer these questions when you apply for such a loan:
—What is your total monthly income?
—Do you have the last three years' income tax statements?
—Can you verify your down payment requirement?
—Have you borrowed any portion of your down payment?

The last question is especially critical; lending institutions want to keep their risk at a minimum. They realize that if an investor has saved at least 25 percent of the purchase price of the property he is buying, he will be less likely to lose the property to foreclosure. If they know that any portion of your down payment has been borrowed, they'll probably try to deny you the loan.

Don't be dismayed. There are specific ways of dealing with lending institutions, even if you have little or no down payment. Let's examine those techniques:

The Second Mortgage Crank. I call this the second mortgage crank because it involves the use of second mortgages and is done in such a way as to allow me to "crank" the required down payment out of the property I want to buy through a refinance. This technique can also be called subordination. When mortgage money is loose, this can be the most powerful technique in your arsenal. The first time I ever tried to use it, I held my breath during the whole transaction. I just couldn't believe it was going to work. But it did!

I called the owner of a twelve-unit apartment building located near a large, local university, to see if he wanted to sell his property. It was the spring of 1976. I had a real estate licence and was farming the area for listings. He wasn't interested.

Several months later he decided that since he lived so far away from his property, he would sell it and invest his money closer to his home. He called an old friend who was in the appraisal business and asked him to do an appraisal on the property. His appraisal came in at $225,000 —an extremely low estimate and a surprise to both me and the seller. He told me that he had to net at least $300,000 or he would not sell. With that in mind, we listed the property for $315,000 with a 5 percent commission to be paid to me if I sold the property.

I did a thorough analysis of the property and determined that the net operating income was about $28,000 per year—quite high because each unit was rented out to six girls—each paying $65 a month. The capitalization rate, then, was almost 9 percent, not bad for a unit located in such a good area. I listed the property, turned the listing over to a colleague, and went to Europe for two months.

When I returned, the unit had not been sold, and no buyers were in sight. Suddenly I realized that I was a better buyer than a seller. I knew that the property was a great buy. I knew that I wanted it badly. But I also knew that I had no money to buy it with.

When the listing expired I began to get imaginative. I attended some creative real estate courses in California to expand my thinking. In the middle of October, while I was in Los Angeles attending one of the seminars, I received a telephone call from the seller. He told me that he had an offer of $295,000 from a neighbor, but he felt an obligation to let me have the first crack. I told him that I would pay $300,000 and that I would fly there and meet with him that weekend.

When I hung up the phone I knew that I had committed myself. Until that telephone call, ownership of that building was just wishful thinking. Now I had to produce. I had no idea how I'd do it.

When I returned to the seminar room I began to concentrate more on what the instructor had to say than I had ever done in any other classroom situation. I began to play with the numbers as I knew them:

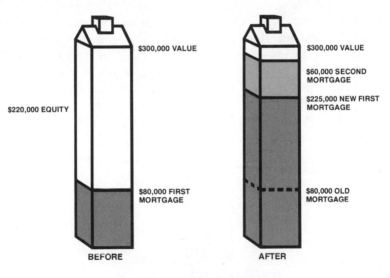

THE SECOND MORTGAGE CRANK

I knew that the seller did not want to receive more than 29 percent of the selling price in any one year because of the tax consequences. Since the seller's equity was a whopping $220,000, I felt that he would be a little more flexible if I could give him most of his equity in cash.

I finally reached a solution. I would go to a local savings and loan association and borrow 75 percent of the purchase price; in addition, I'd ask the seller to accept a second mortgage that would finance the remainder of the 25 percent required down payment. My proposal looked like the "After" drawing in the illustration on page 149.

When I arrived in San José, the seller and I sat in his living room to discuss my proposal. He went along with most of it, but insisted that he would only accept a $60,000 second mortgage instead of a larger one, and he would have to have 12 percent interest. The most important motivating factor for the seller was the fact that he would be receiving $160,000 in cash, so he could afford to give me a break by lending me most of the necessary down payment.

There was a problem: I had wanted to close six months from the date of our conversation, and he wanted to have all of his money by the first of the year. He was concerned that I would tie up his property for six months and then not be able to put the deal together. His worries were probably well-founded: I was a young, single, basically inexperienced real estate agent. He wanted $5,000 earnest money.

I didn't have it. I finally convinced him to let me have six months to try to put the deal together by offering him my duplex—and its $8,000 equity—with no strings attached if I defaulted at the end of six months.

I told him that if I *could* raise the money, he would receive $160,000 in cash plus a note for $60,000 earning 12 percent interest, and I would get my duplex back.

He accepted. We drew up our agreement on a napkin and we both signed. It looked like this:

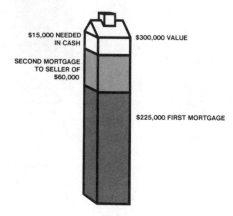

$15,000 NEEDED IN CASH

$300,000 VALUE

SECOND MORTGAGE TO SELLER OF $60,000

$225,000 FIRST MORTGAGE

I still had some monumental financial hurdles: I needed to come up with $15,000 in cash for the additional down payment. And I needed to be able to borrow $225,000 from a savings and loan association.

The first problem wasn't as bad as it seemed. As the new owner, I'd immediately receive approximately $10,000 in rents and deposits. I was only short $5,000.

To solve the second problem, I convinced a good friend who had a strong financial statement to become my partner. He had the ability to get the money; I had the expertise. We applied for the loan together. He was the borrower, I was the co-borrower.

We were extremely lucky. Things fell into place. The money market was loose, the loan officer ignored any extraneous financing we were planning on making, and the building was appraised high enough to qualify us for the loan because I convinced the appraiser with some of my own homework. There were only two remaining obstacles: the $5,000 I was short for the down payment and approximately $7,000 in closing costs.

Our luck held out. My partner and I were able to obtain a six-month loan for the $5,000 on our signatures. That took care of the down payment.

When tenants moved into the building, they were required to pay three months' rent in advance. This is unusual but possible to arrange. As the new owners, we also received that prepaid rent, which amounted to a little over $7,000. Our closing costs were paid.

Let's examine the financing:

Borrowed from savings and loan:	$225,000
First month's rents, deposits:	10,000
Borrowed on signatures:	5,000
Seller's agreed second mortgage:	60,000
AMOUNT OUT OF OWN POCKET:	—0—
Total	$300,000

Incidentally, three months later my partner offered to let me buy him out for $5,000 in cash. Instead, I convinced him to take a recreational acre in a beautiful mountain location that I had $5,000 equity in.

So the property became all mine—with nothing down.

I call this technique the second mortgage crank, because I am able to *crank* out my down payment by borrowing it from the seller. Essential ingredients for a successful cranker are:

—A seller who has a very low mortgage balance and lots of equity.

—A property in a good location.

—A bank willing to loan up to 75 percent of the appraisal price (and, of course, an ample money market).

—A buyer who has a strong financial position or who can find a partner to provide the financial strength.

The illustration below shows what a potential "cranker" property might look like. The property has a low loan and lots of equity. If you could convince the seller to accept only a part of his equity in cash and carry a second mortgage for the balance of his equity, then you have the makings of a nothing down transaction. The first step is to determine how much a local bank or savings and loan association will lend on a potential new mortgage. Generally, on a nonowner-occupied property, most banks lend up to 75 percent of the value of the property. The difference between the potential new loan and the existing loans will be paid to the seller at the time of closing. This is, in essence, a cash down payment. You now only need to convince the seller to accept for the balance of his equity (25 percent in our example) a second mortgage on the property he is selling, with monthly payments or terms agreeable between you. He receives a great deal of cash at closing. The real estate agent involved also receives cash. And you are able to buy a property with absolutely no down payment—although closing costs for your end of the purchase may be as high as 3 percent of the purchase price.

Since most banks will refuse to loan you the money if they think you've borrowed part or all of the down payment, you need to find a way to convince the banker that the down payment has been taken care of. Try one of these ways:

Moving the Mortgage. Ask the seller to place the second mortgage on another piece of property you already own. Use your other property as collateral to the seller until the refinancing is completed. If the bank officer requires proof that the down payment has been made, have the seller draft a letter stating that he has received the amount in the form of an *exchange* for other property or that he has already received "consideration" for his equity.

Uniform Real Estate Contract Method. Ask the seller to sell you the property on a Uniform Real Estate Contract with a $100 down payment. When you go to the bank, you will then be listed as the legal owner of the property, and the loan officer won't question you about a down payment. When the refinancing is complete, pay the seller the remainder of his equity, and negotiate the terms for the second mortgage.

Seller Refinance. If the seller refinances his own property first, before selling to you, the question of down payment is not raised by the banker. When the refinance takes place, the seller deeds the property to you and you take over his payments on the new loan. He gets the cash from the refinance plus a second mortgage from you for the rest of his equity. You get in for Nothing Down.

While using the second mortgage crank can at times be extremely complicated, the paperwork is worth it if you are able to invest in an excellent piece of property. And sometimes the returns are good: I could have sold my $300,000 building one year later for $350,000. After discounting my closing costs and partnership costs, I could have pocketed over $38,000—enough to get me started on my next deal!

If you really want to get fancy, consider doing something like Gary and I did. Gary and I used to have our offices in the same building. He indicated an interest in buying some real estate for his own investment. I told him that I had a full-time "finder," Rex, searching for properties and if I found something I couldn't handle myself I would let him know.

A few weeks later Rex located a four-unit apartment building in a nearby town that was advertised in the newspaper:

Older fourplex.
$55,000; appraised at $58,000. Seller anxious.

Rex visited the seller. He turned out to be a serious don't wanter for the property. His family had just moved to Oregon, and he had stayed to clean up his last-minute red tape messes. He wanted to sell—now!

Rex drove me past the property and I didn't like what I saw. It was a frame structure—I am very partial to brick—and it was in terrible shape. It needed new paint, yard work, and extensive general repair. The stench was incredible. I told Rex I wasn't interested at any price.

But Rex was only paid for finding properties that I bought, so he persisted: "Come on, Bob, surely you would buy the property at the right price. Make him an outrageous offer. You never know—he just might accept it."

So we offered him $45,000 with a $3,000 down payment, and we sent the offer in the mail, never expecting to hear back from him.

To our surprise, he replied immediately. "I will accept $48,000 with $3,000 down," he said over the phone.

I gave Gary a call and told him about the property we had found. I told Gary that the property had real potential but that I didn't have the time nor inclination to clean and repair the building. He drove out to the property with me a few days later and said that he wasn't afraid of the cleanup problems involved if he could purchase the building for an extremely low down payment. We put our heads together and analyzed the details:

Selling price:	$48,000
Seller's loans:	13,000 to a loan company @ 18 percent
	10,000 first mortgage to a bank
Seller's equity:	$25,000

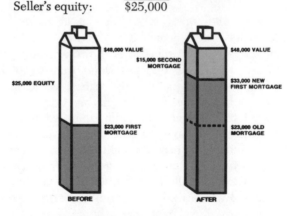

THE SECOND MORTGAGE CRANK

We offered to give the seller $10,000 in cash if he would subordinate $15,000 of his remaining equity on a new first mortgage loan of $33,000. The $15,000 note would be secured against Gary's home until the refinance took place and thereafter would be transferred to the fourplex. The note would bear 8 percent interest with no monthly payments and would come due in five years.

Gary applied for a $33,000 first mortgage loan, but since money was scarce, the mortgage loan was only approved for $28,000. Gary refinanced his free and clear sports car and raised the extra $5,000.

Everyone was happy.

I received a $1,500 finder's fee. I gave Rex $300.

The seller got rid of his property, plus he received $10,000 in cash.

But happiest of all was Gary. He bought a property with little down payment. But there's more: Gary's property was appraised at $58,000, so he made a paper profit of $10,000 the day he bought the property. Within three months of his purchase he began building a new ten-unit apartment building with money he borrowed on the fourplex. It had been appraised at $70,000.

Gary's off and running. You can be, too.

The Overfinance. This is just an extension of the second mortgage crank. It is possible to buy a property and in the process put cash in your pocket using the second mortgage crank technique with a little twist. Suppose we locate a $100,000 building which has a $25,000 existing mortgage. The seller wants some cash but is willing to be flexible with the balance of his equity. We know that we can obtain a new mortgage of $75,000. Obviously, the difference between the new loan of $75,000 and the old loan of $25,000 is $50,000. This money should come to the seller since it is his equity. However, we agree to give him only $40,000 cash from the proceeds and he must agree to accept a second mortgage of $35,000 for the remainder of his equity. This seems fine to the seller. After all, he is receiving $40,000 in cash. Here is how the transaction will look once the refinance is complete:

THE OVERFINANCE

If you look closely you will notice that there was $50,000 cash which came out of the refinance. The seller got $40,000. Where did the other $10,000 go? Into your pocket!

Great!?

No—not so great. While there is a place for this kind of deal, you need to seriously consider the financial burden you assume by promising to repay all of the loans. Unless you have negotiated extremely good terms, the property will probably generate a negative cash flow. You'll need to dig into your own pocket every month until the rents can be raised. The higher the overfinance, the more acute the problem becomes. You should only overfinance a property if you have an absolute profit-maker in which to invest the leftover funds. *Never* spend them on butter.

There is another more serious problem. A seller who finds out that his mortgage may not be completely secured could sue you for fraud. If you do decide to overfinance, *always* explain the benefits to the seller, make sure that he understands the implications, and ask him to sign an affidavit agreeing to the overfinance. (One way to convince him to agree to the overfinance is to offer him security on both his property and on another piece of property you own. You can remove the mortgage from your second piece of property once the seller is satisfied that you'll make payments promptly. This should take no longer than a year.)

Borrow the down payment from holders of existing first, second, or third mortgages, or people who sold on a real estate contract or wraparound mortgage.

How does this technique work?

Suppose you found a seven-unit building selling for $80,000. The seller had an existing loan of $60,000 and wanted his $20,000 equity in cash if possible. If you don't have the $20,000, how can you come up with it?

First, find out about the existing $60,000 mortgage: To whom is it payable? Will the holder be flexible? Is a bank involved?

In our case, the $60,000 mortgage is really a Real Estate Contract payable to Mr. Harrison at $500 a month including 9 percent interest. Harrison bought the property from Mr. and Mrs. Peterson, and he owes them $30,000 at $250 a month at 7 percent interest. Mr. and Mrs. Peterson, who owned the property free and clear, owe no money on the property. The picture looks something like this:

$20,000 EQUITY

$80,000 VALUE

$60,000 CONTRACT OF SALE

$30,000 PRIVATE FIRST MORTGAGE

BEFORE

$80,000 VALUE

$60,000 NEW MORTGAGE

AFTER

DISCOUNTS OF EXISTING MORTGAGES OR CONTRACTS

Further investigation reveals that the Petersons are an older couple who are extremely nervous about the fact that the property they loved so much is not being cared for properly. They are unsure about the security of their $30,000 investment. They complain regularly to the owner, and even tried to repossess the property once due to breach of contract. Every time the property changes hands they become increasingly nervous. It's obvious they might be interested in a payout of their equity.

Harrison purchased the property and sold it to create for himself a monthly cash flow; for the last four years he has enjoyed $250 a month net cash flow. But his business has recently declined, and his wife has asked for a divorce. He couldn't raise enough money to settle with his wife, and he desperately needs extra cash. He doesn't think his mortgage in the building is saleable, and he considers himself stuck.

Armed with this information, do you think it is possible to bargain with the holders of the underlying mortgages, pay the present seller his $20,000 equity in cash, and still purchase the building with no cash investment?

Yes.

There are two possible alternatives available to you. First, you can approach each of the mortgage holders and offer to pay them $20,000 *cash* for their $30,000 mortgages.

Prepare for some moans and groans, but once the dust settles, remind the Petersons that they'd be much better off with $20,000 in cash than with their worries about future security and with the hassle of collecting $250 a month for the next fifteen years. Remind Harrison that the $20,000 in immediate cash will remedy both his business losses and his wife's divorce demands.

Then draft a simple document that reads something like this:

I, ___(seller's name)___, agree to sell my interest in a seven-unit building located at 22556 Peacock Lane, Centerville, Va., for $20,000 cash. The funds should be delivered to Greenacre Title and Escrow Company, where this note and instructions will be held in escrow pending delivery of the required cash by ___(your name)___ (or his/her assigns)___ on or before the 3rd day of September, 1979.

Signed this 1st day of July, 1979.

Notary signature

_____

Get Harrison and the Petersons to sign. You just made $20,000.

But that's not all.

Approach your savings and loan association about getting a new loan on the seven-unit building. Since you paid $80,000 for it according to your agreement with the seller, apply for a 75 percent loan of $60,000. The banker will want to know where your down payment is coming from; just tell him that it is being held in escrow at Greenacre Title and Escrow Company and that the $60,000 mortgage money should be delivered to the title company for final dispersal.

Upon approval, your money will be delivered to the title company. The following events transpire:

—The title company will pay $20,000 to Harrison for his $30,000 interest in the property.

—The title company wll pay $20,000 to the Petersons for their $30,000 interest in the property.

—The $20,000 that remains will be paid to the seller as a $20,000 cash down payment on his $80,000 building.

You just purchased an $80,000 building for a total price of $60,000, and the $20,000 you earned is clear profit.

The only loan you have to pay off is the $60,000 first mortgage. Of course, you will have to pay closing costs on the new loan plus title charges and other miscellaneous expenses, but most of these outlays can be covered by the rents and deposits that you will receive as the new owner. One more thing: there should be a steady, monthly cash flow from the rental units which you can put into your pocket.

The holders of the underlying mortgages might not be as generous as you would like them to be. What happens if both the Petersons and Harrison decide to discount their mortgages by only $5,000 instead of $10,000? You'll be $10,000 short. But your only limits are the limits of your imagination and creativity. Try one of the following alternate plans.

PLAN #1. Convince the seller to receive only $10,000 in cash instead of $20,000, and have him take back a second mortgage of $10,000 as soon as the refinance is complete. The result will look like this:

DISCOUNTS OF EXISTING MORTGAGES OR CONTRACTS

PLAN #2. Convince the Petersons or Harrison (or both) to receive $20,000 in cash and a $5,000 personal note for the rest of their equity. The results are:

$60,000
NEW MORTGAGE

$5,000

PERSONAL
UNSECURED
NOTE TO HARRISON

$5,000

PERSONAL
UNSECURED
NOTE TO PETERSON

PLAN #3. Convince the seller to receive $15,000 in cash and a $5,000 note. Then negotiate with Harrison and the Petersons concerning who takes the discounts and the notes. Perhaps Harrison will take a $10,000 discount, but the Petersons will only discount their note by $5,000. You will still be able to accomplish your nothing down transaction:

$60,000
NEW MORTGAGE

$5,000

PERSONAL
UNSECURED
NOTE TO SELLER

$5,000

PERSONAL
UNSECURED
NOTE TO PETERSONS

You might even be able to crank some cash out of the transaction to put in your own pocket. Suppose that the seller would take a personal note (not secured against the real estate) for $5,000 and that Harrison will discount his note from $30,000 to $20,000 cash. The Petersons will discount their note by $5,000, and they want $20,000 in cash with a $5,000 personal note for the rest.

The results would look like this:

First mortgage proceeds	$60,000
Cash to seller	15,000
Cash to Harrison	20,000
Cash to Petersons	20,000
Total cash paid out	55,000
Your net proceeds	5,000

Situations like this one never just happen. They are *created*. Spend some time and use some imagination, and you'll be able to pocket some cash on most of your real estate transactions.

Buy Low, Refinance High. Of all the techniques we've discussed, this one is easiest to use and simplest to understand for both buyer and seller. In essence it consists of finding sellers who are willing to sell their properties immediately for a substantial discount and all cash.

Here's an example. One afternoon as I was talking with a broker friend, I asked if he had any properties for sale involving a seller who was willing to accept a lower price for his property in exchange for a quick cash-out of his equity. He mentioned that he had recently taken in a home on a guaranteed-sale program, and he was ready to sell it for a great price.

A couple of weeks later his wife showed me through the home and I was flabbergasted. The home had been newly painted and carpeted, and new drapes had been installed. The grounds were beautiful and well cared for. The place was immaculate. It took me about three seconds to make my mind up; a few minutes later I was in his office with an offer.

The property had a new loan on it for $36,000; the seller wanted a $45,000 price and $9,000 cash for his equity. I knew that the market price was at least $55,000 because I was in the process of building some new homes that didn't look as nice and that cost more. Within a few days the seller had his $9,000, and I owned the property with a partner who put up the cash.

How? Our strategy was to get a new first mortgage on the property as soon as possible to refinance our initial down payment. In a situation like this, if you can obtain an 80 percent loan you can obtain a $44,000 loan on a $55,000 appraisal. Most of your down payment will be returned; you can use it on other deals. In addition, rents will cover mortgage payments and other expenses, resulting in a breakeven cash flow.

The basic ingredients of this technique are (1) a seller who wants cash now and is willing to discount his equity for the privilege; (2) a property that can be purchased for 75 percent of what a bank will appraise it for in order to obtain a new first mortgage; and (3) your ability to use your own cash or that of a partner.

There are some twists to this technique. First of all, you don't have to give the seller any cash on the front end if you can convince him that you can raise the cash within thirty days. Every time you talk to a seller ask him, "What is your lowest cash price if I give you all of your equity in cash within thirty days?" For example, suppose that you found a $40,000 house for $30,000 cash. Negotiate with the seller to pay him $30,000 cash in thirty days; then apply for a $30,000 loan from a local lending institution based upon their $40,000 appraisal. Your only investment is to cover closing costs—about $700 in this case.

Another twist is to find a property which, in its present condition, is only worth what the seller is asking but which, with some minor cosmetic repairs, would appraise for a lot higher. Buy the property from the seller at a low price, make some minor improvements, and refinance the higher-valued property for enough money to pay the seller and to cover the expenses you incurred in fixing up the property.

Sometimes the sellers can't wait for thirty days for you to refinance the property. They need their money now. How can you take advantage of a low price? You have to cultivate your cash sources well so that when a "steal" comes along, you will be able to come up with immediate cash. This is one of the main reasons why I always keep my bank lines of communication open. If I need a quick $10,000 for six months, I can get it. It doesn't hurt to have a few partners who can come up with cash within 48 hours' notice. Using the Buy Low, Refinance High technique you could take a $25,000 investment and use it over and over again—buying first one property and then refinancing your cash out again and repeating the process several times a year. You would not need extra capital, and each time you would end up owning a piece of property which had been purchased substantially under the market price. There is no question about the fact that cash is more effective in this circum-

BUY LOW, REFINANCE HIGH

stance. It is like buying real estate at wholesale prices. When you buy real estate with small down payments and high leverage, you generally have to pay top dollar—retail prices. When a lot of cash is involved, the prices come down in a hurry. You can continue to spread your money into as many properties as possible, but if you have the resources, the Buy Low Refinance High technique can make you more "real" dollars in less time than any other method.

How do you raise cash to take advantage of the wholesale opportunities which exist all around you?

—Establish yourself with short-term lenders.
—Explain the program to a partner.
—Sell another piece of property to raise cash.

As you can see, there are all kinds of possibilities. I have the most confidence in the Buy Low, Refinance High technique.

CHAPTER SEVENTEEN

Greed and Need: Using Partners

FRED ASTAIRE and Ginger Rogers. Batman and Robin. Laurel and Hardy. The Lone Ranger and Tonto. Mutt and Jeff.

They're all famous partners. One wouldn't be the same—or as effective —without the other.

The same thing can happen for you in real estate investment. If you need more money than you can get alone in order to purchase that perfect property, consider letting a partner come up with the cash. You'll have to give your partner half the profits, but remember: half a pie is better than no pie at all!

My first experience with partners took place several years ago when I purchased an option on a very valuable piece of apartment ground. At the time I didn't have much experience and was naive enough to think that I could do anything. I found a 3.5-acre piece of ground in an excellent location that was ripe for development. It belonged to a major church organization in the area whose agent was in the process of trying to sell it.

I contacted the agent and established a friendly relationship with him. He had offers on the propety for $150,000, but he thought the property was worth more. I offered to buy the property from him in a year for $200,000; I agreed to give him $2,500 as option money. He accepted. I was bound to keep my part of the bargain.

The deal was a good one. There was only one problem. I didn't have $2,500. At the time, I hadn't established sufficient credit to borrow as little as $500 from my bank. I approached a good friend who had a growing dental practice and drove him over to the property. I convinced him that it was worth the gamble. My friend's banker thought the investment was a stupid one, but my partner persisted and, with some difficulty, was able to borrow the money.

I went ahead with the option and began trying to find a buyer for the property. I had one year. To make a profit I needed to find someone who would buy the property for more than $200,000.

About eight months later we were approached by a builder who was looking for ground; we negotiated a purchase price of $275,000. When the sale was completed I took a check for $10,800 to my dentist partner—his share of the profits. The rest of the money was split with my real estate broker.

The ingredients for success in this story are simple. I found a piece of property that had potential, and I convinced a partner to finance the property. Without the partner I would never have seen any of the $30,000 I eventually put in my pocket.

Start now to cultivate partner relationships. Try to have at least three or four partners in the wings to use when you need them. If you are careful you will *never* have to use your own capital for any real estate venture again. You will always be able to rely on other people to provide all of the investment capital you will ever need.

There are two main motivations that bring people together to form a partnership. It's usually your need for money and his greed and desire to earn more than 6 percent on his invested dollars. If you treat your partners fairly, you will never lack for people who will be willing to lend you money for your investing. The word spreads fast. If you burn anyone, word will get around. But it will also get around if you return good profits.

There are numbers of people who have sizable amounts of money sitting in savings accounts earning 6 percent interest. Your job is to convince them that the returns are higher if they will join with you and invest in real estate. Let's look at the ways to influence partners and to form partnerships, how to treat partners as far as profit is concerned and how to dissolve partnerships when the time comes.

There are some good basic rules concerning partnerships:

1. Don't ever form a partnership unless you absolutely need to. It's too expensive. If you have adequate funds, adequate experience, adequate time, and adequate fortitude to do it yourself, do so. If you're weak in any of those areas, the partnership is probably a good idea.

2. At the beginning of the relationship, define exactly what each person will contribute to the partnership. For example, your partner's responsi-

bility might be to provide the money; your responsibility would be to negotiate, deliver the earnest money receipt, and complete closing procedures. Obvious contributions that a partner would make include cash, equity in other property, the ability to borrow money readily, strong credit history, and good connections in the right places. Obvious contributions you could make include your time, your knowledge, and your fortitude. Whatever you decide on, get it down in writing and make it specific so that there will be no misunderstandings.

One interesting way you can use a partner is to buy his financial statement—in other words, if he's got a good financial statement and a strong relationship with a progressive banker, have him refinance a piece of property. As soon as the refinance is completed, have him give you a quit-claim deed transferring all rights, title, and interest to you, even though his name is on the mortgage and stays there until you are able to assume it. You might pay him $2,000 for the service. It's well worth it.

By the same token, you could make it worthwhile for a seller to take out a loan against his own property and in turn loan you the proceeds. Secure the loan on another piece of property you own, and pay a good rate of interest. The possibilities are limitless.

3. Maintain maximum control of the relationship. If you feel in any way that a partner is limiting your freedom, end the partnership as soon as possible. Don't waste valuable time with a partner who does not trust you or who does not understand a good deal when he sees one. A good relationship sometimes takes time to establish, and the best thing that you can have on your side is a good track record of making profit for both yourself and your partners. When you have established a good track record, you will be able to call one of your former partners and say, "I've found a great buy on a ten-unit building. The required down payment is $30,000. Do you want in or don't you?" It will be that simple. If they have made money with you before, they will find a way to say yes.

4. Keep each partnership on a property-by-property basis. Each project should be evaluated on its own merits, the profits should be split when the property is sold, and the partnership should then be dissolved. This practice allows you to be more flexible when other opportunities arise. For instance, if you have an agreement to buy properties with a partner and he runs out of money, you should be free to look elsewhere for another partner if you run across a good deal. It should be clear from the very beginning that your partnership is temporary.

5. Decide from the outset what procedure you will follow if one of the

partners decides to sell out to the other. Establishing this early will prevent misunderstandings if one partner does decide to sell out.

6. Decide early how you'll divide profits. Try to negotiate the best arrangement you can for yourself while still making it attractive enough for the partner who is putting up the money. Here are some ideas to incorporate:

If you're sure that your project is going to be a winner, don't give large percentages of the profit to your partner. Offer instead to pay your partner 25 percent return on his money. That's still four times what he'd earn in a bank. Most people are very satisfied with 12–18 percent yields on their investment. Be careful of your state's usury laws.

If your partner is financially educated, he will probably wish to forego your offer of a guaranteed percentage return and will opt instead for your less guaranteed program of a percentage of the *profit*. The harder the bargain you drive with your partner, the better off you will be when it comes time to divvy up the profits. I never give away more than 50 percent of the profit to anyone in a partnership, and I try to retain as much as I can for myself. You may say that your partner's dollars are the first to be returned upon the sale of the property, after which, all remaining profits are to be split 60 percent to you and 40 percent to your partner. Or you may decide that a 50/50 relationship is best for both parties involved. Whatever you decide, get it in writing! And whatever happens, guarantee that the partner will *at least* get his original investment back. And then stand behind your guarantee. A partner should understand (and should be guaranteed) that he will not lose one penny of his original investment, regardless of whether or not he makes a profit.

If you plan on being a nothing-down investor, you've got to begin living a borrower's life. The key to maximum leverage is *OPM*—other people's money! You have to learn how to overcome your reluctance to ask people for money. From now on, every person you meet is a potential partner. You are looking for people who will trust you with their money— it's as simple as that.

Let's look at the various sources of investor capital. We'll save the most conventional ones for last.

1. *Relatives.* Most people find it very difficult to borrow from a relative. Granted, it has its drawbacks and could cause serious problems if anything negative happened. But there are also obvious benefits. Relatives are more likely to lend you money because they know you.

2. *Friends and Business Associates.* Word travels fast when you know

what you are doing and you prove it by making money for yourself and others. Talk up your latest adventures with every crowd you have a chance to talk to; someone there will want to spend a little money for a profitable cause. Just make sure you are selective and careful.

3. *The Seller Himself.* The seller ends up lending money to the buyer in over half of the real estate transactions that I am familiar with by agreeing to let the buyer pay him a portion of the remaining equity over a period of time. The borrowed equity is secured by a mortgage on the property purchased, a mortgage on other property, or a personal note. Whenever a seller takes back a second or third mortgage he is, in essence, lending his money to the buyer.

Some methods of dealing with partners will help insure a successful experience.

1. Choose your partners carefully, make sure all of the terms of partnership are in writing, and stand behind your investments. You'll find that teaming up can provide a good solution to an otherwise troublesome money crunch.

2. If necessary, reduce the fears of the partner who needs some added security by placing the property in the name of the money partner. Retain a written agreement with him that whenever the property is sold—and since the property is in his name, he alone can make the decision on when to sell—the profits will be split according to your written agreement. It can be a simple agreement drafted in mutually satisfactory language and signed by both of you, or you can ask your attorney to formulate an agreement. The simple, do-it-yourself method can work just as well and be legally binding.

3. Agree to pay the partner his profit and invested capital first after the sale of the property. He will thus know that your profit is subordinated to his and that you will probably work harder to see that things happen as you say they will.

4. Do not get mixed up in limited partnerships. These are not for the investor who likes to have any control over the situation. The fewer the partners, the better. If you don't have the time to do your own looking for properties, visit a realtor with a C.C.I.M. (Certified Commercial Investment Member) designation in your area. These realtors will give you professional counsel and help you determine the best route for you to take in real estate.

5. Avoid if at all possible investing your own dollars into a partnership. In lieu of cash, give your partner confidence in your ability to raise

cash from other sources. Remember, your contribution to any partnership is the talent, the intangible experience that makes the whole partnership have life and meaning.

6. Partnerships were made for man, not man for partnerships. When you find yourself in a bad partnership, get out as soon as possible. Learn your lesson and don't make the same mistake again.

Let me challenge you to find five people in the next two years each of whom will be willing to lend you $5,000. If you had such a tremendous financial resource at your disposal you could make a handsome living using the $25,000 you borrowed from your partners. And your partners would love you for it because you would be doing something for them that they could not do for themselves.

How do you overcome your fear of asking other people (perhaps even total strangers) for money? Easy! Go out into the real estate market and locate a fabulous property which could be bought for below market value, if you could only raise the cash. Then we'll see how shy you are. At that point you have a very important decision to make. Either you get up the courage to ask a partner to join you in making a tidy profit or you let your fear cost you thousands of dollars. It's up to you. Whenever I talk to a group of people about real estate investing, I ask for a show of hands of those who either have $5,000 in the bank or who could get $5,000 in thirty days if I would double it for them. Generally, over three quarters of the people raise their hands. It's amazing how fast people can come up with money when they smell a profit. This same principle can work for you. If you don't have the money, somebody in your city does—and he's just waiting for you to ask him for it. Show him how he can make a profit and you'll both laugh all the way to the bank. And you'll have a friend for life.

Of course, as soon as you can afford to, get out on your own. Partnerships are great, but if you can afford a whole pie, why should you give half of it away? Until the day that you can go it alone, I challenge you to find five partners who would loan you $5,000 each for real estate investing. I think you could find five partners easily within a two year period of time if you use the techniques outlined in this chapter. Just think of what you could buy if you had $25,000 cash to play with!

CHAPTER EIGHTEEN

Bundles of Benefits: Everyone Wins on Exchanges

EXCHANGE.

A century ago, when an Indian brought his beaver pelts to the trading post and swapped them for a blanket, we called it barter. Today, when we swap services or property—when we get what we want without using money—we call it *exchange*.

For example, if you are a painter, you might offer to paint a dentist's house *in exchange for* having some bridgework done or *in exchange for* outfitting your daughter with braces. There is no reason for you to use cash as long as you can find someone who wants your services more than he wants cash for his own.

You can utilize this philosophy to its fullest in real estate investment. Let me illustrate:

Suppose you own an acre of ground in the country that you bought many years ago. The property has increased substantially in value; since you've decided not to build on it, you have decided to sell it and reinvest the money in a new home in the city. You place an ad in the newspaper to sell the property, and you receive a telephone call from Mr. Bellamy Brown, a local contractor. He owns a new home that he just finished building, and he wants to know if you will exchange your land for equity in the new home.

Let's look at how the exchange would benefit you:

—There is no need for you to search for a cash buyer.

—Since the cash buyer usually wants to dicker for lower prices, you probably would lose part of your equity.

171

—You won't have to look for a new property.

—There are tremendous tax advantages.

There are benefits to the builder, too. He doesn't have to search for a buyer for his home. He doesn't have to look for more land to build on. And he saves time so he can be about his business—which is building, not buying or selling.

Basically, you'd both come out ahead.

Exchange isn't a magic cure-all for every transaction you get involved in, but it can be a valuable tool to use when you need it. Let's examine the basics behind the technique of exchange.

Every piece of property is a "bundle of benefits" that can be sold or traded for other bundles of benefits. In our example, you received a property that had the following benefits:

—It was located in the city.

—It had a house built on it.

—It had equity that approximated the equity of your land.

—It was readily useable.

The builder also received a "bundle of benefits":

—Vacant land that could be built on.

—No need to waste time searching for a building site.

—Disposal of his property.

—Relief from the financial burden of paying a mortgage on the home.

—No transfer of cash.

Both parties are happy. You both received what you wanted—and completely without the use or transfer of any cash.

Since benefits are of such great importance, a successful creative buyer must understand the benefits he is seeking and the benefits he has to offer. It is critical that you understand the seller's situation: Learn what benefits he is seeking. If the seller is seeking relief from the burden of management, step onto the scene as a benefit. Offer to take the property off the seller's hands and thereby relieve the seller of his problem *in exchange for* certain terms.

There is an important point to remember here: there are no problem properties, just problem ownerships. In our example, there was nothing wrong with your property out in the country; you just didn't want it any more because you had decided not to build a house on it, and you didn't see what else you'd need it for. And there was nothing wrong with Brown's house. It's just that he had finished building the house, and he wanted to build another one. To do that, he needed vacant land. There was nothing wrong with the properties; the problems were strictly ownership. Remember—one man's poison can be another man's feast.

1. *Two-way Exchange.* My first experience with exchanging came early in my career when I began calling property owners in a specific area of town to find sellers who wanted to list their property with my real estate company. I found a large company that owned two big apartment complexes in town. They had been managing the properties from out of town and, because of an incompetent resident manager, had found that the management was more than they could handle. In a board of directors meeting they had decided to liquidate the properties and invest instead in other units closer to their base of operations.

I sold one of the units to a group of doctors for cash.

The other apartment complex, a student rental apartment consisting of sixty-five units with space for about 330 students, was a little more difficult to move. It was situated in a marginal location and was an older property that needed a major facelift to make it competitive with newer properties. In analyzing the needs of the sellers, I determined that the major motivations for selling were: (1) the distance factor, (2) the sellers' lack of knowledge about student rental properties, (3) management problems, and (4) needed repairs.

After about two weeks of advertising the property, I ran into a friend, and I told him about the property for sale. Since he was in the market for another apartment complex, he was very interested in examining the figures. He asked me if the sellers would be interested in an exchange for a small mobile home park nearer their home office. I wasn't sure, so I told him to make an offer.

The offer was to exchange the sixty-five-unit apartment building for a fifty-space mobile home park. Since my clients had about $500,000 equity in the apartment building and my friend had only $200,000 equity in his mobile home park, I knew there would be problems.

But my friend came up with a solution: he would bring in a partner who had a smaller apartment complex of thirty units with $300,000 equity. Together they would buy out my client's equity.

The offer was submitted and accepted by all parties.

Let's examine what kinds of benefits each party received. First of all, my client, who happily paid me a fee of $19,000, received the following benefits:

—He rid himself of a deteriorating problem property.

—He rid himself of an unfamiliar and poor management situation.

—He acquired units closer to his home office.

—He was able to start all over again.

My friend, who owned a major interest in a local management firm, received these benefits:

—He rid himself of a mobile home park he had held for years without realizing any substantial cash flow due to a depressed market situation.

—He acquired an ownership position in a unit located closer to his home office.

—He could have needed repairs and maintenance done at wholesale prices.

—He increased his leverage position.

The partner who owned the thirty-unit apartment building was also eventually able to increase his leverage position.

All parties to the transaction came out with a bundle of benefits greater than the bundle of benefits they were leaving behind.

The transaction was a two-way exchange: A took what B had, and B took what A had. Let me give you an example of a three-way exchange.

2. *Three-way Exchange.* Just before I got married a few years ago, my wife let me know in no uncertain terms that she had no intention of living in the small duplex I had purchased only months before. Since I refused to pay rent, I had to find a home we could live in. I had no cash, so I had to find someone who would take my duplex in exchange for a home.

I remembered that a friend of mine was having trouble selling his home, mostly due to seasonal market fluctuations, so I approached him on an exchange. His home was worth $55,000, and he had a loan of $37,000. My duplex was worth $39,000, and I had a loan of $31,000. Here is how the equities paired up:

	Home	Duplex
Value:	$55,000	$39,000
Loans:	37,000	31,000
Equity:	$18,000	$8,000

Since I was $10,000 short I had to come up with something more. I proposed that he accept as part of the equity a $3,000 note which was owed to me. He accepted the note at full face value. I still had to come up with $7,000.

Can you see any solution? I took the obvious: a refinance. Since I was going to live in the home, I could qualify for a 90 percent owner-occupied loan. The loan would pay off the existing first mortgage of $37,000, pay off the $7,000 I owed the seller, and would leave me with $5,500 in cash.

New loan	$49,500
Less old loan	37,000
Cash from refinance	12,500
Less $7,000 to seller	7,000
Net to me	5,500
Less closing costs	1,500
Net cash to me	$4,000

The exchange seemed to be working out so smoothly. But there was one hitch: the house seller did not want my duplex. Here was a case for a three-way exchange:

A wants B   B doesn't want A   C wants A   B wants C

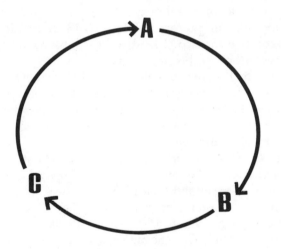

THE THREE WAY EXCHANGE

I brought in a third party who agreed to buy the duplex from the house seller as soon as he received it from me in an exchange. The third party offered to buy the duplex from the house seller for $39,000. The $8,000 equity in the duplex would be given as a note secured by the duplex with a payment of $1,000 in six months and the rest amortized over a two-year period with payments of $100 a month and a balloon payment at the end of the two years. The seller agreed to the three-way exchange and we signed the papers. Thirty days later I qualified for the new home mortgage of $49,500 and the exchange was consummated.

The transaction was completed. I received the house and $4,000 proceeds from a new refinance loan. The house seller received $7,000 in cash, a $3,000 note, and an $8,000 note secured against my duplex. The third party purchased a duplex with no down payment. A got B, B got C, and C got A. Everyone was happy.

3. *Lemonading.* One of my very first exchange clients was a couple who had purchased a piece of speculative real estate years before. It was more a swindle than an investment, and they had experienced little appreciation. What's worse, the property had been up for sale for more than a year with no success. They came to me wanting to see if there wasn't some way to move the $19,000 equity in their land into something more attractive.

I came up with a quick solution by suggesting that they refinance their house and add the proceeds of $30,000 to the equity in the land; with $49,000 equity composed of land and cash, they might have a better chance of moving their problem property.

I made a trip to Phoenix to a Real Estate Exchangers' meeting, and within two days I had twenty or thirty offers to trade for the property. I quickly learned that when a little cash is involved people pay attention. Lemon plus sugar makes lemonade. Add sugar (cash) to your sour investments (lemons) and see how fast they go!

4. *Exchange Cash Generator.* This can be an excellent solution for you. I have even heard of a real estate operator who buys up older homes with little or no down payment and then exchanges them to don't wanters for cash plus their don't-wanter properties. Here's how it works:

Our man buys a home for $35,000 with a $3,000 down payment and a $32,000 mortgage. He finds someone who has a piece of land he doesn't want with an equity of $5,000. He convinces the don't wanter to give him the $5,000 piece of ground plus $3,000 cash in exchange for the house with a $32,000 mortgage. Thus our man gets his $3,000 back and has a $5,000 piece of property as profit. And let's not forget the don't wanter: he is now the owner of a house and is much happier than when he owned the land. Benefits, benefits, benefits.

5. *Anything Goes.* It is not always necessary to trade real estate for real estate. A few months ago I responded to an ad in the newspaper that was

advertising a house for "low down." The agent told me the home had sold a few days earlier for $38,000, and the seller took an older camper as a down payment. I couldn't believe that the seller had taken just an old camper. Then I remembered my own situation with a three-acre parcel of ground: I had been willing to take almost anything as a down payment for my equity in the ground. Almost any don't wanter would be the same.

There are a number of things you can offer as full or partial down payments on real estate:

—Use any dead equities you may own, such as recreational lots you never use and that you shouldn't have purchased in the first place.

—Use mortgage notes that are due you. Suppose you had sold your home a few years ago and you took back a second or third mortgage of $5,000 payable at $50 a month for the next thirty years. Offer it to a don't-wanter seller. Be sure to offer it at face value. You'll benefit, too, because you'll get rid of a "thorn in the side" note you haven't been able to sell on the open market for cash. Double check with your accountant on the tax angles.

—Use any furniture or personal items you no longer have any use for. Give them an assessed value and include them as part of your equity in an exchange. If the seller accepts, you will have solved two problems: clearing out your basement and reducing the amount of equity needed to complete a transaction. I recently met a man who had sold one of his investment houses taking a motorcycle as a down payment. Be creative.

6. *Trade Discounted Paper.* You almost never have to discount real estate notes or mortgages when you use them in a real estate exchange with a don't wanter. This fact implies a great money-making opportunity. One group of smart investors in California buy such notes or paper from anxious people who are willing to take a substantial discount on the face value of their paper in order to raise cash. For example, suppose you were the holder of a $20,000 note second mortgage payable at $214.92 a month including 10 percent interest over fifteen years. If you wanted to sell this note for cash to an investor, you would probably have to sell it for about $13,000 cash, since the investor would want his investment to yield him at least 18 percent. These real estate investors in California buy up these notes for a discount and trade them for real estate equities at full face value. They would buy your $20,000 note for $13,000; they would then trade your same $20,000 note into a $20,000 equity in an apartment building. If they were to sell the apartment building immediately, they would realize a profit of $7,000, a 54 percent return on their investment.

If you'd like to try something similar, you can arrange for a bank line of credit or partnership money to buy older mortgages at a discount. The sky is the limit.

7. *A Bull for a Bear.* If you are a heavy loser in the stock market and want to recoup your losses, offer your depressed stocks to a real estate seller who wants immediate cash and who will discount the value of his property. He will get cash, and you can trade your stocks for equity that is greater than the face value of the stocks you traded. If you know of someone in this situation, offer to buy their stocks for more than what they would sell for. Then find a seller who will discount the value of his property for cash. You make the trade and sell the property for cash, netting you enough money to pay off the owner of the stocks and to put a few thousand dollars in your pocket for your trouble.

Is there good money to be made in exchange transactions?

In the last three months my partner and I have bought five houses and one 10-unit apartment building. Our investment for the $425,000 worth of real estate we purchased was about $60,000, just over 14 percent down payment. Of this $60,000 my portion of the down payment was borrowed on a six-month note at 12 percent interest; I invested no money of my own. It would be a fairly simple matter for us to increase the price of this portfolio of properties by $60,000 up to $485,000 and then to look for a don't wanter with an equity of $120,000 who wanted to pick up some neat, clean, professionally managed investment. Since we bought all of the properties under the market price, we know that we can double our money easily.

Not only can you as the investor increase your equity dramatically using exchanging formulas; you can also pyramid your holdings from smaller properties into larger ones. The classic example of this is the small-fry investor who begins by buying one small investment home with the objective of making cosmetic improvements and trading his increased equity in the now improved property. He searches for someone who is interested in trading a larger property, perhaps a duplex which might have minor problems to solve, for a smaller property which is neat and clean. Once again the philosophy of exchange benefits is important here. The smaller property owner wants to increase his leverage and real estate holdings and is searching for a larger property to exchange for the smaller. The owner of the larger property wants just the opposite. He wants to come "down and out." He is looking for less leverage. He wants a smaller property because he may feel that he can better manage it. Or perhaps he feels that he could sell a smaller property for cash with less difficulty. Once the exchange is completed, the new owner of the duplex begins the same process of fixing up, improving the rental picture, cutting expenses where possible and thereby improving the value of the property. Then he can continue the process of exchanging and pyramiding upward. Perhaps he looks for a four-unit apartment building. He may be able to handle a larger unit. His goal is to find a "don't wanter" of a larger property who wants to come down or who is willing to take other equities in exchange for his own. In the period of only a few short years, a dedicated exchanger might be able to pyramid a meager investment into two or three hundred apartment units. How high can you count? That's your limit.

There is one major benefit of exchanging that we have not touched upon. *Tax advantage!* The IRS has given major tax advantages to real estate owners who want to exchange their properties for larger real estate properties. The section of the IRS code dealing with this is section 1031. Your accountant should be involved in any exchange you enter into because of the complexities of the code. However, let me give you a layman's explanation so that you are at least aware of the general nature of tax-free exchanges.

One of the biggest misconceptions in the minds of beginning investors concerning tax-free exchanging is that they are entitled to sell their investment property on the open market for cash without tax consequence as long as they reinvest the sale proceeds into another larger property within the following eighteen months. This is false. If you sell for cash, you will pay taxes on your gain, no matter what you do with the money. The only way to "defer" taxes is to exchange your equity for a larger piece of property. If you exchange for a smaller property you may still have to pay taxes, and if you receive anything that is not real estate, such as cash or personal property, you may also be liable for taxes on your gain. However, if you exchange into a property of greater dollar value with a higher total mortgage amount without receiving any cash or personal property as part of the deal, you may be eligible for a tax-free exchange. You will not be required to pay taxes on your gains until you either sell the new property for cash (you could exchange again tax-free) or until you die. In this manner, a shrewd investor can defer any taxes he has on the gain in his properties for a lifetime, just as long as he follows the rules set down in section 1031 of the Internal Revenue code. Therefore, not only does his real estate shelter a portion of his personal income tax with depreciation, it also shelters his capital gains. This leaves him with more money to invest. And one of the cardinal rules of any investor is the preservation of investment capital. Now you can see why real estate is such a great investment.

Let me show you some of the ways you can use the above knowledge to your advantage. I own an older twelve-unit apartment building that I bought several years ago for $141,000. In just a few short years the value of this property has skyrocketed. My equity is over $100,000. My initial down payment was only $5,000. If I sell for cash I will have serious tax consequences.

Someone approaches me with a cash offer to sell. I can't accept his offer because of tax problems. How can I use this situation to my advantage? I know that I can't receive cash but I can exchange for a larger building. Using this knowledge, I counter the cash offer with the following terms:

—The buyer will place his $100,000 in escrow pending closing.

—The seller (myself) will look for a larger building to purchase with the $100,000 cash in escrow.

—At the closing the buyer will take title to the new building which I locate and give the $100,000 as a down payment.

—As soon as the buyer takes title to the new property he immediately exchanges the new property to me for my property.

In this way, my buyer ends up with my building. I end up with a new property in a tax-free exchange. And the seller of the new property gets a sale with $100,000 down payment. The exact mechanics of the above transaction can be easily taken care of by your title company or your attorney. Don't try it without advice. You wouldn't want to do it wrong.

How do you find someone who wants to exchange? Any seller is fair game for an exchange. Include exchange items (if it is to your advantage) in every offer that you write. You will find that many sellers are already familiar with the advantages of exchanging—especially the tax advantages—and some sellers will not make a move without exchanging.

On the other hand, most sellers don't understand the mechanics of an exchange. Since a confused mind always says No, you may find that your sellers would rather stick to conventional means of selling, such as all cash, rather than depend on an unfamiliar solution such as an exchange. You may have to do some educating.

If you are currently using a realtor, there is a society of real estate exchangers who deal strictly in creative real estate transactions. Groups of such "exchangers" meet in organized groups all over the country on a regular basis to solve their clients' problems. Usually once a month—but sometimes as often as once a week—these specially trained realtors meet, prepare a copy of the client's property information, and pass these packets out to each realtor present. Then everyone offers his suggestions as to the solution of the client's problem, and generally one or more of the realtors present has a client who wants just such a property. If you have properties you would like to exchange through a realtor, contact your local board of realtors to find names of those persons actively engaged in exchanging. Ask for the name and telephone number of the president of the local or state exchange group. He can tell you where to go and whom to see about your property. If you become more informed and involved, ask him to invite you as his guest to the local exchange meeting. It's a real eye-opener. And a lot of fun.

CHAPTER NINETEEN

Making a Million: The Option Blueprint

WHEN YOU were a child, did you ever sit on the scorching cement on a sweltering July afternoon, patiently hold a magnifying glass over a scrap of last night's newspaper, and stay motionless until the edges of the paper began to blaze? You learned that by concentrating the sun's rays into a limited area, you increased their power significantly.

The same principle applies in real estate. If you concentrate all of your energies and abilities in one limited area of real estate investment, you will increase your power significantly. One such specialty is options.

An option is the greatest form of leverage available to the real estate investor today. It is a simple agreement between the seller and the prospective buyer that says the seller will sell his property to the buyer at a fixed price in the future. In exchange for this "right to buy," the prospective buyer gives the seller an agreed-upon amount of money.

For example, if I give you $1,000 for the right to buy your duplex for $50,000 in two years, if I come up with $50,000 to pay you anytime within the two-year period you *must* sell the duplex to me, even though you might have changed your mind in the meantime.

Why would you give me an option to buy your duplex on such terms? There are three very good reasons:

1. Your property may only be worth $39,000 on today's market, and you might think its value could never increase to $50,000 in the two-year period of time, a figure that would represent 13.23 percent increase annually. If you planned on keeping the duplex for at least two years, taking my $1,000 option money would just be gravy.

"THIS IS A LEGALLY BINDING CONTRACT. IF NOT UNDERSTOOD, SEEK COMPETENT ADVICE."

OPTION

KNOW ALL MEN BY THESE PRESENTS:

That ....
of ...., hereinafter referred to as "Seller, hereby agrees for and in consideration of .... ($................................) Dollars,
paid by ....
of ...., hereinafter referred to as "Buyer", as follows:

1. PROPERTY: Seller hereby gives and grants to Buyer and to his heirs and assigns for a period of .... months from the date hereof, hereinafter referred to as "First Option Period", the exclusive right and privilege of purchasing the follow-ing described real property located at ...., County of ...., State of ...., and more particularly described as follows:

Together with all water rights appurtenant thereto or used in connection therewith.
(Said real property and improvements, if any, shall hereinafter be referred to as "The Property").

2. PRICE. The total purchase price for said property is ....
($................................) Dollars, payable in lawful money of the United States, strictly within the following times, to-wit. All sums paid for this option and any extension thereof as herein provided, shall be first applied on the purchase price, and the balance shall be paid as follows:

3. EXTENSION OF OPTION. Upon payment by Buyer to Seller of an additional sum of ....
.... ($................................) Dollars, cash or by cashier's check, prior to the expiration of the first option period, this option shall be extended for .... months, herein-after referred to as "Second Option Period". Upon Buyer's payment to Seller of a further sum of ....
.... $................................) Dollars, prior to the expira-tion of the second option period, this option shall be extended for a third period of .... additional months, hereinafter referred to as "Third Option Period".

4. EXERCISE OF OPTION. This option shall be exercised by written notice to Seller on or before the expiration of the first option period, or if extended, the expiration of the second or third option periods as the case may be. Notice to exercise this option or to extend the option for a second or third option period, whether personally delivered or mailed to Seller at his address as indicated after Seller's signature hereto, by registered or certified mail, postage prepaid, and post-marked on or before such date of expiration, shall be timely and shall be deemed actual notice to Seller.

5. EVIDENCE OF TITLE.

(a) Promptly after the execution of this option, Seller shall deliver to Buyer for examination such abstracts of title, title policies, and other evidences of title as the Seller may have. In the event this option is not exercised by Buyer, all such evidences of title shall be immediately returned without expense to Seller.

(b) In the event this option is exercised as herein provided, Seller agrees to pay all abstracting expense or at Seller's option to furnish a policy of title insurance in the name of the Buyer.

(c) If an examination of the title should reveal defects in the title, Buyer shall notify Seller in writing thereof, and Seller agrees to forthwith take all reasonable action to clear the title. If the Seller does not clear title within a reason-able time, Buyer may do so at Seller's expense. Seller agrees to make final conveyance by Warranty Deed or ....
.... in the event of sale of other than real property. If either party fails to perform the provisions of this agreement, the party at fault agrees to pay all costs of enforcing this agreement, or any right arising out of the breach thereof, including a reasonable Attorney's fee.

6. CLOSING ADJUSTMENTS. All risk of loss and destruction of property and expenses of insurance shall be borne by Seller until date of possession. At time of closing of sale, property taxes, rents, insurance, interest and other expenses of property shall be prorated as of date of possession. All other taxes, including documentary taxes, and all assessments, mortgage liens and other liens, encumbrances or charges against the property of any nature, shall be paid by Seller except

....

7. POSSESSION. Seller agrees to surrender possession of the property on or before .... days following written notice of the exercising of this option by Buyer.

8. The Seller recognizes .... Real Estate Company (Broker and Agent) through its salesman ...., as the Real Estate Broker with whom Seller listed this property for sale, and Seller agrees to pay a commission to said Broker equal to ....% of the gross sale price; and Seller hereby authorizes the agent to withhold such commission from the proceeds of sale at time of closing.

9. If this option be not exercised on or before the dates specified herein for exercise of same, the option shall expire of its own force and effect and the Seller may retain such option monies as have been paid to the Seller as full consideration for the granting of this option.

IN WITNESS WHEREOF, the Seller hereunto has set his name this .... day of ...., 19..............

SIGNED IN PRESENCE OF:

....

....
                                                                                        Seller

....   Address of Seller: ....

                                                                                        ....

2. The $1,000 option money is not taxable until the year the option is exercised. This means that you could take my money and spend it as you wished without reporting it on your income tax statement. If I exercised the option, you would simply include the $1,000 as part of the down payment and pay the tax accordingly. If the option was not exercised, you would pay capital gains tax on the option money received. It is like receiving tax-free dollars.

3. The innate greed in each of us yearns for an outlet: that outlet is the option. If you feel the value of your property can never increase to as high as the option price, you lose nothing by gambling on me. You are actually hoping that I succeed in paying such a price for the property. It's like having your cake and eating it too. You get to use my $1,000 for two years tax-free, and your chances of getting an outrageously high price for your property are also high. In essence, we make a bet with each other: I am betting $1,000 that your property will be worth more than $50,000 in two years. You are betting the imaginary profit that I am wrong.

So why in the world would I want to take an option to buy your property? Obviously, I don't want to gamble $1,000 of my money on an option unless I am absolutely sure that the property I am buying will be worth *more* than the option price at the end of the option. But suppose I know that your duplex is worth $45,000 on today's market, and you only thought it was worth $39,000. If property increases in value at the rate of at least 10 percent a year over the next two years (which is a fairly safe subjective judgment on my part), your duplex will be worth about $55,000 in two years. If I then sold the duplex for $55,000, I would make $5,000 profit on my $1,000 investment, about 123 percent return on my money.

To pull this off you must be comfortable with several assumptions:

—The property optioned is optioned at the right price; you must know the market.

—The property has potential for increase in value.

There are advantages to options besides profit. The holder of an option does not have to manage the property during the option period, nor is it necessary for him to pay taxes, insurance, or any other expenses. Since the liability of the option holder is limited to the extent of his option money, he does not have to be bothered with large debts or mortgage payments. If at the end of the option period the option holder decides not to purchase the property, he simply fails to exercise the option and loses his initial option money, but he has no legal problems that would have resulted if he had contracted to buy the property. The biggest benefit of all is that the option holder does not have to pay interest.

All in all, the option is simple, easy to use, and very profitable if it is used correctly. It requires very little money and involves very little risk. Let me share with you a success story that illustrates how the use of options can be extremely valuable to the high-leverage investor.

Stewart, a close friend of mine, decided to do some investing in real estate on his own without partners. He discovered a four-unit apartment building the owner wanted to sell for $69,000—definitely under the market price at that time. Stewart contacted the owner of the building and offered to buy his building in four months for $69,000 cash. To bind the transaction he received an option to buy the building at the agreed price. He gave the seller $2,000 option money and placed this ad in the classified section of the newspaper:

Fourplex for sale by owner
$78,000
Call Stewart 555–1234

Within three days he had a buyer who came up with cash. Stewart walked away from the transaction less than three months later with $8,000 in his pocket.

A short-term option like this can only be used if you are absolutely sure that the property optioned is substantially underpriced and if you are absolutely sure that a strong market exists that will enable you to sell quickly. Long-term options involve much less risk.

Another friend of mine did the same thing with a piece of development ground which he optioned for $1 and sold within a few weeks for a substantial profit.

In my travels to various seminars I have had conversations with several investors who spend their entire time studying the values of land in their respective areas and then paying for options on the ground or buildings which seemed to offer the greatest potential for appreciation. They do not purchase any property at all; they just option it. It is a full time occupation and very lucrative. A very astute realtor in my area optioned a large tract of land from a local farmer for a rather outlandish price. I'm sure that the farmer supposed that there was zero possibility of the realtor ever coming through with such a high price. The realtor went to the planning commission and had the property re-zoned for commercial shopping space and resold the package to a developer for at least a million dollar profit—on just one transaction. Ironically enough, the developer who bought the land has resold some of it for an even greater profit. Everyone made money.

Options are powerful, but they aren't easy to come by. It takes weeks or months of evaluating potential pieces of property. And it's usually difficult to convince the property owner that he should let you have an option on his property.

1. *Equity for options.* If you don't have any money to work with and you would like to use options as a tool to increase your net worth, offer a prospective property owner personal property as an option payment instead of cash. I once offered my duplex as an option payment for a large twelve-unit apartment building. If I had not come up with the cash to buy his building within six months, he could have kept my duplex. Needless to say, I hurried. If you have a recreational lot somewhere in the arid reaches of this planet that you bought while you were half-crocked, you could always offer it to a seller as an option on his property. Any equity that you have is usable as an option on another piece of property. If the seller balks at the idea of using your property as an option, convince him that you will cash him out at the end of the option period.

Shouldn't an option involve the least amount of cash possible? Not

always. If it causes the seller to balk at your offer, you may be better off
to raise a larger amount of cash as an initial option deposit in exchange
for more lenient terms for exercising of the option. Once the seller agrees
to the terms of the option, he cannot change his mind later on, so work
the option to give the best leverage at the end, not the least cash at first.
You should always try to structure the option so the terms will be enticing
to a new buyer if you need to sell your position to someone else during
the term of the option.

What happens if when the term of the option arrives, you don't have
the money to cash out the seller? You need to provide for this eventuality
in the original option by negotiating a rolling option: state in the option
agreement that the option can be extended for another year by the
additional payment of $10,000 (or some amount agreeable to the seller).
If you really want the property, it would be easier for you to come up
with an additional $10,000 than to have to come up with the entire
purchase price. In addition, you'll have an additional year to come up
with the necessary money. Negotiate two or three such terms of extension
if the seller is agreeable.

The rolling option is also used extensively in land transactions when
a developer does not want to buy a large piece of ground all at once.
The interest charges on a large piece of undeveloped property would eat
a developer alive within a short period of time. Instead, a developer can
negotiate to buy a smaller portion of the ground for cash and option the
remainder of the ground at higher prices for later on. If the project does
not go as well as the developer desires, he can drop the options, lose a
small amount of money, and go on to another project. But if the project
is a success, he can option the remaining ground as the need arises. In
effect, he rolls his option from one piece of ground to the next until the
entire property is purchased and developed.

There are two especially creative ideas that use the option philosophy:

2. *The "earnest money" option or "offer to purchase" option.* Whenever
you purchase a piece of property, you normally use a standard Earnest
Money Receipt or offer to purchase signed by you and the seller to bind
the transaction. The earnest money agreement establishes the terms of
the sale and the completion date, which is usually thirty to sixty days in
the future. If someone should come along within this thirty- to sixty-day
period and offer you more money for the property than you had committed to pay for it, is there any reason you could not sell him your
interest in the earnest money agreement for a profit?

Suppose you found a twelve-unit apartment building that was priced $30,000 under the current market rate for such units. If you could find someone who wanted to buy the building from you for a $10,000 profit before the closing date, there is no reason why you could not do so. It is totally legal and honest. You have given the seller a check for earnest money that will be forfeited to the seller if you are unable to complete the transaction according to terms. If the seller gets his terms, it doesn't matter *who* ends up with the property.

Whenever you find a property that is substantially undervalued, make an offer on it subject to an earnest money agreement to perform within sixty to ninety days. Then you have two to three months to convince someone else that the property is a good buy, and you can pick up extra cash by selling your interest in an earnest money agreement.

I first used this technique about a year ago when I found a choice apartment building for sale offered on excellent terms and for an excellent price. I did not hesitate. I made an offer to purchase, and the sellers accepted my $500 check as earnest money. The closing date was scheduled seven weeks later. I immediately contacted a client and convinced him that the property was an excellent buy—for $10,000 more than I had agreed to buy it for. He checked with his advisers and verified my claims. When the original closing date rolled around, he gave me the money to close the transaction in my name. As soon as I legally owned the building, I sold it to my client for a nice $10,000 profit.

Note some important factors about this deal. First, I did not have the $50,000 needed for the down payment that I had agreed to pay in the earnest money agreement. But I *had* given $500 to the seller, which I would have forfeited if the deal had fallen through. You don't have to have cash in your pocket in order to tie up property. Use the earnest-money option technique.

I could have been able to avoid the hassle of closing the above transaction in my name if I had written the original earnest money or offer to purchase correctly. I had agreed to close in my name in the original offer to purchase. However, if I had written that I "or my assigns" would close, then I would have been able to let my client come in with the down payment on closing day. He would have bought the property with the written understanding that as soon as he received title to the building he would transfer the $10,000 profit to my account. This kind of transaction can be accomplished without ever having to notify either the buyer or the seller of your intentions. The seller does not have to know that you are immediately reselling his property for a profit, and the buyer does not have to know that you don't own the property he is buying (you merely control it with an earnest money option). This is best accomplished by setting up separate accounts at two different title companies. In the first title company you deposit your earnest-money check and your earnest-money agreement or offer to purchase. You give instructions to the closing officer that you will be depositing the down payment for the closing on or before the day of closing and that the money will be coming from another title company. At the second title company, you instruct your new buyer to deposit his down payment (which is enough to cover your down payment negotiated with the seller of the property and a little extra to cover the profit you wish to make on the transaction). The buyer does not need to know that you are making a quick profit. He just expects that when he deposits his down payment, you will be transferring to him the title to the property. In actuality, the closing officers of the two title companies confer on the phone about how the title is to be transferred from the seller to you to the new buyer. This is called a simultaneous closing, or a double escrow. The result of the double escrow is that the money from your new buyer is used to pay off the seller and you keep whatever profit you earned for putting the two people together. The mechanics of the double escrow are well known to the title companies in your area. If you have any questions about how this works, you might give one of these companies a call before you use the earnest-money option technique.

I read about a couple in Texas who began optioning ground a few years ago and who made more than a million dollars in five short years. How did they do it? They copied from the county records the names and addresses of all property owners who lived out of state. They reasoned that these people would be less likely to have kept track of the rising values of their property. They were right. They sent out form letters to hundreds of out-of-state owners, offering to buy their property for cash with a 90- to 120-day closing. A large percentage of the owners offered to sell at a price that was usually below current land values.

Once an affirmative letter was returned, the man and wife would go inspect the ground to see if it really was worth buying. If they felt that a profit was probable, they would send a $500 earnest-money check to the owners and would have them sign the agreement binding the transaction. Then they would place ads in the local newspapers announcing a sale of the property. They tried to price the property just under current market prices to insure a good response. As soon as a buyer was located for the higher-priced land, they closed the transaction, using a double escrow, and kept the difference as profit. As an example, suppose the couple found eighty acres below the market at $3,000 per acre. If the going market rate was $5,000 per acre, they could tie the property up with a $500 earnest money agreement and proceed to sell the ground for $4,000 per acre. It would not take long to sell the property for cash at such a good price. Their profit would be $1,000 per acre—a total of $80,000 on one transaction. This is not impossible.

You can do the same if you can find a seller who does not realize the value of his property and who is willing to give you a longer than normal time period for closing the transaction. In one of my seminars, I discussed the use of the earnest-money option, and two of my students took my techniques to heart. One father and son partnership began researching the county records in a sparsely populated county of Utah, and to their surprise they found hundreds of properties belonging to out-of-state landowners who had held their land for years without realizing its value. They have made thousands of dollars buying ground from out-of-state owners and selling the property in smaller pieces to in-state owners on good terms. Another law student used the same idea and took the county records which showed the out-of-state owners of improved property. He wrote thirty-five letters, received eight replies, and affirmed two offers to sell. A lady called him long distance to tell him that she owned a triplex for several years and wanted to sell at a price and terms which he could dictate within reason. This young student didn't have any money, but he did have a good idea, and it paid off for him.

In another example, I'm familiar with a group of realtors who recognized the potential of a particular piece of ground and approached the seller of the ground with an offer to buy. They requested a closing date nine months in the future, to give them time to come up with the money. The seller agreed and accepted $200 as a deposit. In the next nine months these enterprising men had the property re-zoned from agricultural to multiple residential dwelling land. They took an architect in with them who drew up plans for a beautiful condominium project. With these plans, the city gave them preliminary approval for the development. Then, they found a local building contractor who showed an interest in the property and sold the ground to him for $125,000 more than they had agreed to pay the original seller. They did this without ever having to own the property physically . . . they just controlled the eventual sales price with an offer to purchase. When the time rolled around to close with the original seller, the new owner, the building contractor, simply completed the transaction in the place of the realtors. Obviously, this is a powerful technique.

3. *Lease with an option to purchase.* Another creative way to use the option technique to lower your down payment requirements is to use the "lease with option to purchase" technique. Let's look at an example that shows the benefits of such a technique.

While searching for property to buy, you find a man who has a house up for rent. It is a four-bedroom home located in a decent neighborhood. It is worth $40,000. The owner is trying to rent because his home sat on the market for six months, priced at $45,900, with no takers. Since the owner had already bought a new home and had moved into it, assuming the additional mortgage payment and all other home-owner bills, he decided to put the home up for rent or lease rather than go into the hole every month to pay the $275 per month mortgage on the existing $30,000 mortgage balance.

Obviously the owner doesn't need a lot of cash, since he has already purchased his new home and has already adjusted to making a higher mortgage payment. But he is definitely concerned about having to fork out an extra $275 a month until his old home is either leased or sold. This seller is a special kind of don't wanter. He doesn't want the hassle of managing his own property, and he wants to save himself from a negative cash flow situation.

Offer him a solution to his problems and create an advantage for yourself: offer to lease his home from him for five years. Tell him that you will handle all maintenance and that he will never get a call from you— only a regular monthly check. In return, ask him for an option to buy his house from him in five years at a price of $51,000, which is an increase of about five percent a year on a $40,000 price. You should also require that 25 percent of the lease payment be applied to the eventual purchase price. In this case that 25 percent would amount to just over $4,000 and would lower your option price from $51,000 to $47,000.

Suppose that the seller decided to accept your offer of a firm price of $51,000 within five years, but with no lease credit. If property values increase at an annual rate of between 10 percent and 15 percent as they have been over the past few years, then your home will be worth between $64,000 and $80,000 by the time the option is ready to be exercised. The seller can sell the home to anyone he wants to in the meantime, but the

RESIDENTIAL LEASE WITH OPTION TO PURCHASE

RECEIVED FROM_____

_____ hereinafter referred to as _____

the sum of $_____DOLLARS),

evidenced by _____, as a deposit which, upon acceptance of this Lease shall belong to

the Owner of the premises, hereinafter referred to as Owner and shall be applied as follows:

	RECEIVED	PAYABLE PRIOR TO OCCUPANCY
Rent for the period from _____ to _____	$_____	$_____
Last_____month's rent	$_____	$_____
Security Deposit	$_____	$_____
Key Deposit	$_____	$_____
Cleaning charge	$_____	$_____
Other	$_____	$_____
TOTAL	$_____	$_____

In the event that this agreement is not accepted by the Owner or his authorized agent, within _____days, the total deposit received shall be refunded.

Tenant hereby offers to lease from the Owner the premises situated in the City of _____, County of_____, State of_____,

described as_____

_____

and consisting of_____

upon the following TERMS and CONDITIONS:

TERM: The term hereof shall commence on _____, 19____, and continue for a period of _____months thereafter.

RENT: Rent shall be $_____per month, payable in advance, upon the _____day of each calendar month to Owner or

his authorized agent, at the following address: _____

or at such other places as may be designated by Owner from time to time. In the event rent is not paid within five (5) days after due date, Tenant agrees to pay a late charge of $10.00 plus interest at 10% per annum of the delinquent amount. Tenant agrees further to pay $5.00 for each dishonored bank check.

UTILITIES: Tenant shall be responsible for the payment of all utilities and services, except: _____

which shall be paid by Owner.

USE: The premises shall be used as a residence with no more than _____adults and_____children, and for no other

purpose, without the prior written consent of the Owner.

PETS: No pets shall be brought on the premises without the prior consent of the Owner.

ORDINANCES AND STATUES: Tenant shall comply with all statutes, ordinances and requirements of all municipal, state and federal authorities now in force, or which may hereafter be in force, pertaining to the use of the premises.

ASSIGNMENT AND SUBLETTING: Tenant shall not assign this agreement or sublet any portion of the premises without prior written consent of the Owner which may not be unreasonably withheld.

MAINTENANCE, REPAIRS OR ALTERATIONS: Tenant acknowledges that the premises are in good order and repair, unless otherwise indicated herein. Owner may at any time give Tenant a written inventory of furniture and furnishings on the premises and Tenant shall be deemed to have possession of all said furniture and furnishings in good condition and repair, unless he objects thereto in writing within five days after receipt of such inventory. Tenant shall, at his own expense, and at all times, maintain the premises in a clean and sanitary manner including all equipment, appliances, furniture and furnishings therein and shall surrender the same at termination hereof, in as good condition as received, normal wear and tear excepted. Tenant shall be responsible for all repairs required for exposed plumbing or electrical wiring and for damages caused by his negligence and that of his family or invitees or guests. Tenant shall not paint, paper or otherwise redecorate or make alterations to the premises without the prior written consent of the Owner. Tenant shall irrigate and maintain any surrounding grounds, including lawns and shrubbery, and keep the same clear of rubbish or weeds, if such grounds are a part of the premises and are exclusively for the use of the Tenant.

ENTRY AND INSPECTION: Tenant shall permit Owner or Owner's agents to enter the premises at reasonable times and upon reasonable notice for the purpose of inspecting the premises or showing the same to prospective tenants or purchasers, or for making necessary repairs.

INDEMNIFICATION: Owner shall not be liable for any damage or injury to Tenant, or any other person, or to any property, occurring on the premises, or any part thereof, or in common areas thereof, and Tenant agrees to hold Owner harmless from any claims for damages no matter how caused.

POSSESSION: If Owner is unable to deliver possession of the premises at the commencement hereof, Owner shall not be liable for any damage caused thereby, nor shall this agreement be void or voidable, but Tenant shall not be liable for any rent until possession is delivered. Tenant may terminate this agreement if possession is not delivered within _____ days of the commencement of the term hereof.

DEFAULT: The failure by Tenant to pay rent when due, or perform any term hereof, shall, at the option of the Owner, terminate all rights of Tenant hereunder. In the event that Tenant shall be absent from the premises for a period of 5 consecutive days, while in default, Tenant shall, at the option of the Owner, be deemed to have abandoned the premises and any property left on the premises shall be considered abandoned and may be disposed of by Owner in any manner allowed by law. In the event that Owner reasonably believes that such abandoned property has no value, it may be discarded. All property on the premises is hereby subject to a lien in favor of Owner, for payment of all sums due hereunder, to the maximum extent allowed by law.

Recovery of the premises by Owner shall not relieve Tenant of any obligation hereunder, and Owner may let the premises to others upon such terms and conditions as he deems proper, and recover from Tenant sums due hereunder, less any consideration received from others for the use of the premises, for the remaining term hereof, after paying expenses.

SECURITY: The security deposit set forth above, if any, shall secure the performance of Tenant's obligations hereunder. Owner may, but shall not be obligated to, apply all or portions of said deposit on account of Tenant's obligations hereunder. Any balance remaining upon termination shall be returned to Tenant.

DEPOSIT FUNDS: Any returnable deposits shall be refunded within two weeks from date possession is delivered to Owner or his Authorized Agent.

ATTORNEYS FEES: In the event that Owner shall prevail in any legal action brought by either party to enforce the terms hereof or relating to the demised premises, Owner shall be entitled to all costs incurred in connection with such action, including a reasonable attorney's fee.

WAIVER: No failure of Owner to enforce any term hereof shall be deemed a waiver, nor shall any acceptance of a partial payment of rent be deemed a waiver of Owner's right to the full amount thereof.

NOTICES: Any notice which either party may or is required to give, may be given by mailing the same, postage prepaid, to Tenant at the premises or to Owner at the address shown below or at such other places as may be designted by the parties from time to time.

HEIRS, ASSIGNS, SUCCESSORS: This lease is binding upon and inures to the benefit of the heirs, assigns and successors in interest to the parties.

TIME: Time is of the essence of this agreement.

HOLDING OVER: Any holding over after expiration hereof, with the consent of Owner, shall be construed as a month-to-month tenancy in accordance with the terms hereof, as applicable. No such holding over or extension of this lease shall extend the time for the exercise of the option unless agreed upon in writing by Owner.

CONTINUED ON REVERSE SIDE

OPTION: So long as tenant is not in default in the payment of the rent provided for, Tenant shall have the option to purchase the real property described herein for a PURCHASE PRICE OF $_____DOLLARS), upon the following TERMS and CONDITIONS:

ENCUMBRANCES: In addition to any encumbrances referred to above, Tenant shall take title to the property subject to: 1) Real Estate Taxes not yet due and 2) Convenants, conditions, restrictions, reservations, rights, rights of way and easements of record, if any, which do not materially affect the value or intended use of the property.

The amount of any bond or assessment which is a lien shall be ☐ paid, ☐assumed by _____

EXAMINATION OF TITLE: Fifteen (15) days from date of exercise of this option are allowed the Tenant to examine the title to the property and to report in writing any valid objections hereto. Any exceptions to the title which would be disclosed by examination of the records shall be deemed to have been accepted unless reported in writing within said 15 days. If Tenant objects to any exceptions to the title, Owner shall use all due diligence to remove such exceptions at his own expense within 60 days thereafter. But if such exceptions cannot be removed within the 60 days allowed, all rights and obligtions hereunder may, at the election of the Tenant, terminate and end, unless he elects to purchase the property subject to such exceptions.

EVIDENCE OF TITLE: Evidence of Title shall be in the form of ☐ a policy of title insurance, ☐ other:_____to be paid for by _____

CLOSE OF ESCROW: Within _____ days from exercise of the option, or upon removal of any exceptions to the title by the Owner, as provided above, whichever is later, both parties shall deposit with an authorized escrow holder, to be selected by the Tenant, all funds and instruments necessary to complete the sale in accordance with the terms and conditions hereof.

PRORATION: Rents, taxes, premiums or insurance acceptable to Tenant, interest and other expenses of the property to be prorated as of recordation of deed. Security deposits, advance rentals or considerations involving future lease credits shall be credited to Tenant.

EXPIRATION OF OPTION: This option may be exercised at any time after_____, 19____, and shall expire at midnight_____, 19____. unless exercised prior thereto. Upon expiration Owner shall be released from all obligations hereunder and all of Tenants rights hereunder, legal or equitable, shall cease.

EXERCISE OF OPTION: The option shall be exercised by mailing or delivering written notice to the Owner prior to the expiration of this option and by an additional payment, on account of the purchase price, in the amount of

$_____(_____DOLLARS) for account of Owner to the authorized escrow holder referred to above, prior to the expiration of this option.

Notice, if mailed, shall be by certified mail, postage prepaid, to the Owner at the address set forth below, and shall be deemed to have been given upon the day following the day shown on the postmark of the envelope in which such notice is mailed.

In the event the option is exercised,_____ percent from the rent paid hereunder prior to the exercise of the option shall be credited upon the purchase price.

The undersigned Tenant hereby acknowledges receipt of a copy hereof.

_____Agent   DATED: _____

By: _____   _____Tenant

Broker: _____   _____Tenant

_____Address   _____Address

_____Phone   _____Phone

ACCEPTANCE
The undersigned Owner accepts the foregoing offer.

BROKERAGE FEE: Upon execution hereof the Owner agrees to pay to _____ the Agent in this transaction, the sum of $_____(_____DOLLARS) for leasing services rendered and authorizes Agent to deduct said sum from the deposit received from Tenant. In the event the optin is exercised, the Owner agrees to pay Agent the additional sum of $_____(_____DOLLARS). This agreement shall not limit the rights of Agent provided for in any listing or other agreement which may be in effect between Owner and Agent. In the event legal action is instituted to collect this fee, or any portion thereof, the Owner agrees to pay the Agent a reasonable attorney's fee and all costs in connection with such action.

The undersigned Owner hereby acknowledges receipt of a copy hereof.

DATED: _____

_____Address   _____Owner

_____Phone   _____Owner

option will remain in force, and the new owner will have to honor the contract that the seller had with you.

The only investment you will have in the option is time. Once you have negotiated your option, you will have to find a renter so that you don't have to make the $275 monthly payments on the lease. As soon as you locate a renter, your only responsibility will be to make sure the renters treat the property carefully and that the property always stays rented.

As the second and third year roll around, you will be able to increase the monthly lease payments by as much as $100 a month. Every time a new renter moves in, the rent can be increased. If you have five or more "lease/option" properties, your monthly cash flow could easily be more than $500 after only two years of operation.

You're probably wondering where to find people who will lease their property with an option to buy. Think about it for a second. If you were in the same situation, what would you do? Advertise! Turn to the "Homes for Rent or Lease" section of your daily newspaper classified ads and see how many ads are there. Call every person listed in the ads and ask, "Are you interested in giving an option to buy your property if I lease your home?" Don't forget to ask if some of your monthly rental can be applied toward the eventual option price.

Most people won't be interested. Don't get discouraged. This is a numbers game. You may have to call every night for a week or more. You'll soon be able to recognize the old ads and save time. Even of the people who are interested in your offer of a lease option, only a small percentage will finally agree to let you have a long-term lease of up to five years. Of those who accept the long-term lease, only a few will agree with the option price necessary for you to make a profit. Some people will be well aware of the increasing values for local real estate, and will insist that the option price be determined by evaluating the current market value of the home (perhaps determined by appraisal) and increasing this value by 10 percent or more per year until the option date. Forget dealing with this kind of seller. You won't see a penny of profit, so why should you handle maintenance and find renters for someone else?

Even though a good lease/option property is rare, it is well worth it. What are the benefits of this lease/option wealth blueprint?

1. It lets you become a future owner of real estate now without the outlay of a large amount of cash.

2. It provides a future cash flow situation as the market rents increase.

Depending on the number of homes you have lease/optioned, you can have hundreds of dollars of positive cash flow from property you don't even own!

3. You don't have to fight the constantly increasing tax and insurance costs. Your lease should be for a constant sum for a five-year period. If you negotiate otherwise, be sure there are enough benefits in the property (such as a low option price or the ability to apply lease payments toward option price) to insure that you will benefit in the long run.

4. Usually people who are lease/optioning their property are trying to avoid a constant mortgage payment figure. This mortgage payment will often be much lower than the property rental value. Since the mortgage is seasoned, the interest rate on the mortgage is probably lower and the payment is much lower than a monthly payment to amortize the selling price. The difference can be as great as $100. Thus, you avoid having to charge higher rental rates that would render you less competitive.

5. You have locked in a price based on a future value. If the property is well selected, you may make much greater returns than normal, especially if the property can be converted to a different use, such as commercial or office space. The option can be sold at any time for as much as you can negotiate. It could provide a handsome cash flow to you as you sell off your options to other investors.

There are some negatives. You cannot retain any tax advantages from such optioned properties. The seller still owns the property; you have just negotiated a future sale. You will have to spend hours managing your properties and leasing them to new tenants. You will also have to be responsible for all major repairs and minor maintenance unless you specify otherwise in your lease agreement.

Here are some general guidelines to follow in the lease/option game:

1. Don't lease a property unless you can get a long enough lease to make it worth your while—preferably three to five years. Always begin with a five-year option, and don't come down unless your other benefits are great.

2. Make sure that the future option price allows you enough room to make a profit. I usually try to keep the eventual price less than 5 percent per year compounded increase, whereas I am counting on at least a 10 percent per year annual compounded increase. You can lower the option price by having the seller credit part of your monthly lease payment toward the eventual option price, a technique that can defray the bite of a large future option price.

3. Only option properties that are in a good neighborhood and that have potential for steady increase in value. If the neighborhood is deteriorating, you will be working for nothing. Also choose properties that are easily maintained, such as those constructed with brick.

4. Call your local rental agency and offer to pay them a finder's fee for every property they refer you to that you eventually lease with an option to buy. Try placing an ad in the newspaper requesting "a lease with an option to buy." Keep at it and you'll eventually get results.

Investing in real estate through options is a five-year retirement plan that is feasible and possible with determined effort. Don't be discouraged if people are not thrilled to lease their properties for five years. Start out with a few shorter-term options, and look for the kind of a don't wanter who will let you write the terms of the lease/option to suit yourself. Your knowledge and confidence will grow as you become more familiar with the option market. I'll wager that five years from now your hobby of buying with options will be a full-time one, and you'll be on your own as a free-lancer.

CHAPTER TWENTY

Born-again Property: Consider Conversions

ONCE YOU have invested in real estate property, consider increasing your return on the investment by using the method of conversion.

Everywhere you look you will see buildings that are functioning in a completely different capacity than that for which they were designed. Homes have become office buildings. Old churches have lost their congregations to dance schools or restaurants. Apartment buildings have become condominiums. Gas stations have become retail stores. Farm land is now prime residential and commercial ground. To convert a property is to change its use from one utility to another. This is done for three reasons:

1. A building or piece of land has outlived its originally intended use.

2. A building or piece of land has failed in its originally intended use. For instance, a gas station can't compete with the other two gas stations on the block, so it is converted into a retail store.

3. It has become economically infeasible to operate the property as was originally intended. Maybe a farmer is not able to return enough money from his crops, so he sells to a commercial developer, who builds a shopping mall on the site of the old farm.

Conversions provide limitless possibilities for the creative real estate investor. Look at the relative values of a typical acre of ground under different uses:

A typical acre of raw undeveloped ground (43,560 square feet) used for grazing of animals or left unused could go for as little as $100. This converts to less than one fifth of a cent per square foot—.0023 cents per square foot, to be exact.

199

If this same property were sold as farm ground or converted to farm ground, it would sell for up to $2,500 per acre, or about 6 cents a square foot.

If this same land were converted to subdivision lots, it would sell for as high as $25,000 per acre, or just under 60 cents per square foot. In some cases the same subdivision land could sell for as high as $2 a square foot.

If the subdivision ground could be used instead for apartment ground, the seller could reap more than $75,000 an acre in some cases.

The highest priced ground is land used to build shopping centers and office buildings—land that sells for up to $250,000 per acre.

The chart below shows the relative values of each of the different types of property:

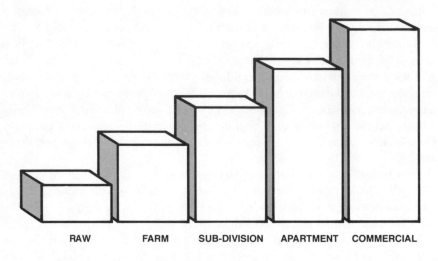

RAW   FARM   SUB-DIVISION   APARTMENT   COMMERCIAL

PYRAMIDING LAND VALUES

Between any two categories of ground there lies an absolutely fantastic opportunity for profit: all you need to do is convert land from one use to another.

Unfortunately, it is not easy to do in the conventional real estate market. To convert raw land to farming ground takes ingenuity and guts. One of my closest friends has hired a full time legal leg man to file claims with the Idaho state government that will enable him to homestead the vast unusable tracts of Idaho desert. Once the ground is in his name—perhaps 5,000 acres at a time that he acquires for little or nothing—he purchases one of those massive circular sprinkling systems. He files for a well permit and proceeds to irrigate the property; eventually it is suitable farm ground. If he converts only 1,000 acres a year and sells it for $1,000 an acre or less, he can make up to $1,000,000 at a time. Not many people are doing this; not many people have the guts or the creativity. But it only has to happen once to put you over the hump.

Converting farm ground to subdivision ground is a little bit easier, since any ground within a two-to-five-mile limit of your town, if you live in such an area of the country, is fair game for a future subdivision. If you can buy the ground for $5,000 an acre and resell it to a builder for up to $25,000 an acre, you will turn a tidy profit, multiplied by the number of acres you buy.

In cities where houses in depressed areas are abandoned for tax reasons, there may be an excellent profit opportunity for an apartment building developer who is looking for new ground to build his next project on. If you can purchase contiguous homes at a good price, you might be able to assemble a package of ground large enough for a good-sized apartment complex. The homes can be torn down, making way for a beautiful project.

I heard of two investors who approached the owners of old, rundown houses in an area zoned for apartments. Most of the owners were widows who could not take adequate care of the property; the investors offered them a brand new apartment for a home and an ownership position in the new apartment complex, which would be built upon the ground where their homes now stood.

These two men convinced a sufficient number of people to go along with their plan, applied to the city for a building permit, and built a beautiful unit where the new owners of the property were able to live for the rest of their lives rent free.

Since the land was donated to the partnership, the two developers did not have to invest any money on the front end in order to build the property. They ended up with a major ownership in the complex without any cash investment. This is a classic example of the conversion of land from one type of use to another, more profitable use.

How do you know how to take advantage of these changes? It is very simple. Just go down to your city's planning department and ask for a zoning map; the map indicates how each area is zoned. Apartments are usually zoned into one specific area, commercial space into another. Any property that is in an area zoned for different properties can be converted. For example, any home along a major artery leading into a major shopping district has potential as either an office or a shopping space. Of course, the property must be in an area that is zoned for commercial use, or you'll have to apply for a zoning change—something that is difficult to obtain and that takes time and effort.

Another potential conversion exists when one property lies directly adjacent to another zone of higher use. When an older apartment building is directly next to an office zone, for example, there is the possibility that the apartment building could be converted to offices.

Let's look more closely at two conversion possibilities.

Conversion of an apartment building to an office complex. I own a beautiful old twelve-unit apartment building in the center of my city of 60,000 people. It is a classic building with a fifty-year-old brick veneer and stately white balconies. I am now renting out the building for about $150 per month per unit, a price that gives me $18,000 a year with a net operating income of about $12,600. If the capitalized rate is 7 percent, the building is worth about $180,000 as an apartment complex.

But I have other plans. The building is located directly across from the county courthouse, which provides peripheral business opportunities for title companies, lawyers, office supply stores, and others. Suppose I convert my building to office space to house these peripheral businesses?

Will I benefit? To analyze the benefits I will need some important information. Here are some of the questions I will need answered:

How many square feet are usable as office space on each floor? Approximately 3,000 square feet each for three floors.

Is there adequate parking for office space? Checking with the city, I learned I will need one parking space for each 500 square feet of office space. I'll need eighteen spaces. I have thirteen spaces now, and I can rent an additional five spaces from a neighboring office building.

Is the property zoned for the intended change? The city master plan shows that my building is in a professional office zone. The city planner indicated that there would be no problem with the proposed conversion, but that I would have to submit my plans to the city council for its approval.

Is there an adequate market for office space? I called one of the county commissioners and found out that they needed extra space for some of their county offices. In fact, they had recently purchased some buildings across the street from my unit for some badly needed office space. One of the tenants in the buildings that the county bought needs a new office and asked about my rates. Others also expressed an interest. Before proceeding further, I need to get firm commitments for at least two-thirds of the space I am planning to convert; these signed leases will give me added borrowing power at the bank.

What about costs? I hired a local architect to make a study on the kinds of improvements that will have to be made to the building; his cost estimate is $50,000. This will include new carpet, paint, and furnaces.

What about the bank? Will they lend the money? My banker, on the strength of the pre-signed leases, would agree to lend me $80,000 to pay off an existing second mortgage and to complete the renovation. The payments on the bank's second mortgage are steep, but I can still show a good cash flow.

Here is how the building looks before and after the proposed conversion:

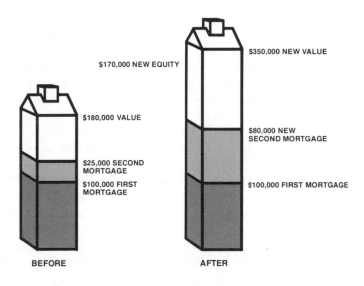

CONVERSION OF APARTMENTS TO OFFICE SPACE

The first mortgage payment was $850 at 7 percent interest. With the new $80,000 second mortgage (12 percent interest over a twenty-five-year period and a ten-year balloon), my payments are $842 per month. This makes a total mortgage payment of $1,692; my previous payment was $1,280.95.

The difference comes in the income picture. Previously the gross annual income was $18,000. Now, with office space, the income is much higher. I can lease out office space for about $5 per square foot per year with 3,000 square feet per floor, I can lease out 9,000 square feet, I can bring in $45,000 a year for total occupancy as an office building. Here are the details:

Gross income	$45,000
Expenses at 33 percent	15,000
Net operating income	30,000
Mortgage payments	(20,304)
Net income	$ 9,696

I borrowed $50,000 to make the necessary renovations, and after the building is leased up, I can put about $10,000 a year in my pocket. The apartment building was only a break-even situation.

There is another reason why the conversion is profitable. I gave the apartment building a value of $180,000 based on its new operating income capitalized at 7 percent. With the office building having an annual net operating income of $30,000, I have substantially increased the value of my building. If I capitalize the building's income at 7 percent, the value is $30,000 ÷ .07 = $428,571. If this figure seems unrealistic, try to capitalize the net operating income at 9 percent for a value of $333,333. Even on those terms the building is worth over $300,000 because of the conversion. Since I have a mortgage of $180,000, I will be able to sell the building and reap about $150,000 for my efforts.

Condominium conversions. My first positive experience with condominium conversion happened only a few short months ago. My partner and I were able to locate a choice ten-unit building in an excellent location. Four of the units were being rented out as commercial office space. The remaining six units were apartments containing about 1,000 square feet of space with two bedrooms. We negotiated a purchase price of $208,000 with a down payment of $30,000 and a land sales contract of $178,000, with monthly payments of $1,524.36 until paid in full. Once we owned the building we contacted our attorney and had him prepare the necessary documents for the conversion of the ten units into ten condominiums. In essence, this would convert the individual units from a rental status to an ownership status. In order to accomplish this, certain items had to be taken care of. First of all, the city had to give authorization for the change in use. Our attorney met with the city planners to explain what we intended to do. They asked to see our condominium documents and a new survey of the property. Once they were satisfied that the papers were in order, permission was granted to sell the individual units. With the help of a real estate company, the units were placed on the market for a price of $32,000 per unit. All the units were sold quickly because of our easy financing; we agreed to accept a $5,000 down payment and to carry the financing ourselves for the balance of the $27,000 owing. Here is our profit picture:

Sale of ten units @ $32,000	$320,000
Less:	
Commissions	$20,000
Survey	$1,000
Attorneys' fees	$2,500
Miscellaneous sales costs	$1,500
	$(25,000)
Net sales proceeds	$295,000
Less cost of building	$208,000
Profit	$87,000

The interesting part of the story is yet to come. We required a down payment of $5,000 per unit with a total cash down payment for all units equally of $50,000. When we deducted our $25,000 costs of conversion (commissions, attorneys' fees, etc.) from the total down payment, we came away with $25,000 in cash. This returned to us almost all of our original down payment of $30,000. Then, where is the benefit for converting the units to condominiums? As you remember, our monthly payment on the property when we bought it was $1,524.36. By selling the units as condominiums and carrying back the paper ourselves, we created a situation whereby the new owners made a total monthly payment of approximately $2,500 per month. With this money we make the payment of $1,524.36 and keep the difference of almost $1,000 a month for the next twenty-five years. In summary, we bought the building with a $30,000 down payment, sold the units as condominiums, got back $25,000 in cash at closing, and a monthly cash flow of approximately $1,000 a month for twenty-five years. We did not have to make any extensive improvements in the property—we simply sold the units "as is." The attorney did most of the work for us. The real estate company took care of the sales. All that was necessary for us to do was to come up with the idea in the first place and to delegate the details to the professionals. Profit was created because we knew that people will pay more for a condominium than they will for a rental apartment unit. If you're like me, you'll be out looking for an apartment building just waiting to be converted. Mark my words, condo conversion is just in its infancy in this country. It is the wave of the future.

Land subdivisions. Another form of a conversion from one use to another is converting land that has been kept vacant for farming or other reasons into a land subdivision. Your land is a prime candidate if it is near a growing metropolis. The increase in price from one use to the other is dramatic.

Let's look at a ten-acre parcel of ground that has been used for raising corn. The farmer is getting older and wants to retire; he has watched the sprawling city slowly encroach and almost completely surround his small farm. Since his livelihood has been derived in part from his land, he has resisted the offers of previous land subdividers; now, with retirement in sight, he begins to contemplate selling his property so he can enjoy the life he has always wanted.

Along comes a creative real estate investor—we'll call him Bob. Not much money jingles in his pockets, but his ideas won't stop. Since Bob has done his homework, he knows that farm ground in the county has been selling for $2,000 to $3,000 an acre; however, ground this close to the city limits has recently sold for $12,000 to $15,000 an acre. The farmer has kept close track of the higher price land sales, and he wants at least $15,000 an acre for his ground. He must have $150,000 or nothing at all.

When Bob begins to negotiate, he must have all of the facts at his fingertips. He checks with the city to determine the difficulty of obtaining building permits on any subdivision lots that would be created. Is there adequate water, sewer, and fire protection? Is the city going to cause any trouble when a final plan of the subdivision is submitted to the planning department for approval? Is the land properly surveyed? Is there a market for property in this area? What size lots can be sold and at what prices?

Bob checks with a reputable land surveying company and asks the surveyor these questions; he has most of the answers.

In the case of the ten-acre parcel, all of the signs are GO. Building lots have sold for as high as $18,000 a lot within the last three months. The surveyor draws up an inexpensive preliminary subdivision plan showing that once roads and sidewalks are accounted for, there will be about thirty lots ready for sale.

Bob is able to obtain a firm bid from a local contracting outfit (recommended by the surveyor), which has agreed to do the improvements on the property such as roads, sewer, water lines, and sidewalks. Here is the financial picture:

Cost of the land	$150,000
Cost of the improvements (at $3,500 per lot)	$105,000
Sales costs at $1,000 per lot	$ 30,000
Total costs	$285,000
Gross sales of 30 lots at $18,000	$540,000
Less total costs	$285,000
Total profit	$255,000

The profit picture is outstanding for such a small piece of ground, ten acres, for a year's work. You would also be wise to sell the lots on a wholesale basis to a local builder who needs land for his next home subdivision. You may be able to sell the whole thirty-lot package for $15,000 per lot and end up with a profit of $165,000. The profit is quicker this way and does not involve advertising campaigns. I've done subdivisions both ways, and I think I will always pick the quick profit over the long-term method.

What about financing the land in the first place? Use the subordination technique discussed earlier. The seller is going to have a tremendous tax consequence if he receives all of his $150,000 in one year. Convince him that he should only accept 25 percent of the money during the first year of sale. His accountant will then call this an installment sale and will verify that the seller did not receive the entire amount in one year. A 25 percent down payment amounts to $37,500; the rest ($112,500) should be subordinated to a construction loan which you have obtained to make improvements on the property. Since the improvements will cost about $105,000, you will need to find a bank that will give you a development loan; some will lend up to 75 percent of the value of the developed building lot.

Every year thousands of homes are being built, and land is needed desperately by growing building companies. You can fill a need by bird-dogging the land for them and reap a profit in the process!

Keep your eyes open. Make conversions like this one and the others we've discussed work for you.

CHAPTER TWENTY-ONE

Creative Self-unemployment: How to Retire in

Five Years on a Tax-free Income

ORTY-FIVE-MINUTE lunch hours.

Traffic jams in the mornings—and in the afternoons.

Working twice as hard as the guy in the next office for half the pay.

Punching a time clock.

Two measly weeks of vacation in return for fifty weeks of hard labor.

The incessant clang of the alarm clock.

Hand-to-mouth existence.

Shackled.

Aren't you sick of it all?

It's time for you to say good-bye to a job you don't enjoy. Use your knowledge of real estate and your creative abilities to become financially independent. The time is right. The opportunities are there. *You* can do it. You have been successful in your real estate investment program even though you were doing it on a part-time basis. Just think what will happen if you can devote full time to it.

Declaring your financial independence by quitting your job is a lot like jumping off the edge of the world. Make sure you look before you leap—and consider the following elements:

Cash Flow. As soon as your last paycheck arrives, you are on your own. Unless you have established a monthly income stream from some other source, it won't be long before you will be in trouble. As a rule, you should not quit your job until you have at least six to twelve months of living-expense money in the bank (or until you have an adequate outside monthly cash flow). Remember—quitting your job is supposed to provide you with more time to cultivate your real estate investments. If you're not financially prepared, you'll waste your time worrying about money— or scrambling for money. Don't leap until you have a parachute of some sort, even if it's only a small umbrella. Can you imagine how embarrassing it would be if you had to come crawling back to your employer—all because you didn't plan your "escape" well enough and weren't prepared to handle cash flow problems?

We'll never know how many prospectors closed down their mines because they ran out of money when they were only days away from discovering a rich vein of gold. Don't let it happen to you. Have a one year supply of either food or money on hand before you quit.

Office Space. If you have been used to working in an office that your boss provided for you free, you will be shocked to discover just how much it costs to rent and maintain your own office space. You won't need much —perhaps 100 square feet in a corner somewhere—but you'll need something. I work out of my home, but children, your spouse, and other family concerns can really cut into your productive working time. If you are doing your job, you will be out looking at real estate much of the time, but there will be times when you'll need quiet time to concentrate. Do what seems best for you.

Time Management. If you have trouble managing your time, you will find all kinds of excuses not to be out there hustling all day long. It takes tremendous discipline to overcome a streak of laziness or fear. Set rigid goals for yourself on a daily basis: "I'll visit ten homes or apartment buildings today. I'll present five offers today. I'll buy something today. I'll talk to ten realtors today. I'll read up and study today." I recently read a story about an investor who woke up one morning and decided to see just how much money he could make that day from dawn to dusk. He began his search, located a property, tied up the property with an option, sold the option to a group of investors—all within the prescribed time limit—and netted for himself over *two million dollars.*

Loss of Company Benefits. You must realize that you are probably going to leave behind a group health insurance program, some kind of retirement benefits, the use of the company car, and all those other goodies that come with the corporate life. These are called "Golden Handcuffs," and more than one potential free-lancer has not answered the knock of opportunity because of them. These benefits are designed especially to keep the best employees from moving on to other jobs. They are meant to shackle you. You must recognize them for what they are: the bars that invisibly keep you a prisoner in a job that makes you unhappy.

Lack of Borrowing Power. As soon as you quit your secure, steady-paying job, you are also cutting yourself off from the help of the bank. If you are planning to do any refinancing of properties or borrowing for down payments, you will be wise to do as much of it as you can *before* you quit your job. After you quit you will have to rely on partners with strong financial statements to help you until you are strong enough on your own.

Okay. So there are some disadvantages. You can counter them with adequate planning and conservative judgment if you are aware of the disadvantages and if you are determined to overcome them.

There are also some huge plusses.

Time. All day long—every day, if you wish—you can be free to seek your fortune however you wish. That's the biggest plus of them all. No longer will you have to "push someone else's pencil." No more "Yes, Massa; no, Massa." You will be amazed at how quickly your net worth increases when you work full time at it. A sense of accomplishment will swell inside of you until you feel like bursting. You will be building your own empire instead of building someone else's. You will be leaving a legacy to your children. This sense of freedom was the foundation upon which our great nation was built. Fifty-six brave men signed their own death warrants when they affixed their names to the Declaration of Independence in 1776. Where would we be now if they hadn't? The freedom to spend one's time in whatever manner one wishes is sacred ground. Don't let someone deprive you of it.

Money. The risks of self-employment are tremendous, but the rewards are well worth the trouble. When the money starts to flow, it will come in larger amounts than you had thought possible. In the meantime, hang on—by your fingernails if necessary. Stay rational. Don't make any hasty decisions.

You must realize that in order to increase your ultimate financial freedom you will have to cut back on your expenditures for a short period of time. As the chart below illustrates, when you become your own boss your standard of living sometimes has to be adjusted downward in comparison to your neighbors, the Joneses. They spend almost every dollar they earn on "butter" and have nothing worthwhile to show for it. You must learn to sacrifice immediate pleasures for the long-range satisfaction that financial independence provides. There is no other way. You either pay the price now for a short period of time (and live the rest of your life in financial independence) or you pay the price later, when you reach age sixty-five and have nothing to show for your butter lifestyle and must rely on social security for the rest of your days. It's your choice.

Up to where the lines cross on the chart your lifestyle is lower than the Joneses' because you have chosen to take a gamble and to invest full time in real estate. S.P. stands for starvation period. After the lines cross you are financially independent. The Joneses still struggle. You don't.

A ship in a harbor is safe, but that's not what ships were built for. What were *you* built for? Think about it as you drive to work tomorrow morning.

Security. Security? That's right. Security for the future—security that your wise investments of today will afford you, a great deal more security than the retirement program you're now paying in to. Security that says you won't be laid off by a supervisor if the budget gets cut. Security that says your income will always keep pace with inflation. It's a solid kind of security, better than the "security" of having a steady—albeit small—income.

What can you do to make your free-lance experience successful? A successful free-lance experience, of course, is one that provides enough cash flow to meet the costs involved in living expenses and to provide the cash you want to continue in your investment program. Let's look at how you might obtain such a cash flow.

PLAN #1. *Buy low, sell for nothing down with high price.* This consists of finding an undervalued property that is also available for a small down payment. These kinds of properties are difficult—but not impossible—to find. They are generally those that require quite a bit of fix-up and cosmetic work. Buy the property, clean it up, and sell it for a nice profit. You might do something like this:

Four-unit Apartment Building

Purchase Price	Sales Information
Cost: $120,000	Sales price: $142,000
Down payment: $10,000	Down payment: $12,000
Mortgage: $110,000	Mortgage: $130,000
Payable at $849 per month with 8 percent interest	Payable at $1,181 per month with 10 percent interest
Fix-up expenses: $2,000	Net to you: $12,000 cash
Total cash: $12,000	You will also receive the difference between the old and new loans: $332 a month.

This $332 cash flow comes in each month and gives you a source to help you with living expenses. You still have your $12,000 capital to invest in another project. If you "roll your money over" several times like this you might be able to generate enough cash flow from your properties to give you the courage you need to quit your job and devote full time to your real estate ventures. As I mentioned in the previous chapter on conversions, on one project alone my partner and I were able to create a cash flow for ourselves of almost $1,000 per month by converting a small ten-unit apartment building into condominiums. We bought low and sold high and kept the profit in the form of a steady monthly cash flow.

PLAN #2. *Triple net lease.* If you are just starting out and you would like to delay buying real estate until you know the ropes, try the triple net lease approach to making steady monthly cash flow. You simply need to approach owners of apartment buildings or of office space in your area who are especially tired of managing their properties and agree with them to pay them a certain guaranteed income from their properties if they will allow you the privilege of operating their building for them.

For instance, suppose you find an elderly gentleman who has owned and operated a twelve-unit building for twenty years, owns it free and clear, and does not have the time or energy to manage his property any more. He doesn't want to sell it, and he doesn't know management firms exist. Your main selling point would be to relieve him of his headache and give him a guaranteed, steady, hassle-free cash flow each month. If the building rents for $2,400 a month ($200 an apartment) and the expenses are running at 40 percent of the gross income—about $1,000 a month—then he normally receives $1,400 a month net cash flow before taxes. Offer him a net $1,200 a month for a five-year lease on his apartment building. This would give you $200 a month for your efforts in the first year. In later years as rents increased and you were able to keep expenses to a minimum, you might get up to $500 a month from your lease contract.

This income will not come without some work on your part. You will have to keep the units rented at all times and take care of maintenance problems. But once you understand the building and how to run it efficiently, you can turn it over to one of the building tenants in exchange for a partial rent reduction. Then you can keep the excess income and spend your precious time on other projects.

The leasing of single-family residences with options to buy (as discussed in the chapter on options) can also provide additional monthly income. I have heard of some investors who have taken this technique seriously and have leased dozens of houses with a small monthly cash flow. A portfolio of nine or ten leased houses could possibly generate enough positive cash flow to support a modest living budget for the potential full-time investor.

PLAN #3. *Buy low, sell high all cash.* In real estate, a smart investor can make as much money in one transaction as the average American makes working for fifty weeks a year (at a job he can't stand, I might add). The skill comes in recognizing which property has potential and which property does not. The more you know your real estate marketplace, the easier it will be to recognize the "once-in-a-lifetime deals" that seem to pop up about every other week. In this book I have given examples of transactions where the buyer made tens of thousands of dollars in only *one* transaction in less than a year's time. These are not isolated examples. They are happening every day—around you, in front of your very eyes. On your way to work each morning you are driving by dozens of properties which are crying out for someone with vision and courage to buy them. The next move is yours.

Let's go through a quick example. Suppose you are working nine to five at a job you are not in love with. You agree with the principle of becoming your own boss but realize that you don't have any money saved up to make the break on your own. You begin studying and researching the real estate market to find out how it operates. At this point, you should be looking for a property that needs some minor cosmetic repair—a "sleeper" that most people have overlooked because of its condition. Suppose you locate a shabby four-unit apartment building with a price tag of $80,000 and a down payment of $10,000. With a little work, you surmise that it could be placed back on the market for $100,000 with a cash down payment of $30,000. You tie the property up and use one of the techniques outlined in this book to come up with the cash. Then you begin to make the necessary improvements. Since you do a lot of the work yourself, the fix-up job is completed in about six months at a total cost of $2,500. At this point you have $12,500 invested in the property. You place the property back on the market listed at $100,000, and six months later the building closes and the new buyer gives you a down payment of $30,000. You may have to return the $10,000 and the $2,500 you borrowed plus interest—but even at that you are left with at least $15,000. Not bad for a few extra hours and a part-time effort. If you look at what you accomplished with only minimal effort, you may begin to ask yourself, "Why don't I do this full time?" Remember that you will need a cushion to start with—but isn't $15,000 in the bank enough? It should be adequate to keep you alive for a year until you locate your next property and turn it over for another profit. One cardinal rule to remember is that each time you sell a property for a profit, you should always try to buy a property to keep. Take a portion of your earnings and reinvest it into another property, which you will leave in your portfolio for long-term growth. If you follow this pattern it won't be long before your money worries will be gone forever.

PLAN #4. *For property owners only.* If you have property that you've owned for some time, you might be lucky enough to have a cash flow from your units. If you raise rents regularly on a competitive basis, there will come a time when the building will generate a rather substantial monthly cash flow. There are two other ways to realize cash from properties you already own: refinance the property and reinvest the profit, or sell the property. But why should you sell your property if you don't have to?

Let's look at a really exciting prospect—retirement in five years with a tax-free income—without selling your property.

Of all the formulas mentioned in this book, this one has the most promise, is the easiest to accomplish, and requires the least amount of time.

This plan centers around single-family residences. Why? Because they are in the greatest supply; most people understand the methods of home purchasing because they've gone through the process at least once. And single-family residences are usually easiest to buy for the small investor. (Of course, you can work this same plan with any investment medium, but for our purposes we will discuss only single-family residences. You may apply the principles any way that will benefit you most.)

Suppose you were able to devote one full day a week—say Saturdays— to looking for real estate investments. Since you have fifty-two Saturdays a year, you should be able to find and purchase just *one* property, one small home valued near $40,000, from a seller who is anxious to sell and will accept a $35,000 price with a $2,500 down payment. This will take some looking, but remember you have a year to find it. When you find the right property, buy it. If necessary, borrow the down payment, using one of the creative methods discussed earlier in this book. Then rent the house.

The next year, do exactly the same thing. Buy just *one* property valued below market price with a small down payment. Again, rent the house; you'll have to be able to rent the house for enough money to cover mortgage payments, including taxes and insurance. The tenants will pay all utility bills and minor maintenance bills. In the first year or so the rental income will be tight, but after several years you will begin to experience a steady positive cash flow.

In the third year, do the same thing. And so on until the fifth year, when you'll own five rental homes, all rented out, with no negative cash flow. If you have chosen the property well, there is a good chance that it will double in value in this five year period (appreciation of at least 14 percent per year).

Let's look at our equity position in these five houses:

	1st Home	2nd Home	3rd Home	4th Home	5th Home
Value	$80,000	$69,960	$60,800	$52,900	$46,000
Loans	31,640	31,960	32,250	32,500	32,775
Equity	$48,360	$38,000	$28,550	$20,400	$13,225

How do you make the money? Do you sell? No. You refinance. And you attempt to find the highest possible loan on your properties. Help yourself to do just that. Paint the trim on the houses, maintain the yard, or consider new carpeting or draperies. You might even paint the interior throughout the entire house. Do as much as possible with as little money as possible. Your aim is to get the highest appraisal possible for your invested cosmetic dollar.

Then do your homework. Be prepared to convince the appraiser that the value of the home is twice what it was five years ago. If you are able to obtain a new loan of 75 percent of the value of the appraisal, you should be able to refinance your first property for at least $60,000:

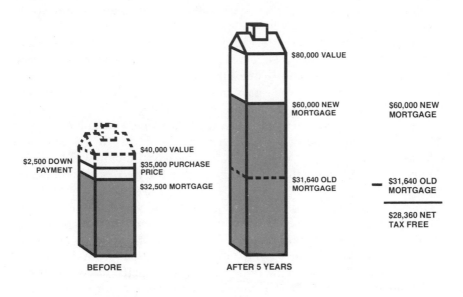

$80,000 VALUE

$60,000 NEW MORTGAGE

$60,000 NEW MORTGAGE

$2,500 DOWN PAYMENT

$40,000 VALUE

$35,000 PURCHASE PRICE

$32,500 MORTGAGE

$31,640 OLD MORTGAGE

$31,640 OLD MORTGAGE

$28,360 NET TAX FREE

BEFORE

AFTER 5 YEARS

5-YEAR RETIREMENT PLAN

If your existing loan is $31,640, your net proceeds from the new loan will be $28,360, less loan fees, which may be as high as $1,500. So you should be able to keep at least $26,000 of the new loan, a figure that represents the equity that belongs to you and that, as such, *is not taxable*. You will not have to report this income to the government as long as you don't sell the property (one good reason not to sell!).

Can you now rent the property for enough to pay the mortgage payment? A mortgage payment on a $60,000 mortgage at 10 percent interest for twenty-five years would amount to $545.52 plus taxes and insurance—

perhaps as much as $650 a month total. Sound impossible? Remember, you're looking at rents five years down the road; they're bound to be considerably higher.

Still uncomfortable? Hold out $2,000 from your refinance profits. That will give you $166 a month to apply toward the mortgage payment. You'll still have $24,000 left over to spend as you want to, *and it's tax free*. Kick off your shoes and pursue a full-time real estate investment hobby. In the sixth year of your program, the second investment home is now ready for refinancing after your having experienced five full years of appreciation.

Do this with one house each year. Refinance in January, and you're set for the year.

Is your program finished after you have refinanced the fifth investment home (in the tenth year)? Of course not! Your very first home, which you refinanced (harvested) in the fifth year of your program, has now had five more years to grow a new crop. It's ready to be harvested once more. And so you start all over again. Ad infinitum.

If you want to retire with an even higher income—insurance against inflation—buy *two* houses a year. Then, at the end of five years, start refinancing *two* houses a year. It's twice the work, but it will be twice the income. And you'll still have plenty of time for your new hobbies and lifestyle.

For those property owners who don't want to wait for five years to take advantage of the five-house retirement plan, there are ways of pulling all of the equity out of properties you own without having to sell them. Let me illustrate. Whenever you are paying mortgage payments to a private party who holds a mortgage on your property, there exists the possibility of flexibility. One of my first purchases was an older twelve-unit building which I bought with $5,000 down. As in the illustration below, I now am paying on a $125,000 contract for twenty years. The underlying $100,000 portion of the contract is held by an elderly woman who sold the property years earlier carrying back a first mortgage of $100,000 at 7 percent interest. Her sons have since realized that the income from the mortgage (about $850 a month) is really not adequate for their mother. They approached me with an interesting proposition. They encouraged me to refinance the property and place a new $150,000 loan on it. Normally, the proceeds of the new loan would go to pay off all underlying indebtedness—thus paying $100,000 to the woman in cash. The sons agreed that if I were to place a new loan on the property, they would split the proceeds of the money their mother would receive—therefore, she would only receive $50,000 in cash and I would get the remaining $50,000 in cash. This latter amount would be lent to me at a higher interest rate and would be secured by a second trust deed on the twelve-unit building. It is easy to see the rationale behind this offer to refinance the property. The sons would thereby obtain at least half of the outstanding $100,000 debt. Their mother would be able to improve her lifestyle and enjoy herself more—and in addition, she would increase the interest rate on the $50,000 portion that she did not receive. Likewise, it is easy to see the rationale behind my desire to go along with their plan. I could refinance the property and thereby borrow out 100 percent of my equity and still be able to retain ownership of the property. I would walk away from the refinance with $75,000 cash in my pocket, with which I could go out and buy more real estate. The only thing I would have to worry about in the above situation is negative cash flows. And this would have to be structured to my satisfaction before I would agree to refinance.

$200,000 VALUE

$75,000 EQUITY

$50,000 NEW SECOND MORTGAGE

$200,000 VALUE

$150,000 NEW FIRST MORTGAGE

$100,000 PRIVATE FIRST MORTGAGE (7%)

$125,000 CONTRACT OF SALE (9.7%)

BEFORE

AFTER

PULLING CASH OUT OF BUILDINGS YOU ALREADY OWN

Apply these solutions; commit yourself to a lifestyle that will afford you ultimate freedom and security. Begin planning now for the day you will walk up to your boss with a smile on your face and a letter of resignation in your hand. Dream about it. Plan for it. Make your goal specific; mark the day on your calendar. Do these things faithfully, and you will reach your goal. You're one step closer just by deciding to do it!

Your goal might seem unusual to some, and there will undoubtedly be those who will try to deter you from your course, just as there were those who tried to talk Columbus out of sailing for the New World. Thank heaven he did. And you'll thank heaven you did. Take the road less traveled by—it *will* make all the difference!

[I'd like to thank Jack Miller and John Schaub for sharing the basic idea for the five-year retirement plan in their nationwide seminar entitled "Making It Big on Little Deals."]

CHAPTER TWENTY-TWO

To Sell or Not to Sell? A Few Tips on Selling

Wᴇ ʜᴀᴠᴇ concentrated our attention on everything you should know about buying properties effectively and for maximum gain. There are times, however, when it is overwhelmingly advantageous to sell. It is critical that you know when it is in your interest to sell and when you should hang on to your property at all costs.

What are some of the reasons you shouldn't sell?

1. If you've made any profit at all during the period you've owned the property and you've had the property for more than one year, you'll have to give part of that profit to the government in the form of capital gains taxes when you sell. If you've owned the property for *less* than one year when you sell it, your taxes will be even higher. And one of the reasons you invested in real estate to begin with was to avoid paying your profits to the government. If you don't want to give some of your marbles away, then you might consider refinancing the property or exchanging it instead. More on this later.

2. Selling your property means you will need to invest precious time locating another property in which to invest. You'll need to find the right property, and you'll need to find a don't wanter. That takes time—sometimes a great deal of time. And you'll need to be prepared to spend it.

3. Selling a property ruins your investment program unless you immediately reinvest your profits into other comparable buildings. Your accumulation goal is fixed, specific. As soon as you sell a piece of property, you alter that accumulation plan. It is often difficult to reinvest quickly enough to preserve what you've worked so hard to gain.

4. As soon as you get all of that money in your hands, you will

221

probably be tempted to spend it on just a little bit of butter—a new stereo, new carpeting for the house, a boat, a vacation. You can easily lose everything you've worked to gain. It's often better just to leave the equity in the property where it will grow—untouched—and where it will help you reach your financial goals.

Those are all good reasons for not selling property, and they apply most of the time. There are some cases, however, when they *don't* apply, and those are the times when you should consider selling your property.

Let's consider those cases.

1. *You need money for an excellent investment opportunity.* Every once in a while you might run across the chance to make an investment that will significantly advance your financial goals. The property might be at the right price and the right terms, but you don't have the money you need to make the down payment. For any number of reasons you might decide against involving a partner or applying for short-term loans from a bank or lending institution.

In a situation like this one, you might consider selling one of your properties to raise the needed down payment for the new investment. By selling, you take a step up: you might move to a larger apartment building from a portfolio of smaller properties, consolidate various diverse equities, or increase your leverage position.

For example, suppose you locate a beautiful thirty-unit apartment building that is selling for $600,000. The seller wants a $100,000 down payment. You decide that having the apartment building will be more beneficial to you than owning the three houses and the duplex you already have, and you can't raise the $100,000 any other way, so you liquidate the three houses and the duplex. You sell them, and you reinvest the money in the apartment building. Your management problems are now centered in one location, you have better leverage, and you've increased your cash flow. You've improved your investment position.

That's the key I always consider: if a sale of property will better my investment position, I sell; if the sale will not better my investment position, I seriously consider all alternatives before I decide to sell.

There's an avenue you should always consider when you do decide to sell and reinvest in another property: exchange. If you sell your property, the government will tax you on it. If you exchange your property, you will not be taxed as long as (1) the property you exchange into is of greater value than the property you are exchanging out of, (2) there is no mortgage relief (in other words, the mortgage you assume on the new property is greater than the old mortgage on your previous property), and (3) you don't receive any cash—or any other non-real estate property—in the exchange along with the property.

Sometimes a seller will be glad to accept your smaller equities in exchange for his property; you might have just the solution he's been looking for. Other times a seller will insist on cash. If he does, try to tie up his property subject to finding cash buyers for your smaller properties. The transfer of titles would then be a three-way exchange—a little more complicated, but certainly less expensive tax-wise. See more on this in Chapter Eighteen.

Make sure you're ready if the opportunity to sell and reinvest ever arrives. Keep a list of all those who contact you to ask if you're interested in selling. You might not be interested at the time they ask you, but you can refer to the list if you ever *do* decide to sell. Those names might come in very handy.

2. *You have reached your financial goals and have decided to follow the "Doomsday Philosophy."* Someday you'll reach your financial goals; you'll have completed your investment program. In order to retire and reap the benefits of your investment plan, you may need to sell some properties to provide a cash flow to meet your living expenses.

In my own investment program, I intend to sell some of my properties and invest the proceeds into paying off the mortgages on one of my choicest apartment buildings. This will leave me in a free and clear position on that one building, which will provide a handsome cash flow for my retirement. At the same time, I'll retain some of my highly leveraged properties, a situation that will give me tax breaks that will ensure long-term growth.

At that point I—and you, if you use a similar plan—will be in a secure position in case of a financial crisis. (We've called fear of and preparation for such a financial crisis the Doomsday Philosophy.) I will have a steady cash flow from my apartment building, and, because it's completely paid for, I don't run the risk of losing it for failure to make mortgage payments.

My goal under this plan is to have a beautiful home free and clear and a large apartment building free and clear that will provide me with my needed cash flow. In this way I can derive the utmost amount of security. You may have to take your lumps tax-wise, but the security is well worth it.

3. *You are selling to generate cash flow.* We've discussed a number of techniques that can be used to generate cash flow: the earnest money option, the buy low/sell high plan, and the technique of splitting the property. They depend upon the sale of some of your property.

If your goal is to retire as early as possible, you may need to sell some properties to generate the cash flow you need to accomplish your goal. Selling should be a last resort, but, in this case, it may work well for you.

Ultimately, you should try to keep as many properties in your portfolio as possible. You should sell only to better your investment picture. Remember, it's the long-term appreciation growth that makes you rich, not a large cash flow.

If you do decide to sell, follow these general guidelines:

1. If you are in a market where properties are in high demand, try to sell the property yourself instead of paying a realtor a commission. If you do decide to list with a real estate agency, find one that is aggressive in their advertising approach and that has many sales agents; the more exposure you can get in the same office, the better.

Research your area for the peculiar rules of your local real estate agencies before you list. Find an agency you have confidence in before you list.

When you do list, leave yourself as much flexibility as possible. Never list for six months; a one-month listing should be sufficient. And remember, if you are dissatisfied with the service you receive from the agency, get the listing agreement rescinded for lack of performance. You can usually do so by visiting your local county board of realtors. You don't have to wait out a listing agreement if you feel you are being mistreated.

If you are in an area where there are many properties and few buyers, of course, you should always hire a realtor rather than waste your precious time trying to sell your property.

2. Whenever you carry a second mortgage as you sell a property, always include a clause in the mortgage stating that all of your remaining equity in the note will be due and payable if the property is ever sold to a person other than the one you are selling to. The clause is called a "due on sale clause" and will protect you if the property is sold again before you are paid for it. If you decide later that you would rather receive monthly payments after all, you may choose to ignore the clause, but never limit your flexibility by eliminating the clause from your agreement.

3. Always try to get a third party escrow agent—usually the title company that handles the sale papers—to hold all of the documents, deeds, and mortgage papers. Then if the buying party defaults, you can get back all of the deeds and papers for your property.

4. Use an accountant to help you structure your sales so you can get

the maximum tax benefits. Consult him and review all details with him before you sign anything. He might be able to suggest ways to avoid or reduce tax losses—such as agreeing to an installment sale so that you receive less than 30 percent of the sale price in any one year, a technique that will exempt you from excessive taxes.

5. Establish a good relationship with an attorney and let him prepare and/or review any documents you use in the sale of your properties.

6. Always use trust deeds (if they are available in your state) because they are easily foreclosed upon if the buyer defaults. A mortgage is more cumbersome and usually takes longer to foreclose.

7. If the buyer is assuming your existing mortgage and paying your down payment in cash, make sure he follows through. Never transfer the title to him until you are sure he has assumed the mortgage and made the down payment.

8. Try to retain a long-term option to repurchase the property you are selling. You always have the chance that the property will increase in value and that the buyer will want to sell, and you can make money again on the same piece of property.

Make sure you're selling for the right reasons, make sure you are bettering your investment position, and follow the guidelines listed here. This will insure a successful selling experience.

CHAPTER TWENTY-THREE

Home Buyers—For Private Use Only

Maybe you're not interested in buying hundreds of thousands of dollars worth of real estate. You realize that the excitement of investing is keen and that the returns are incredible, but, well, it's just not for you. You just want to buy a home, something you can live in happily and that you can afford easily. Great! The techniques described in this book still apply to you because they can help you invest in that home even if you don't have a large down payment in the bank. And even if you do have cash, the creative techniques described here may help you to locate and negotiate a better deal.

Maybe you've been discouraged about trying to buy a house. There are two major problems that affect many young Americans today: many are unable to qualify for a loan (because their incomes are too low or because their credit rating is poor), and many are unable to pay the required down payment. These problems are real. The goal and dream of the last generation was to pay off their mortgage. The goal and dream of this generation is just to *get* a mortgage.

But that ever-elusive creature called a mortgage can be yours even if your income is low and your credit rating isn't quite up to snuff. Your greatest asset is the knowledge that you can buy a home without even involving the bank. You can buy directly from the seller, and you can have the seller carry the loan himself on a land contract, a contract of sale, or a wrap-around mortgage. There are many sellers who will agree to do just that—some to avoid tax problems, others to create a monthly cash flow during retirement—so you should be out there looking for that new home!

Let's look at a good program to follow. Before we begin, one word of advice: your best bet as you begin your search will be to hire a competent realtor. He knows all of the ins and outs, and if he's someone you can trust, he can help you in countless ways. So let's see how you should go about finding your new home.

You may not be in a position financially to buy your dream house right now. But, the home you are about to buy can be a stepping stone to a bigger and better home somewhere down the road. Don't let your pride get in the way. Each step you take, just like each step you take up a mountain, will bring you closer to your destination. Each time you buy a smaller house you will be building up equity for that larger ideal house. Move through several homes, possibly making several thousand dollars in profits on each move, until you are able to invest in your dream home —free and clear. It's well worth it.

If you have absolutely no down payment to work with, find a realtor who is willing to receive his commission from the sale in the form of a note. Many won't agree to do that; if you can't find one who is willing to help, try to learn as much about real estate as you can, and go it on your own!

If you don't have a realtor, you'll have to do a lot of searching yourself. Try to find a don't wanter—someone who will be flexible in the terms of the sale, someone who will agree to carry a loan instead of insisting on a large cash down payment. Especially look for people who are managing properties from out of state; they're usually the ones who are weary of the management hassle and who will agree to your terms.

Don't despair. Finding the right combination—a don't wanter, a property that suits your needs perfectly, and terms that fit your budget— takes time. Don't give up; the home you are looking for may be just around the corner. Keep looking until you find it.

If you find a good bargain with a seller who is willing to be flexible but who insists on *some* cash as a down payment, and if you don't have that cash, consider bringing in a partner. Your partner provides the cash down payment. You agree to make the mortgage payments, keep the property in top condition, and even make improvements while you live there. Then, when you sell the house, you'll make a hefty profit because of your hard work, and you'll split that profit with your partner. Convincing a partner that his investment is safe may take some effective talking, but you'll probably be able to show him a 25 to 30 percent return on his investment. Use all of your knowledge of real estate to persuade him to help with the cash outlay.

You might try the earnest money option: find a property that's a good bargain, tie it up with an earnest money receipt, find another buyer immediately, and resell the property for a profit. There—you've earned your down payment!

If you belong to a credit union, you might consider borrowing the down payment. This might mean that your payments are higher until you repay the loan, but it is better than waiting to save for a down payment— something that usually never happens! You might have to hang on by your fingernails until you get that loan paid off—but under present market conditions prompt action will pay you many times over.

Look for properties where the seller is delinquent two or three mortgage payments. These sellers are often flexible in their terms.

Search for a house that is up for lease; persuade the seller to give you an option to buy within a certain period of time. This technique locks the price in *now* and gives you the opportunity later (if you have negotiated a hard bargain) to sell the home for a price well above the option price. Again, you've just earned a down payment for the next purchase!

As a last resort, find an individual with a strong financial statement who is willing to cosign on your loan.

Any of these techniques can be used to come up with the down payment. You also ought to be aware of special programs available to home buyers.

The FHA (Federal Housing Authority) guarantees loans for people who don't have large down payments. Under FHA loans, which can be obtained through almost any savings and loan association in this country, you verify that you qualify for a low down payment loan. Depending on the price of the home, you could obtain a loan with a down payment as low as 3 percent; loans of up to $60,000 are currently available. The interest rate is generally lower than borrowing with any other arrangement. There are a few disadvantages: the loans take longer to obtain, and the appraisals are usually low (something that can cause problems at closing).

The Veteran's Administration also sponsors a program for veterans; if you've served in the armed forces, you can buy a home with no down payment. You will have to be prepared to pay closing costs, however.

Local savings and loan associations often make special offers to home buyers; a qualified buyer can often buy a home for as little as 5 percent down. It's worth your time to check around your area and see if any such programs are available.

So quit gazing in despair at the empty columns on your savings pass-book. There is a home out there just waiting for you to move in the sofa, dust off the mantel, and mow the front lawn. Take a good look at this book again. We've talked in terms of large investments, but the principles are universal. They apply to you too. And they'll work for you. Study them again, and a few months from now you might be pruning your own fruit trees while your wife drinks lemonade on your own back porch.

CHAPTER TWENTY-FOUR

How to Grow to One Million, Realistically

YOU'VE SET a goal.

Let's say that your goal is to invest in a million dollars worth of real estate in the next five years, with little or none of your own money.

That goal *is* possible to attain.

I have given you principles, suggestions, food for thought in this book. I have tried to include enough examples to illustrate my investment guidelines. But there is still that one last hurdle: grasping the abstract and making it mean something in your life.

To help make the whole spectrum of real estate investment less abstract, I have created what I feel is a realistic picture of how you might build your million-dollar pyramid. Study it. Then apply it and tailor it to your own situation.

Dedicate yourself to make your plan work, and it will.

Find out where you are and where you are going. I am going to make some assumptions about a typical small investor, give him a name, and empower him with all the information in this book. His net worth statement looks something like this:

Name: Jim Wilson
Age: 33
Marital status: Married
Dependents: Two children, ages six and two
Income: $1,500 a month with a bonus of about $500 every December

Assets		Liabilities	
Cash and checking:	$ 350	Mortgages:	$44,000
Savings accounts:	1,250	Notes (School loans):	2,500
Real estate owned:	55,000	Loans on life insurance:	0
Securities:	1,000	Unsecured debts:	500
Notes receivable:	0	Car loans:	4,500
Bonds:	0	Furniture loans:	1,500
Furniture and personal		Master Charge:	400
possessions:	5,000		
Automobiles		TOTAL LIABILITIES:	$53,400
'76 Monte Carlo:	4,500		
'71 Volkswagen:	1,500	NET WORTH:	$17,200
Life insurance cash value:	1,000		
Boats, trailers:	1,000		
TOTAL ASSETS:	$70,600		

Jim is a middle-management employee of a manufacturing company and has been with the company for over six years. His salary is steady and increases to keep pace with the consumer price index. The loans he took out to put him through school are payable at $75 a month. His stint in the army before he married gave him veterans benefits and the possibility of low down payment loans through the Veterans Administration.

After meeting his monthly mortgage payment of $400, he has living expenses and taxes to pay. He has tried to put at least $50 a month into his savings account and has used the yearly $500 bonus to pay off furniture or car loans. When his wife's father died two years ago, he and his wife inherited $5,000, which they invested in the stock market on the advice of a stock broker friend; the value of their stock has dropped to about $1,000.

The home the Wilsons bought four years ago on a VA loan for $45,000 has increased in value to $55,000, and its value could be higher if Jim would finish off the basement (currently about 80 percent completed). This is not their final home, and they would reinvest and move if the right deal came along.

Jim was given a paid-up $2,500 life insurance policy by his parents when he graduated from college with his master's degree. He thinks he could borrow about $1,000 against it at 6 percent interest if an emergency ever came up.

He has finally made the last payment on a boat he and his wife bought three years ago. They seldom use it anymore—the thrill just wore off. It sits in the garage gathering dust.

Jim is becoming increasingly aware of the hopelessness of his financial situation. He has read several books on real estate, and recently bought a book titled *Nothing Down*. He has decided to try his hand at this approach, more out of curiosity than anything else. He and his wife set a financial goal to have one million dollars in equity by Jim's forty-third birthday, about ten years from now. He figures that if he can buy one million dollars' worth of real estate within the next five years, he will have a million dollar equity long before the ten years are up.

Let's follow Jim on his investment journey as he progresses year by year.

Jim's first year was a good one. His wife, Nancy, was just as excited about Jim's investment program as he was. In fact, she found their first property while Jim was out of town, a $42,000 house with two bedrooms, some special amenities, and a large yard. The owner lived out of town and couldn't manage his property; he was a don't wanter. Nancy offered him $2,000 down on a thirty-year contract with monthly payments of $322, with Jim's inspection and approval. The seller accepted Nancy's offer; when Jim returned they retrieved the down payment out of savings and a few other miscellaneous sources. The mortgage payment was taken care of because they rented the home, located in an excellent neighborhood, for enough to cover expenses.

Jim and Nancy started looking for another investment. In their search they found a beautiful $60,000 house, something they wanted to live in themselves. The seller was a don't wanter, and he agreed to accept a $5,000 down payment with the Wilsons assuming the underlying mortgage of $55,000 at 8.75 percent interest, subject, of course, to the Wilsons selling their own home. They sold their home quickly for $56,000, and they received $11,000 cash from the closing. They used $5,000 of that money as a down payment on their new home; the remaining $6,000 was put in savings for future investments.

Next the Wilsons bought a solid eight-unit apartment building consisting of 1,100-square foot units. The owner was too busy to take care of maintenance problems, and he wanted out—fast. The Wilsons offered him $144,000—$7,500 in cash with a contract for the remaining $136,500 at 9 percent interest payable at $1,100 a month over thirty years.

How did they get the $7,500? Rents and deposits from the building itself supplied part: eight units at $210 a month rent supplied $1,680; deposits of $100 each supplied $800. The Wilsons had almost $2,500. They withdrew $5,000 from their savings account to total the required $7,500 down payment. They used the remaining $1,000 in their savings account to do some touchup painting and to take care of numerous deferred maintenance items.

At the end of the first year, the Wilsons' investment picture looked like this:

Investment home	$ 42,000
Personal residence	60,000
Eightplex	158,000
Total gross value	$246,000

The Wilsons decided to take a breather for several months to establish their cash flow and to get settled into their new lifestyle, which now required extra time for the overseeing of their two investment properties as well as time to care for their home. During those months they studied several books explaining the techniques of managing and operating apartment buildings.

Year Two opened with an interesting twist: Jim found a don't wanter who was willing to sell a $56,500 house (appraiser-verified) for $48,000. Jim tied up the house on an earnest money option with $500 earnest money (borrowed from his bank). He immediately found a new buyer for the house by advertising "$3,000 below appraisal," and he sold the house forty-five days later for $53,500. After closing Jim collected $4,500 in cash; he paid off the $500 loan from the bank and paid off his furniture loan. He and Nancy spent $500 on a nice vacation and returned excited about the possibilities for investing the remaining $2,000.

Soon after returning from their vacation they found a serious don't wanter who was willing to take $2,000 and the Wilsons' old boat (worth $1,000) as partial down payment for a $60,000 duplex with a $40,000 underlying loan on it. What about the rest of the down payment? The seller agreed to accept a $17,000 secured note for the rest of the equity. The note carried no monthly payments and had a balloon payment due in seven years. He also agreed—in writing—that if the Wilsons found another piece of property, he would be willing to move his $17,000 note to the new building if the interest rate on the note would be increased from 8.5 percent to 9.25 percent; he signed a "substitution of collateral" agreement.

As Nancy was reading the newspaper one night, she saw the following ad:

Nice ten-unit building
Owner will trade for
smaller units
Call Joe, 555–6789

Nancy called Joe and found out that he didn't have time to manage the property he owned, but that he did not want to get out of real estate completely. Joe looked at the Wilsons' duplex and said that he would be interested in an exchange. The Wilsons valued the duplex at $65,000 with a $40,000 underlying loan. Joe's property had a $175,000 loan and a value of $200,000. The equities were equal at $25,000. (The Wilsons' equity was $25,000 because of the $17,000 note the original owner held and that he was willing to move to the new ten-unit building; the Wilsons did not have to come up with any cash.)

Result? The Wilsons made $5,000 in equity profit through the exchange, but they won't have to pay taxes on the money because the transaction was a tax-free exchange.

At the end of the second full year, the Wilsons' investment picture looked like this:

Investment home	$ 46,000
Personal residence	66,000
Eightplex	158,000
Ten-unit building	200,000
Total gross value	$470,000

(All first-year property appreciated within one year at the rate of ten percent.)

As the third year began, the Wilsons didn't have any money left in their savings account, but they were still looking for good investment properties. They found a $50,000 house that had a $13,500 loan balance outstanding. The Wilsons used a second mortgage crank: they agreed to put a new 75 percent loan on the property if the seller agreed to accept a 25 percent second mortgage subordinated to the new first mortgage. The seller agreed; he received $24,000 cash from the refinance. It took considerable searching, but the Wilsons finally found a bank that gave them a $37,500 non-owner-occupied loan. The seller agreed to accept a $12,500 loan at 8.5 percent interest with no monthly payments and the entire balance due in seven years.

The Wilsons rented the home for enough to cover mortgage payments.

While talking to his dentist, Jim happened to ask him about his tax situation. Moaning, the dentist replied that he'd love to find some kind of tax shelter. Jim said he hadn't paid taxes for two years because of the real estate he owned, and they talked about forming a partnership. They decided Jim would locate the good buys, and the dentist would come up with the down payments (from $30,000 he had in a pension and profit-sharing plan).

Jim located a beautiful twenty-four-unit building for $450,000; the seller required a $20,000 down payment. The $420,000 loan had monthly payments of $3,600 resulting in a $300–$400 monthly negative cash flow. Jim was able to take the $6,000 in rents and deposits that he got when he bought the building and use it to upgrade the property exterior and to replace some wornout items. Then he raised the rent enough to get into a positive cash flow position.

At the end of the third year, the Wilsons' investment picture looked like this:

	Value After Two Years at Ten Percent Appreciation
Investment home	$ 51,000
Personal residence	73,000
Eightplex	174,000
Ten-unit building	220,000
Investment house	50,000
24-unit apartment building (Jim's half)	225,000
Total gross value	$793,000

(The net worth on the properties was over $140,000!)

Jim became a little bolder during the fourth year, so he decided to convert the apartments in the first building into office spaces. The building was well located on a major street, and the area was zoned for either professional offices or apartments.

Jim checked with some expanding companies in the area and found a tenant who would rent one whole floor of the building if the conversion was accomplished; Jim approached a money lender about getting a new first mortgage loan on the building. He was able to arrange a new $150,000 loan based on an appraisal of $200,000. The holder of the mortgage of $135,000 had an underlying loan of $80,000, and agreed to take a second mortgage subordinated to the new loan of $25,000 for the remainder of his equity if Jim would give him $30,000 from the proceeds of the new refinance loan.

The refinance was completed. Jim grossed $40,000, out of which he paid $3,000 closing costs and pocketed a net profit of $37,000. He used that money to tear out walls, demolish kitchens, and take out unnecessary bathrooms. Jim added new carpets, a parking lot, and new furnaces. Total cost of remodeling was $22,000, and he had to make mortgage payments totalling $5,000 during the remodeling. After several months the building was ready to lease, with 8,000 square feet of rentable space on two floors. He found two reliable tenants; each took one floor of office space at $5 a square foot. Jim collected $40,000 gross rent per year. And he had $10,000 left over to invest in something else.

Here's how he did it:

Gross rents	$ 40,000
Less expenses	$15,000
Net operating income	25,000
Less mortgage on both first and second	19,000
Cash flow	$ 6,000

So Jim ended up with a positive cash flow of about $500 a month for as long as he kept the office building rented. But there's an added plus: he increased the value of the building to $312,500 (and his total loans are $175,000).

While the conversion was being handled, Jim found another property for sale: a home priced at $47,000 with a $41,000 mortgage. The seller agreed to receive his $6,000 equity over a year's period of time at the rate of $500 a month with no interest. Jim used the cash flow from his new office building to buy the house.

At the end of the fourth year, the picture looks brighter:

	Value	Loans	Years of Appreciation at 10%
First investment home	$ 56,000	$ 39,000	Three
Personal residence	80,000	54,000	Three
10-unit building	242,000	197,000	Two
Investment house	55,000	50,000	One
24-unit apartment building (half)	247,000	210,000	One
Office building	312,000	175,000	
Last investment home	47,000	47,000	
Totals	$1,040,000	$772,000	

TOTAL NET WORTH: $268,000

The fifth year is one of consolidation and review. Jim tried his hand at land purchases using the earnest money option technique; he found two pieces of well-priced property that he turned over during the year at a cash profit of $29,000. The extra cash flow from the office building was used to pay off the loan on the last investment home, so there is little cash flow from the buildings. But Jim still had the $10,000 from the office conversion and the $29,000 from the earnest money option technique in a savings account in the bank, a total of $39,000 that gives him the security he needs and the courage to quit a job he had grown to detest.

Look at Jim's position as the sixth year began:

He had $500 a month from the office building plus another $500 a month from the increased rents on his properties. He used this $1,000 a month cash flow to cover living expenses until he increased his earnings through real estate.

He had $39,000 in the bank that he could devote to real estate investments. Jim was now able to spend full time on his real estate ventures.

He owned over a million dollars worth of real estate and had a net worth of over $350,000. In less than five years, even if he makes no further investment, Jim's property will increase in value enough to make him a millionaire. But Jim determined to cut that time in half and could probably succeed by spending full time at it.

At the end of the five years, Jim's picture looked like this:

	Purchase Price	Value	Loans	Number of Years Held
First investment home	$ 42,000	$ 61,500	$ 39,000	Four
Personal residence	60,000	88,000	54,000	Four
10-unit building	200,000	266,000	195,000	Three
Investment house	50,000	60,500	50,000	Two
24-unit apartment building (half)	225,000	272,000	210,000	Two
Office building	144,000	343,750	175,000	One
Last investment home	47,000	52,000	41,000	One
Totals		$1,143,750	$764,000	

TOTAL NET WORTH: $379,750 (Achieved in five years)

How did Jim achieve his million-dollar goal?

In those five years he purchased a total of thirteen properties. He sold five of them for cash or trade. Of the eight he kept, he converted one into an office building.

The remarkable thing is that Jim is by no means unique. I've personally known numbers of people just like him who have set high goals, have given themselves a time limit, have used these "nothing down" techniques, and who have achieved those goals.

I receive calls almost every day from the graduates of my Nothing Down Seminar who tell me about their successes. Several of my very first students have, in less than two years, already bought over a million dollars' worth of real estate. I ran into one of my graduates last year who had made more than $300,000 in one year from the properties which he purchased with the nothing down techniques described in this book. One of my students in Baltimore owns a seven-unit building and twenty investment homes. He did this in less than six months after learning of the concepts in this book. And with little or none of his own money! A broker in Oklahoma City called me to tell me that before he learned about creative financing he made most of his income from selling. Now he concentrates on buying with nothing-down techniques and makes more money. Dozens of my graduates have purchased hundreds of thousands of dollars' worth of real estate apiece. Hundreds have bought their first piece of real estate and are actively pursuing their second investment property. These are ordinary people with extraordinary commitments for reaching financial independence. And they will succeed! No one can tell me that these techniques don't work. I've seen them work in my own life and in the lives of hundreds of my students. Even in the cities where real estate prices seem to be out of this universe, these techniques work. Just a week ago a man came up to me and told me his story. He had heard my lecture in San Francisco, where I had demonstrated a few of my creative financing techniques. He decided to try them for himself. He located a three-unit apartment building, which he bought with nothing down. He was so excited that he could hardly get through the story. He was an immigrant from Taiwan and his English was rather hard to understand, but he had not let this stop him.

Don't let anyone convince you that real estate investing is no longer possible unless you have a lot of cash in the bank. Right this very moment, in your very city, there are properties you can buy using the techniques outlined in this book—with little or nothing down. The ball is in your court.

CHAPTER TWENTY-FIVE

Fear: The Ugliest Four-letter Word

As you finish this book and prepare to begin investing in real estate, there's something you must come to grips with: fear.

In these pages I've stressed the advantages of creating a highly leveraged position, of purchasing the most real estate possible with the least cash possible. I've shown you how to invest in real estate with little or none of your own money. This kind of a program works, but it does require that you live under a mountain of staggering debt. Unfortunately, that can be scary. It can breed fear. And fear is the ugliest four-letter word.

Fear can stop you cold. It can clutch at all your good resolves and send you, trembling, to hide from your goals. It can keep you trapped in a job that you hate or in one that is getting you nowhere.

There are eight reasons why people don't achieve success, reasons why people don't reach their goals. All those reasons stem from fear. Let's look at them, and what to do about them.

1. *A confused mind always says no!* If you are confused about how you are going to be able to accomplish your goals, you won't accomplish them. Fear and confusion are the exact opposite of faith and confidence. Without faith and confidence you have a less than one-in-ten chance of reaching your goals. You can't reach them because you don't think you can.

Get your thinking straight. Think your program through. Reduce your goals to single components that will seem more realistic. Read more, study more, and then get out there and get your feet wet.

2. *The paralysis of analysis.* When a child is afraid of the dark, he

usually thinks some scaly monster is hiding under the bed, ready to grab him and strangle him. The only solution is to turn on the light and get the child to look under the bed.

There's an adult counterpart, but it doesn't work as well. It says that if you're afraid, read up. A certain amount of reading is good, because it helps eliminate confusion. But don't get paralyzed. In other words, don't read *too* much. Get out and do something.

3. *Procrastination.* If you keep putting it off, you'll never get anywhere. Don't laugh. Procrastination is not funny. It can get you into hot water. What's worse, it can get you nowhere. Fast.

Ask yourself, "What are the consequences of my non-action?" Every day you are growing poorer—due to inflation—when every day you could be growing richer—due to real estate investment.

Go on, chart it out if you have to. Draw a literal picture of how much buying power you're losing now. Then draw a literal picture of how much money you could be earning through an investment, even a small one, in real estate. Then get your act together, get out and do something.

4. *The conservative investor.* I ran across a friend one day who was lamenting his financial situation; seems he couldn't quite seem to decide on "the right investment."

"I wish I had your guts," he sighed.

It doesn't take guts. It takes brains. Real estate is a *smart* investment; more important than that, it's a forgiving one. If you make an unwise investment, all you have to do is wait around for a few years—or even months—and property values will catch up. You'll be redeemed.

Don't worry about "gambling" on real estate investments. The worst gamble of all is to be too conservative and to talk yourself out of investing at all. It is foolishness to play a waiting "game," looking for the right investment.

5. *Fear that the economy will fail.* When Boeing laid off thousands of employees in Seattle several years ago, someone placed a billboard along a thoroughfare that read, "Will the last person to leave Seattle please turn off the lights?" The banks had such problems with delinquent mortgage payments on homes and apartments that they foreclosed buildings right and left and offered them to any investor who could come along and pay even the mortgage payments with no down payments. Seattle is on the rebound. Homes and apartments are full again. And those investors are very rich people.

Remember that real estate is the one thing that always appreciates despite a fickle economy.

But, for the benefit of any pessimists reading this book, I'll say this: What do you lose if there is a crash?

Nothing.

That's all you had when you began. That's all you invested into each building you purchased along the way. You bought with nothing or very little down.

Most importantly, you gained experience. So what if there's a crash? You've lost nothing. And when things pick up again, you've got the experience, the know-how, to take advantage of low prices and great availability.

Then you've got everything to gain.

So get out there and do it! Don't be like Chicken Little, strutting about the barnyard and announcing, "The sky is falling!" You might be right—but you might be wrong. There may be a 25 percent chance that there will be a crash, but there's a 100 percent chance that real estate will continue to skyrocket in value. It's simply a matter of placing your bet on the most likely thing.

6. *Head-in-the-sand syndrome.* People who are afraid to do anything do nothing. And so they get nowhere, which is really where they wanted to be in the first place. They'd rather stand around all day with their heads in the sand. It's more comfortable that way. They don't have to think much. Enough said.

7. *Fear of asking for what you want.* Some people are afraid of asking for a bank loan. Afraid of making an offer on a piece of property. Afraid of buying the unknown. Afraid of talking to sellers. Afraid of asking for what they want.

Try this: Walk up to a friend. Ask him to raise his right hand high into the air. Then, ask him to touch the tip of his left ear with the forefinger of his outstretched hand.

He'll do it. It's amazing what people will do if you only ask them.

Remember this: you'll never know until you ask. The worst thing that can happen is that someone will say no. That never hurt anyone. The best thing that can happen? The sky is the limit. You've got the world to gain and nothing to lose.

Get out there and do it!

8. *The fear of being wealthy.* Sounds absurd, doesn't it? Replace that fear with a fear of being poor. You can become wealthy with as much or as little effort as it takes to be poor. Remember that financial bondage is *not* fun.

You've got the knowledge. Do your homework; set up your goals, find some good properties, negotiate, buy. Every time you go through that process you come one step closer to financial independence. You become a little more secure. You've got what it takes. The only thing that can hold you back now is fear. And you're a much better person than that.

I challenge you to quit stalling your financial freedom until it is everlastingly too late. I challenge you to commit yourself to buying at least *one* property each year until you reach your financial goal. Others have done it. So can you.

Go out and do it!

A RELUCTANT INVESTOR'S LAMENT

I hesitate to make a list
Of all the countless deals I've missed;
Bonanzas that were in my grip—
I watched them through my fingers slip;
The windfalls which I should have bought
Were lost because I overthought;
I thought of this, I thought of that,
I could have sworn I smelled a rat,
And while I thought things over twice,
Another grabbed them at the price.
It seems I always hesitate,
Then make my mind up much too late.
A very cautious man am I
And that is why I never buy.

When tracks rose high on Sixth and Third,
The price asked, I felt, was absurd;
Those blockfronts—bleak and black with soot—
Were priced at thirty bucks a foot!
I wouldn't even make a bid,
But others did—yes, others did!
When Tucson was cheap desert land,
I could have had a heap of sand;
When Phoenix was the place to buy,
I thought the climate was too dry;
"Invest in Dallas—that's the spot!"
My sixth sense warned me I should not.
A very prudent man am I
And that is why I never buy.

How Nassau and how Suffolk grew!
North Jersey! Staten Island, too!
When others culled those sprawling farms
And welcomed deals with open arms . . .
A corner here, ten acres there,
Compounding values year by year,
I chose to think and as I thought,
They bought the deals I should have bought.
The golden chances I had then
Are lost and will not come again.
Today I cannot be enticed
For everything's so overpriced.
The deals of yesteryear are dead;
The market's soft—and so's my head.

Last night I had a fearful dream,
I know I wakened with a scream:
Some Indians approached my bed—
For trinkets on the barrelhead
(In dollar bills worth twenty-four
And nothing less and nothing more)
They'd sell Manhattan Isle to me.
The most I'd go was twenty-three.
The redmen scowled: "Not on a bet!"
And sold to Peter Minuit.

At times a teardrop drowns my eye
For deals I had, but did not buy;
And now life's saddest words I pen—
"IF ONLY I'D INVESTED THEN!"

—Anonymous

If you haven't caught on by now, let me tell you what the secret of this book is:

DON'T WAIT TO BUY REAL ESTATE
BUY REAL ESTATE AND WAIT!